TROPE

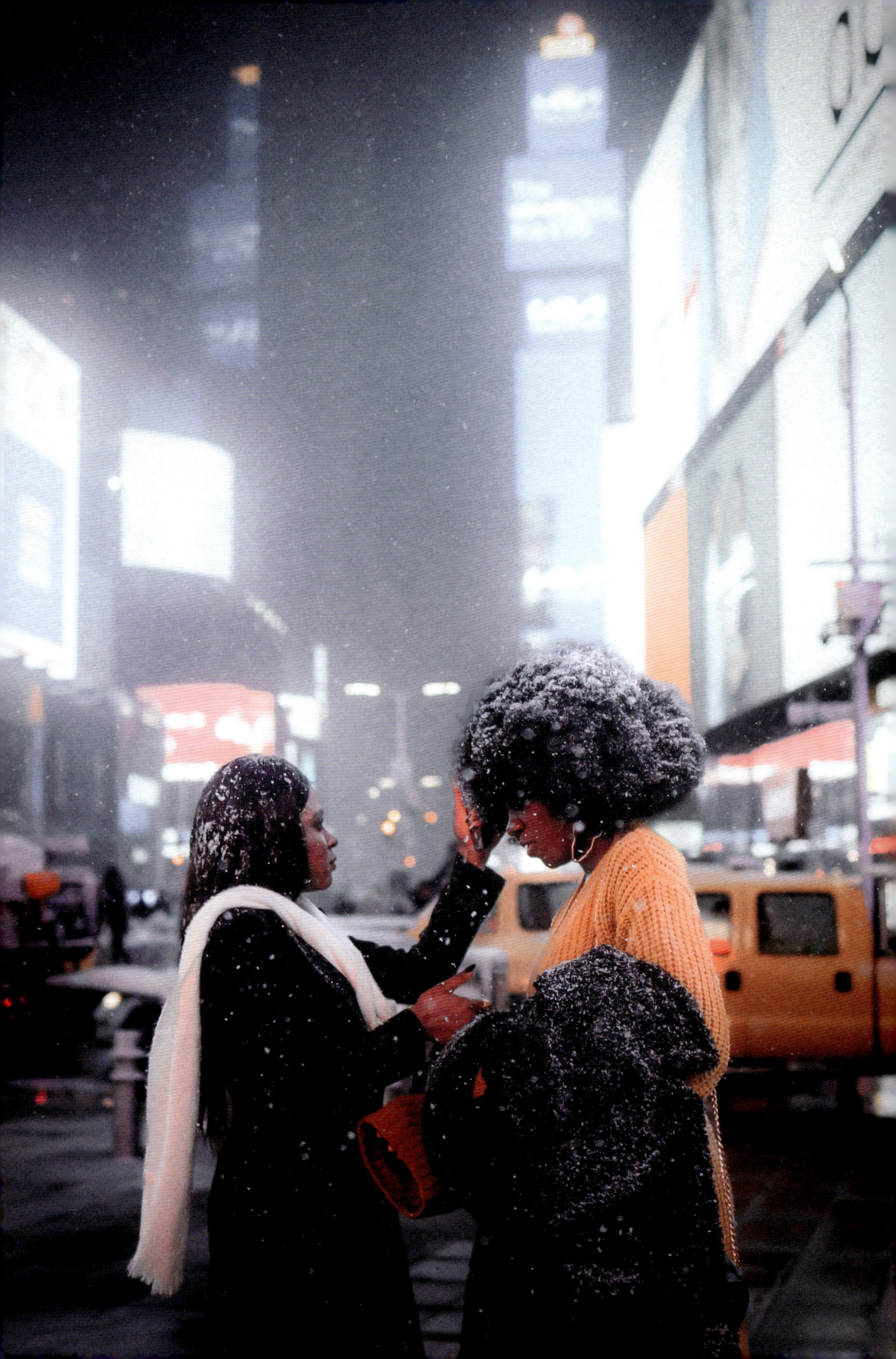

NEW YORK AFTER DARK

PHOTOGRAPHS BY
SANMI KRUEGER,
DECLAN MCWHINNEY,
AND CYRIL MOUTY

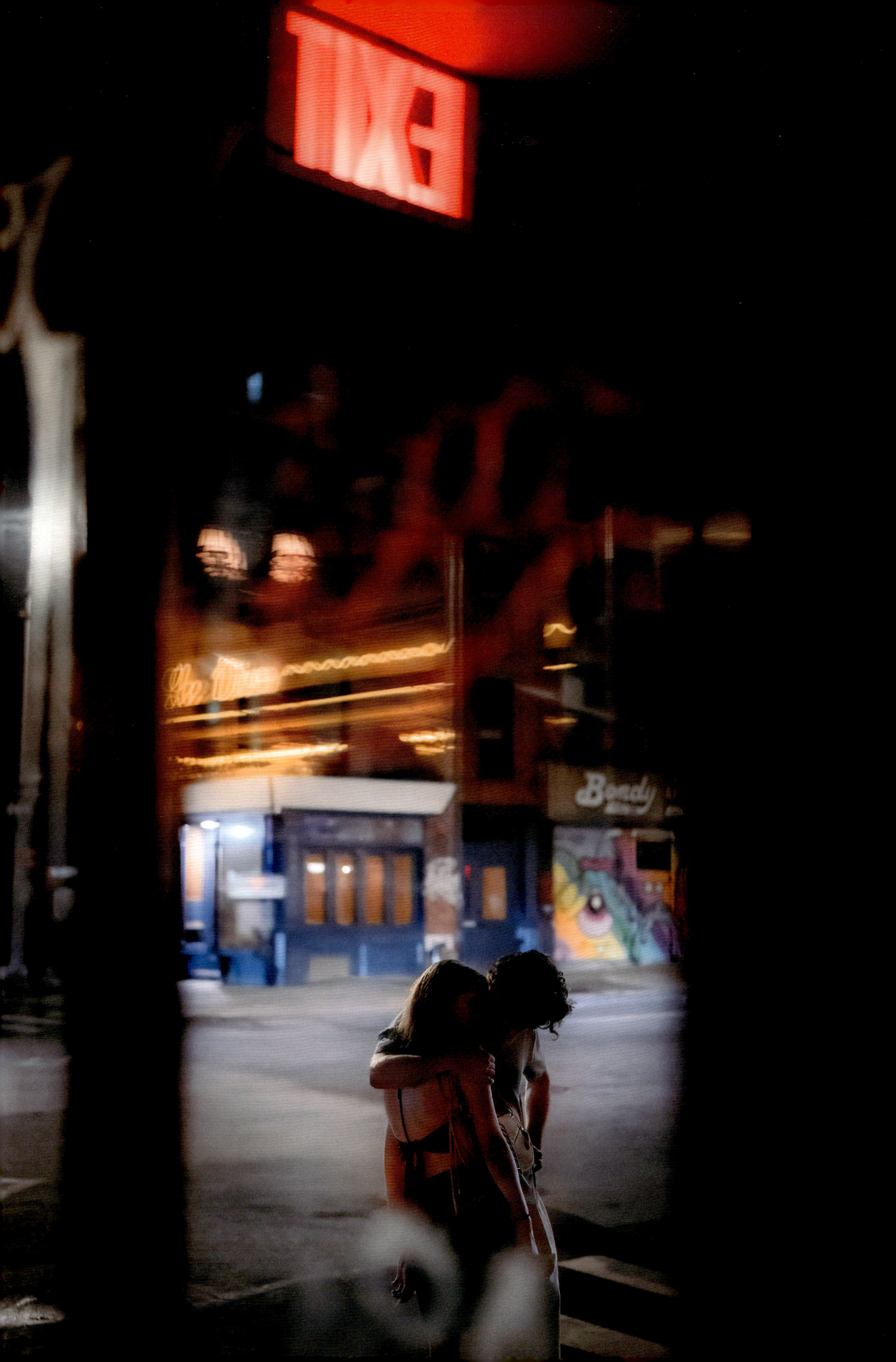
Bondy

Growing up in Malmo, Sweden, New York City wasn't just a place. It was an ideal, the city we all aspired to visit someday. My friends and I knew the city through movies and late-night television shows. Like so many others, I grew up with the dream of New York City in my head, but it wasn't until I moved here at 24 years old that I realized the dream was actually a living, breathing reality. It was better than I could have imagined. I thought my time in New York would be brief. I originally came to experience the city's energy for a season, and yet, decades later, I am still here.

There is a specific universe that explodes in New York the moment the sun sets. While half the world goes to sleep, New York's late-night soul wakes up—the cocktail lounges, the music venues, and the clubs that hum until dawn. But the "city that never sleeps" isn't just a cliché; it's a reputation that we, the people who live here, have a collective duty to uphold.

Whether you are a delivery driver weaving through traffic or a hospitality veteran serving patrons well past midnight, there is an unwritten responsibility to keep the gears turning. Every person, from the early morning commuters to the late-night cab drivers, plays a part in creating this world. It's a legacy built by people from every corner of the globe who arrived with the same thought I had: *I need to be a part of that.*

After years of living in the thick of it, you can sometimes grow numb to the magic of New York's nighttime energy. It's easy to take for granted the ability to walk down the streets late at night and still be surrounded by people. Or how you can get a slice of pizza at 3am in almost every corner of the city. Or that there is public transportation to take you home no matter what time the night ends. It's only when I leave New York that I'm hit with the understanding that I never want to stay away for long. In New York, the middle of the chaos is where I feel the most comfortable. It is where I finally learned to relax.

When I left the hospitality world to open BonBon, I knew we had to honor that spirit. To be a true New York institution, you have to be there when the people are out. And that meant staying open until midnight, seven days a week. We opened our doors to match the rhythm of the city, proving that in a place this vibrant, there is always someone looking for what you're offering—even if it's Swedish candy at midnight.

Selim Adira
Co-Founder, BonBon - A Swedish Candy Co.

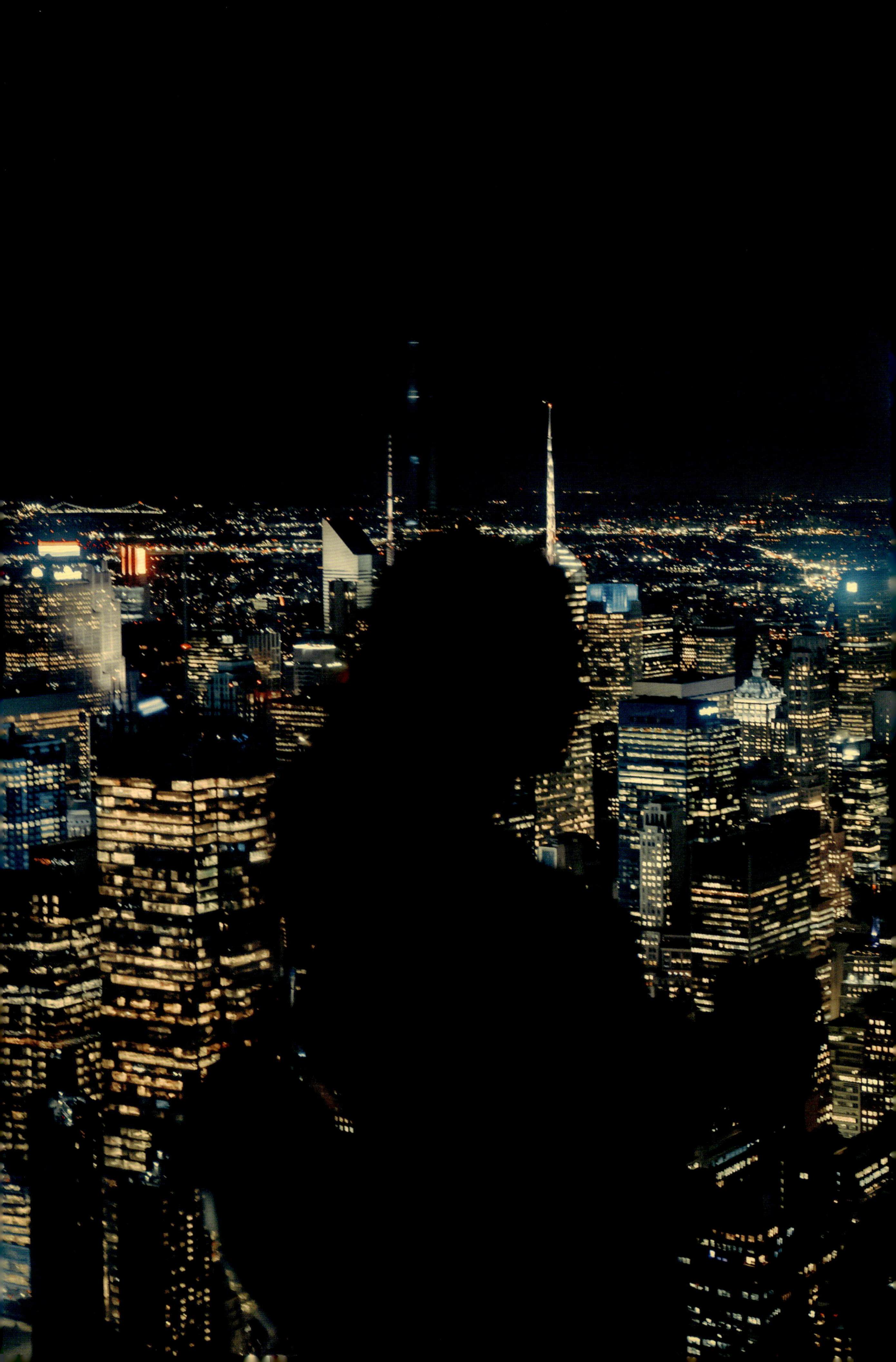

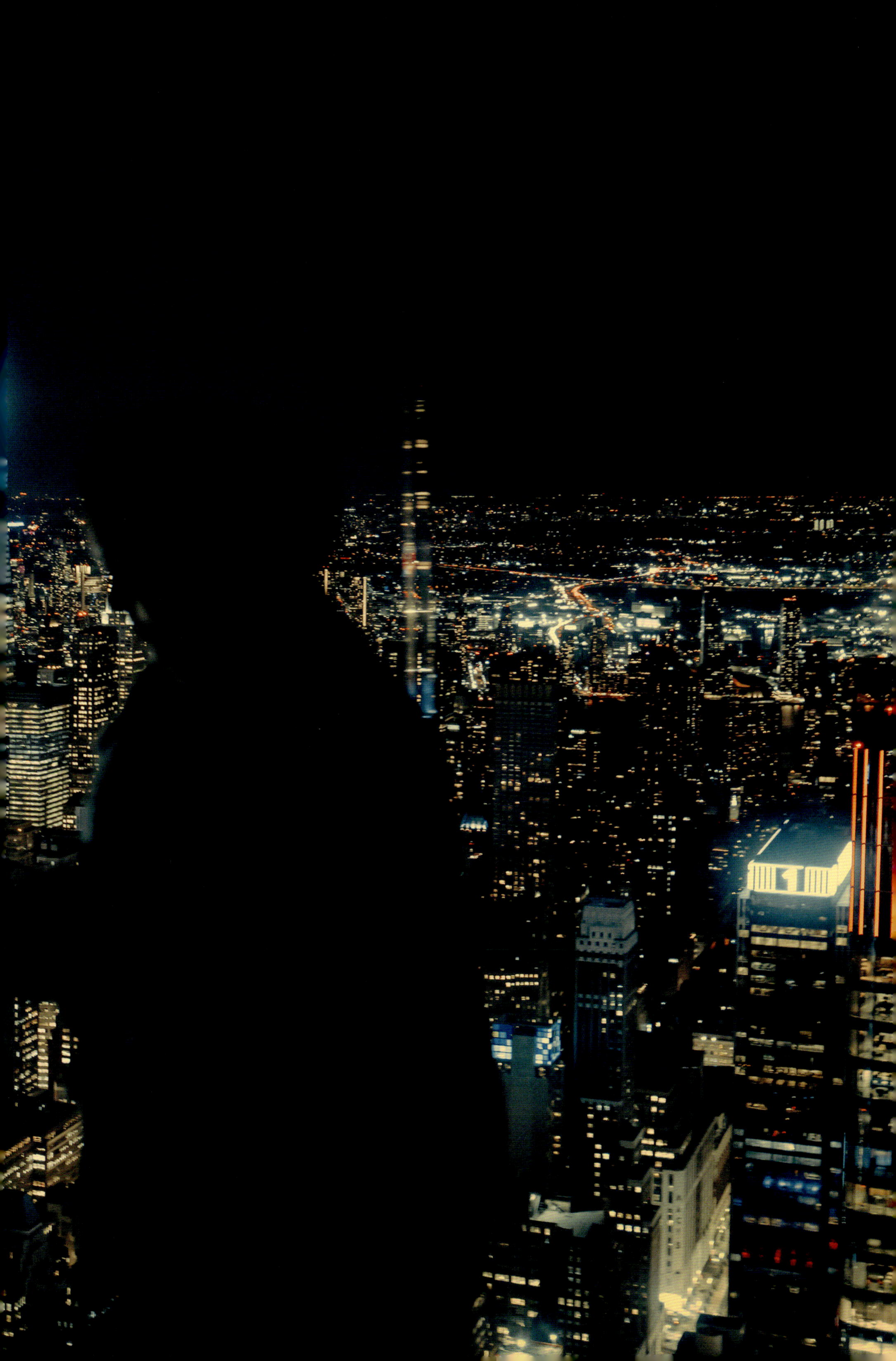

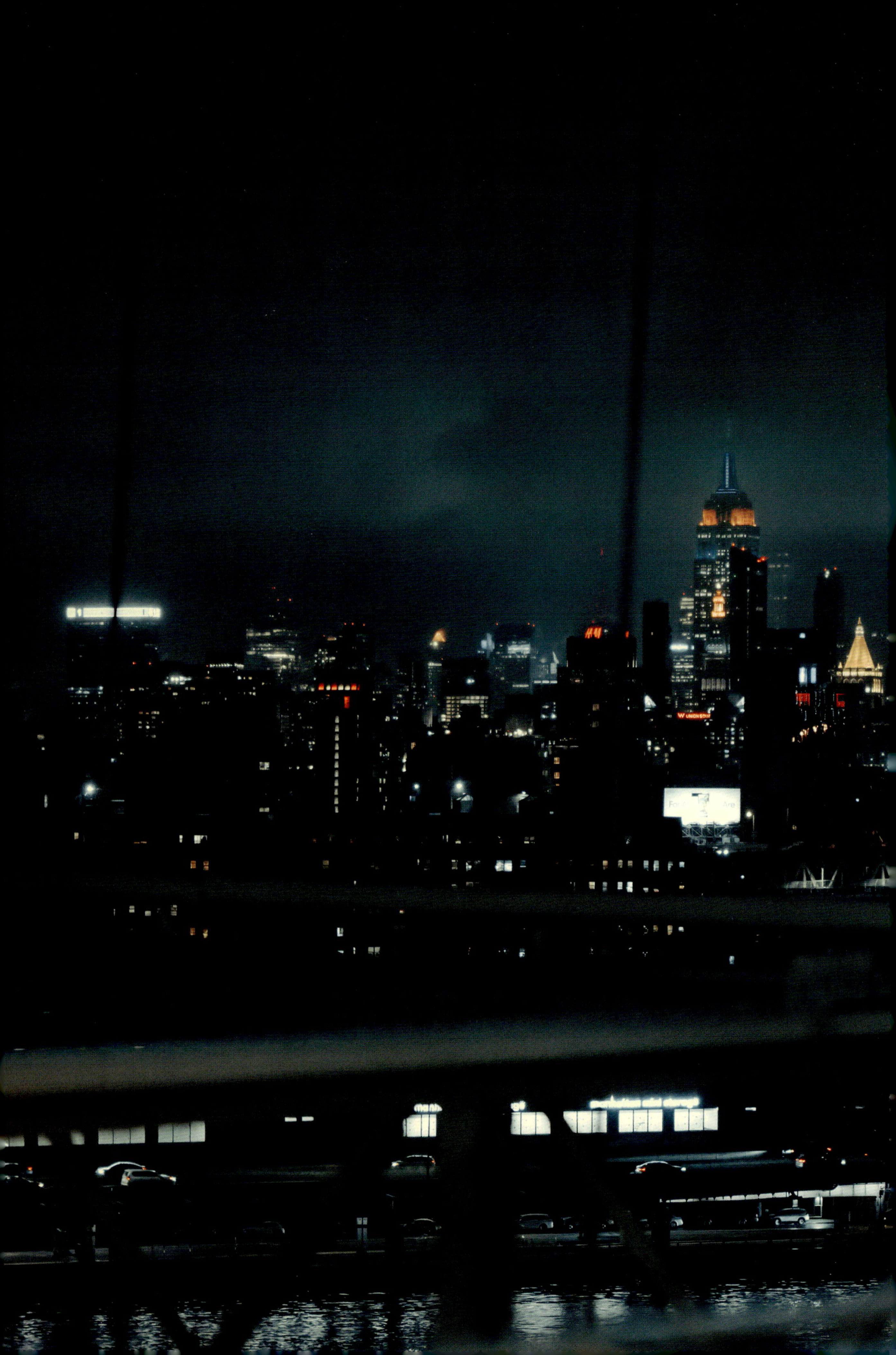

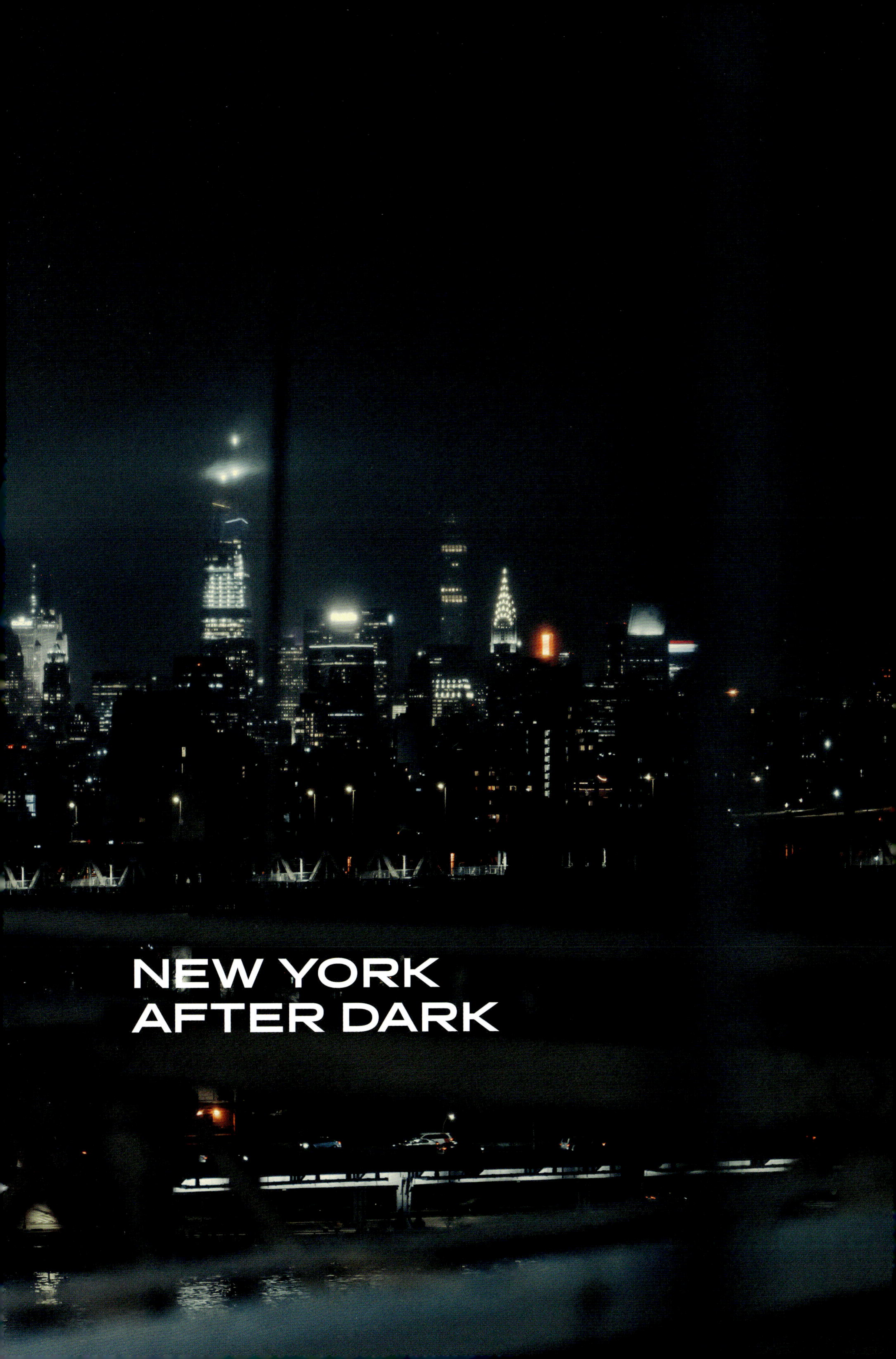

NEW YORK AFTER DARK

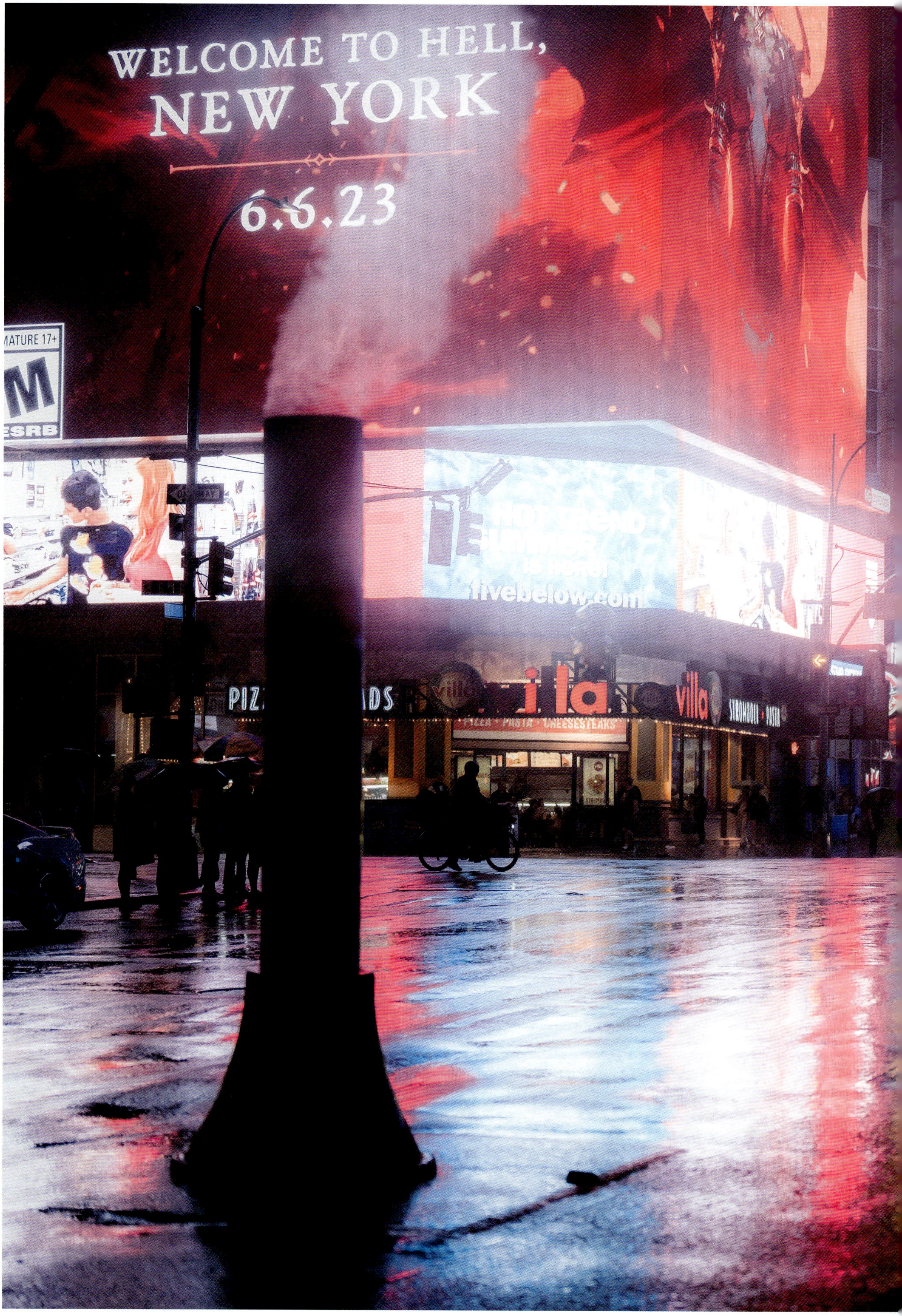

TIMES SQUARE

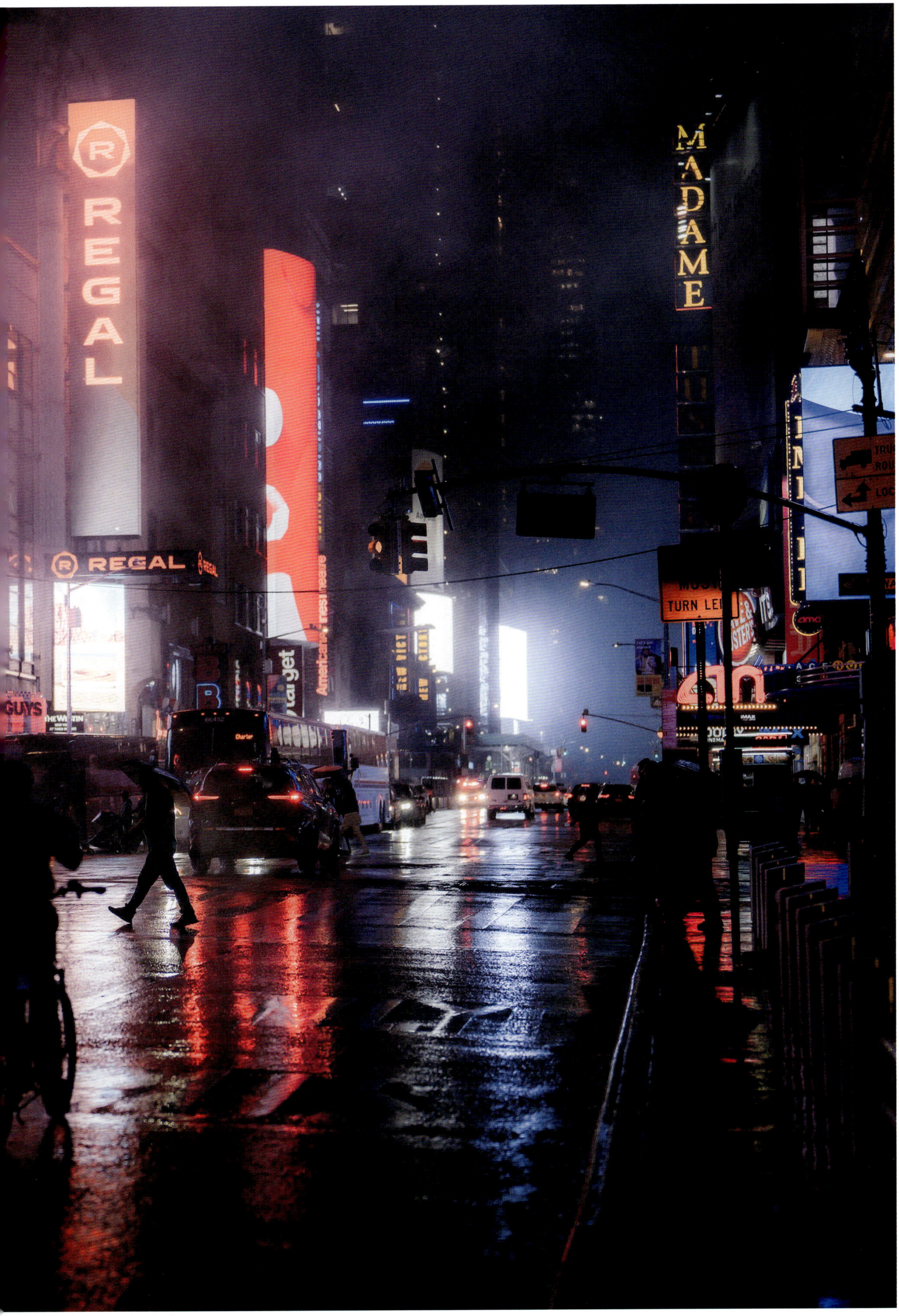
REGAL
REGAL
MADAME

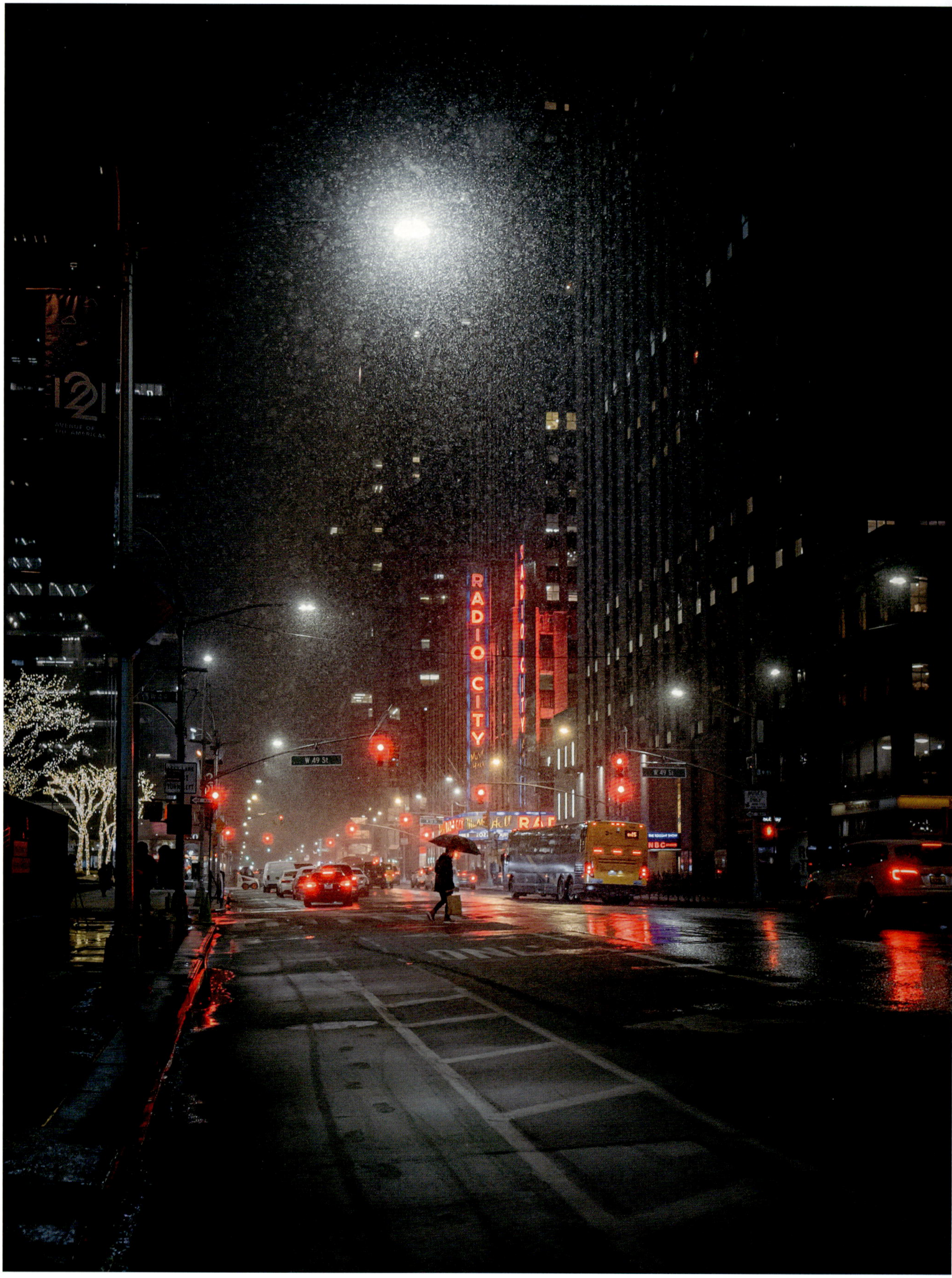
RADIO CITY
W 49 St
NBC

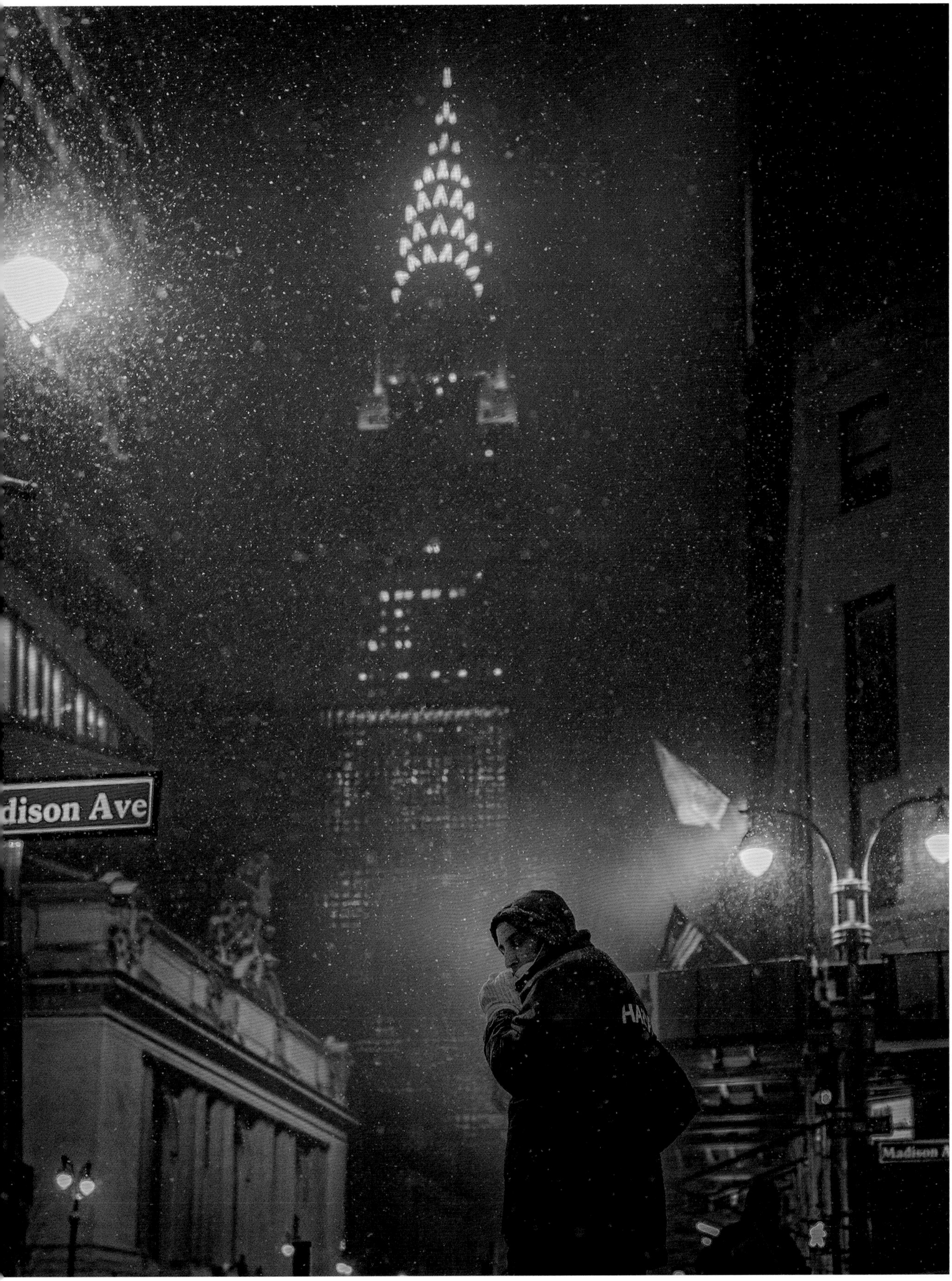
dison Ave
Madison A

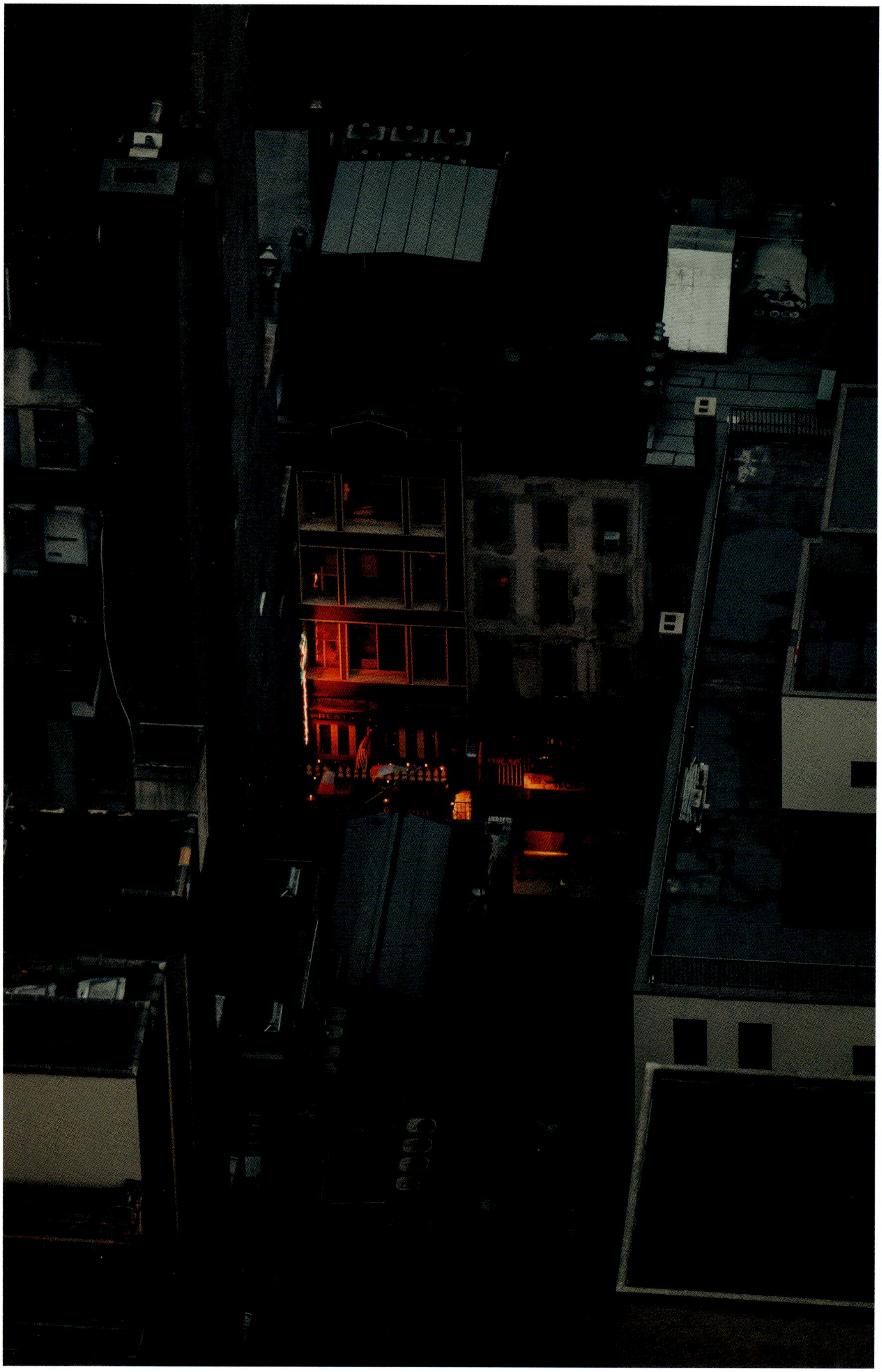

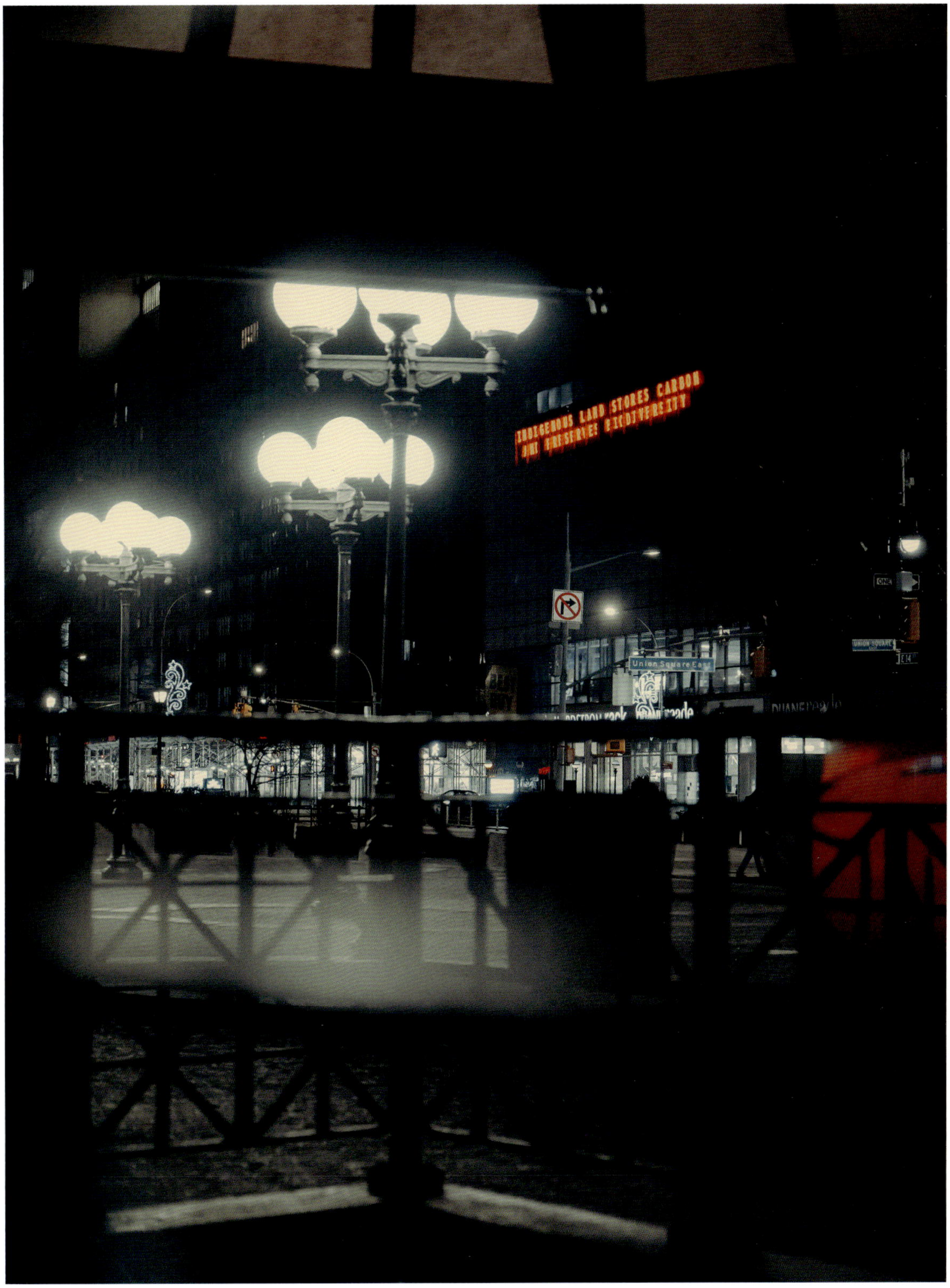
INDIGENOUS LAND STORES CARBON

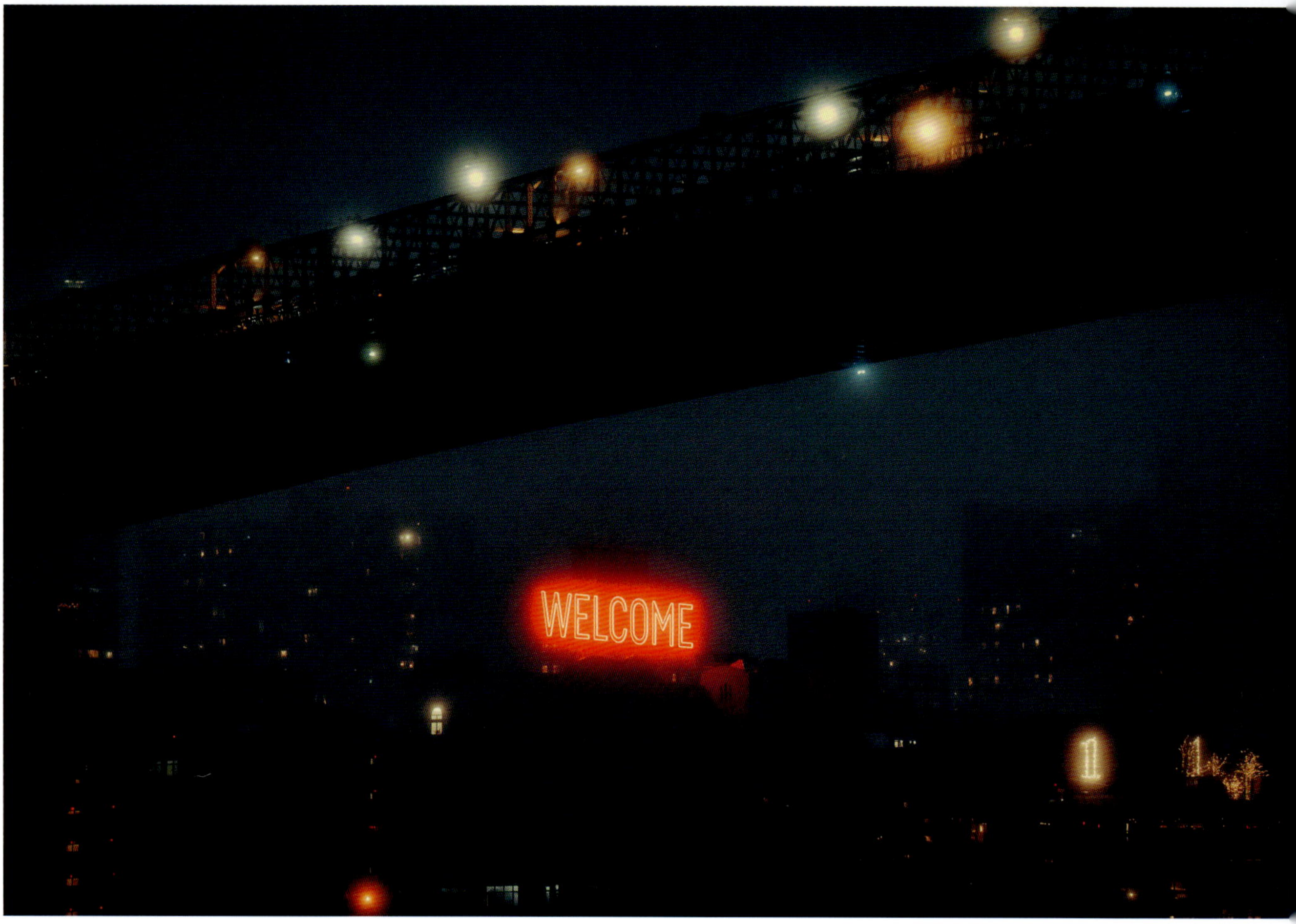
WELCOME

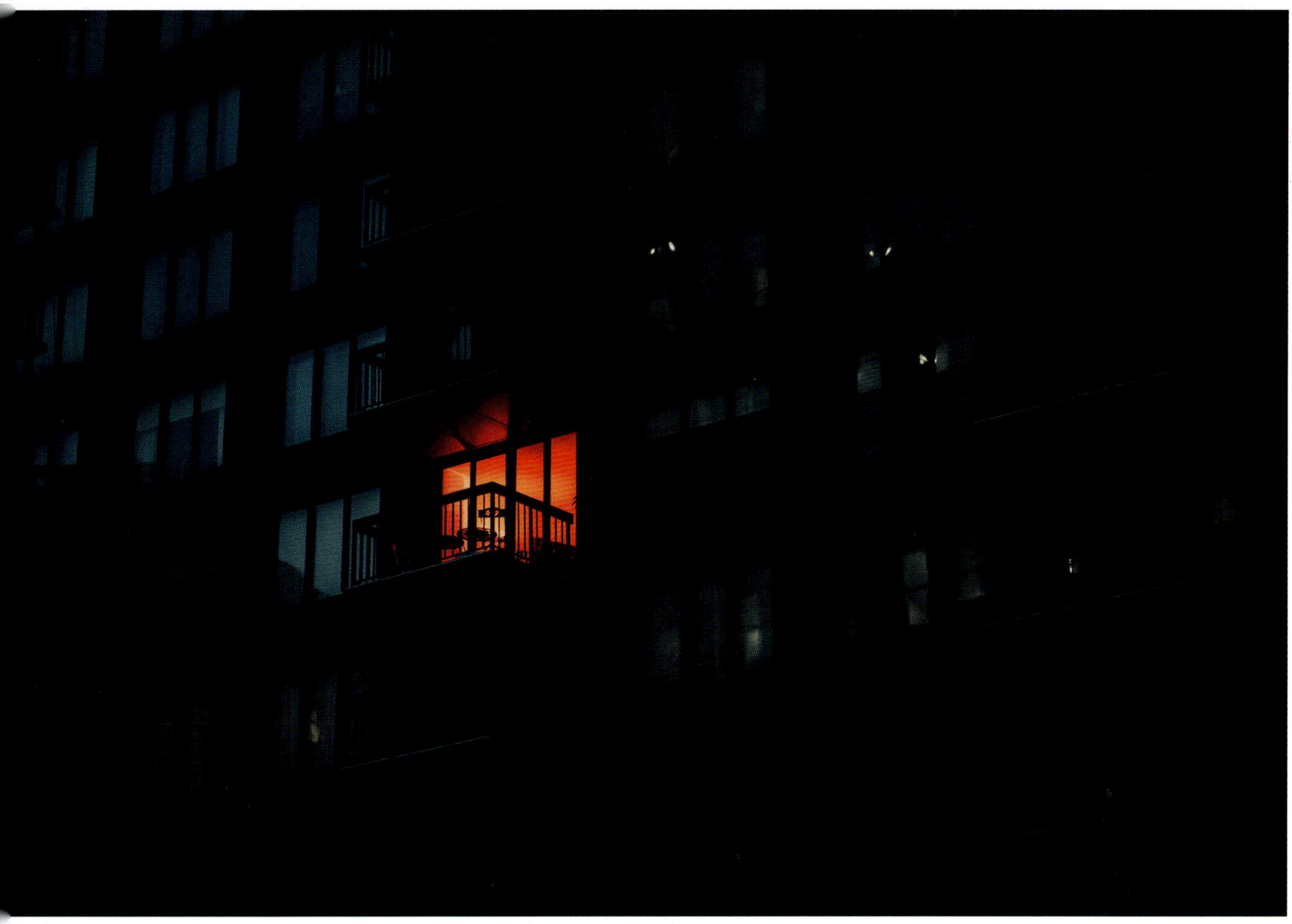

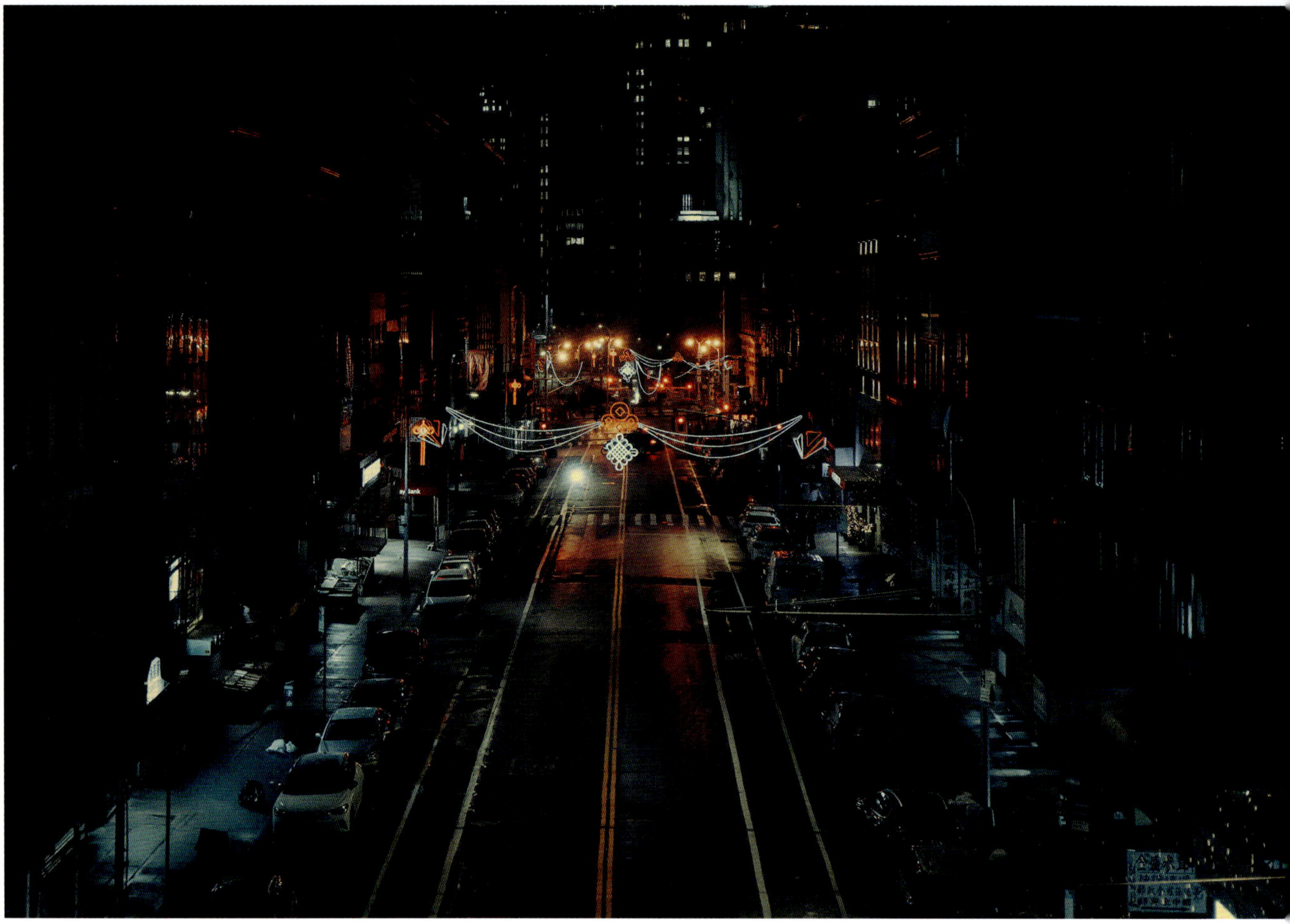

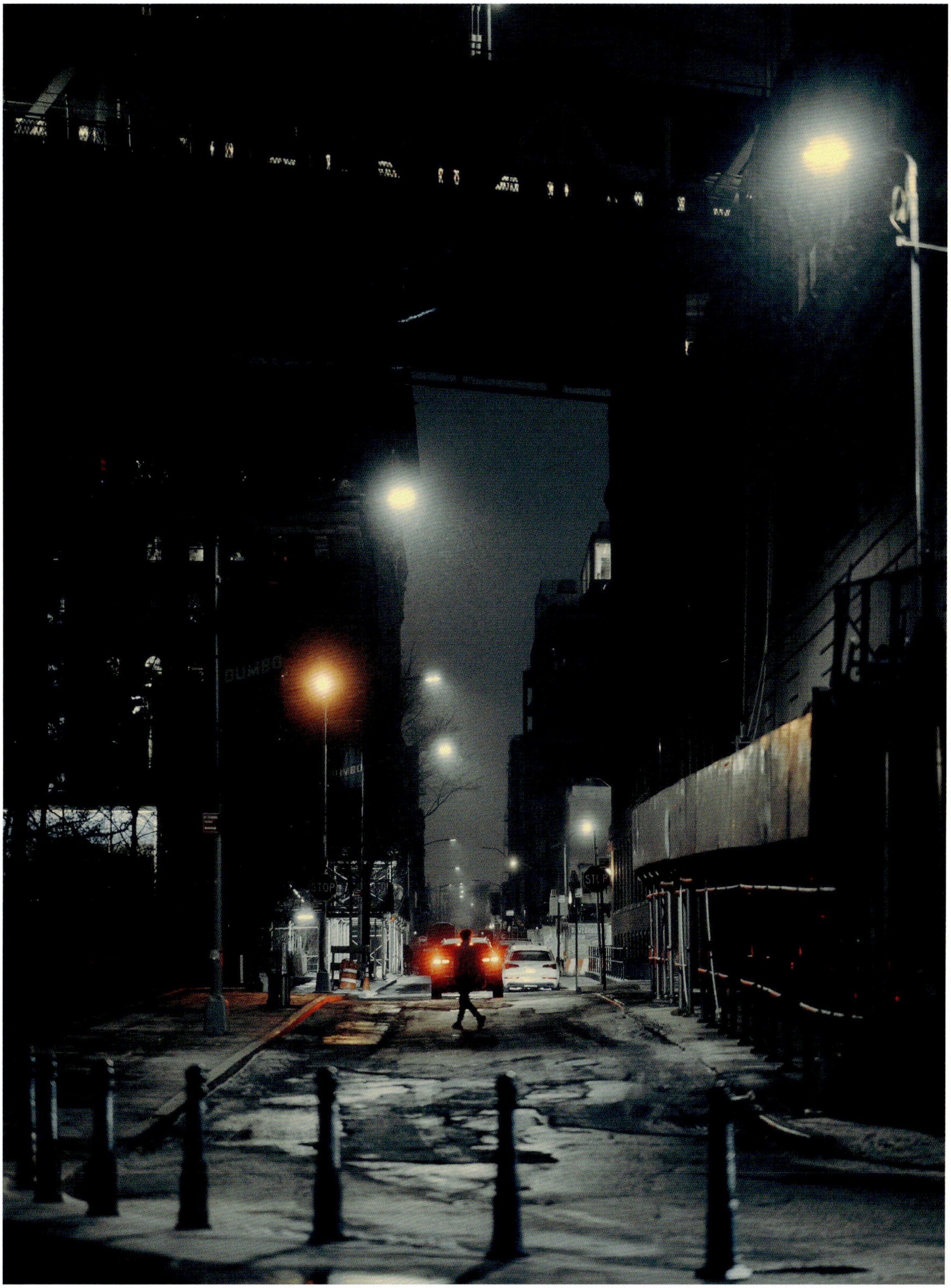
STOP

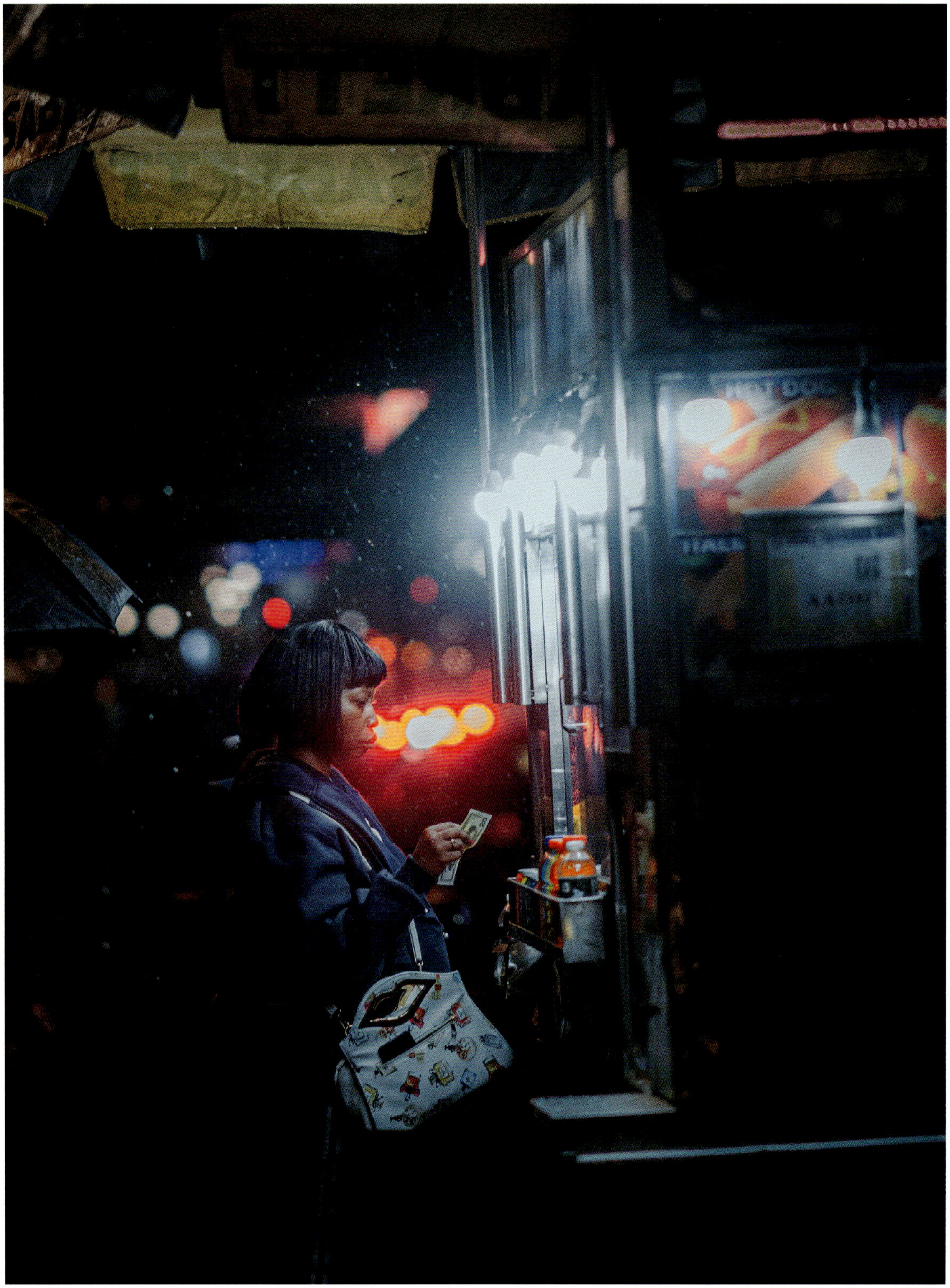

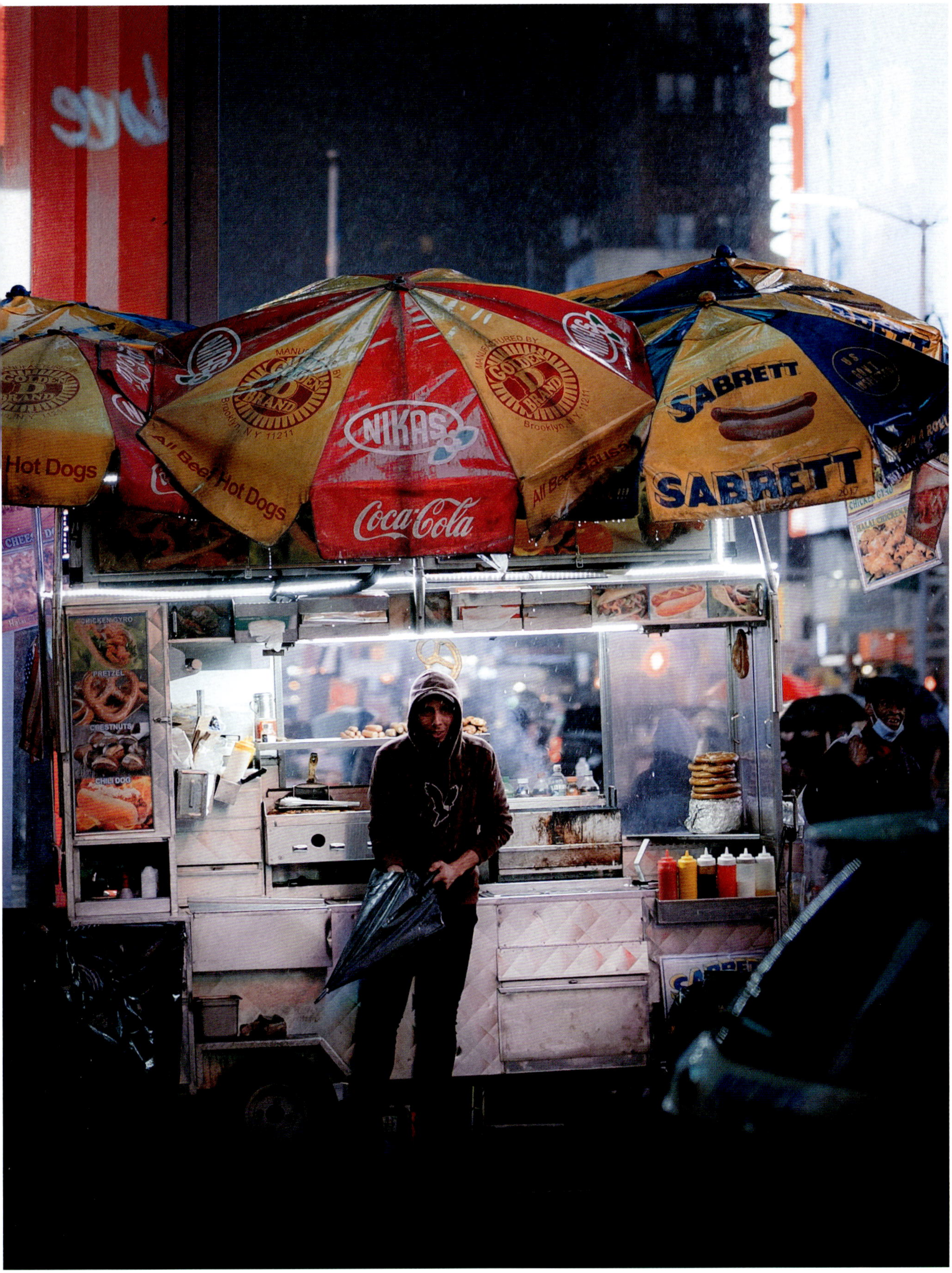
NIKAS
Coca-Cola
All Beef Hot Dogs
Hot Dogs
SABRETT
SABRETT

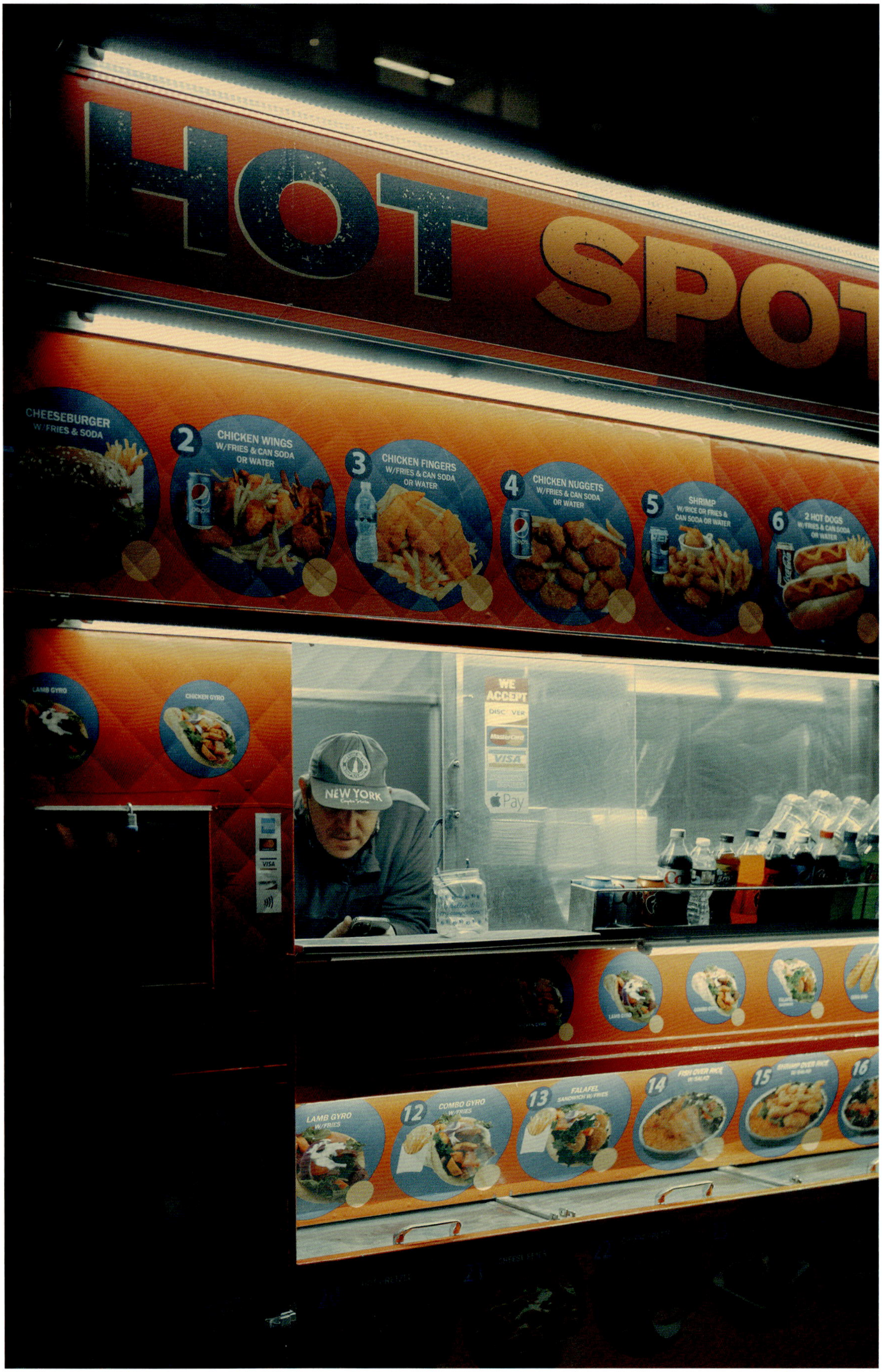
HOT SPO
CHEESEBURGER
W/ FRIES & SODA
2 CHICKEN WINGS
W/FRIES & CAN SODA
OR WATER
3 CHICKEN FINGERS
W/FRIES & CAN SODA
OR WATER
4 CHICKEN NUGGETS
W/FRIES & CAN SODA
OR WATER
5 SHRIMP
6 2 HOT DOGS
LAMB GYRO
CHICKEN GYRO
WE ACCEPT
DISCOVER
MasterCard
VISA
Pay
NEW YORK
LAMB GYRO
W/FRIES
12 COMBO GYRO
W/FRIES
13 FALAFEL
14
15
16

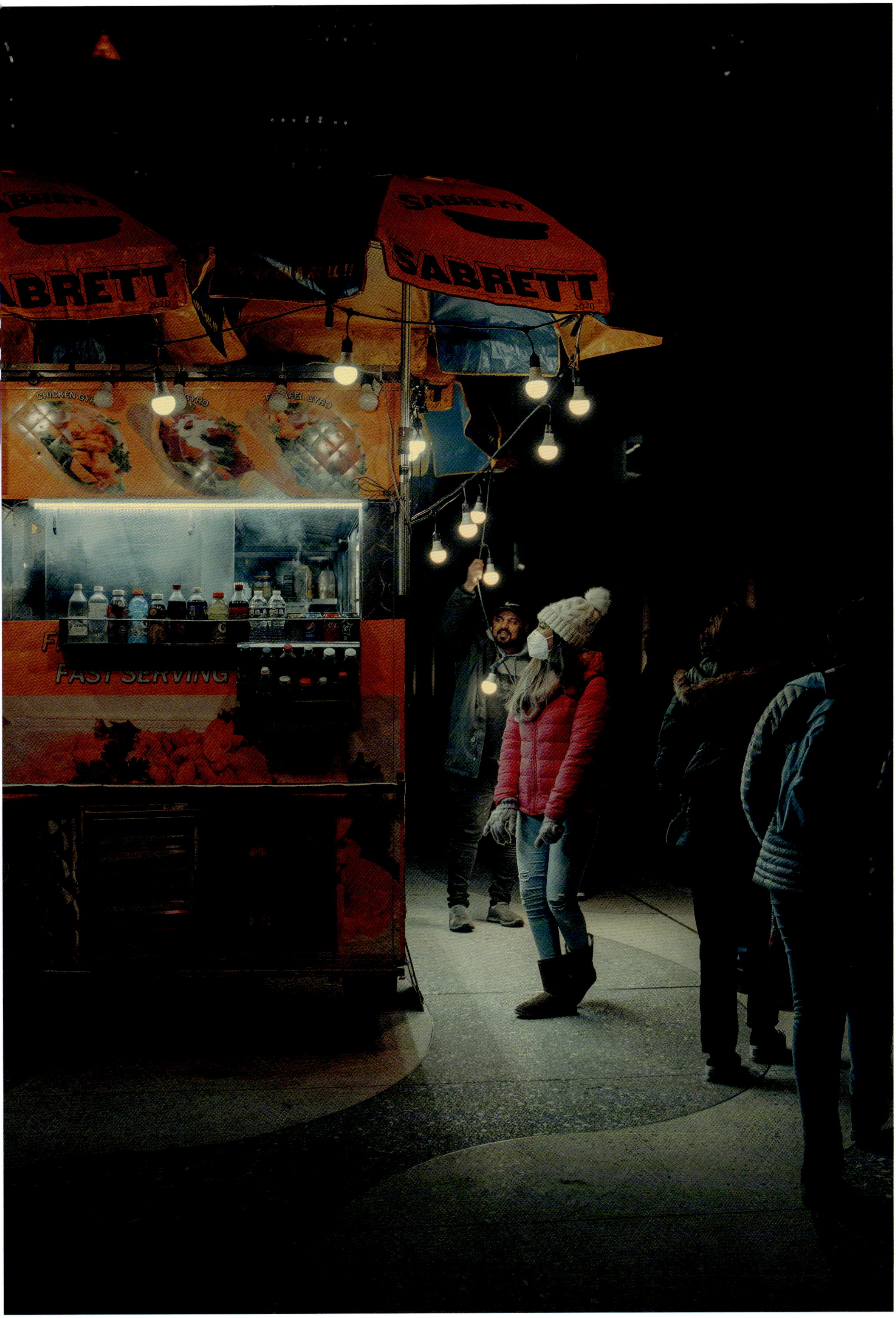
SABRETT
SABRETT
FAST SERVING

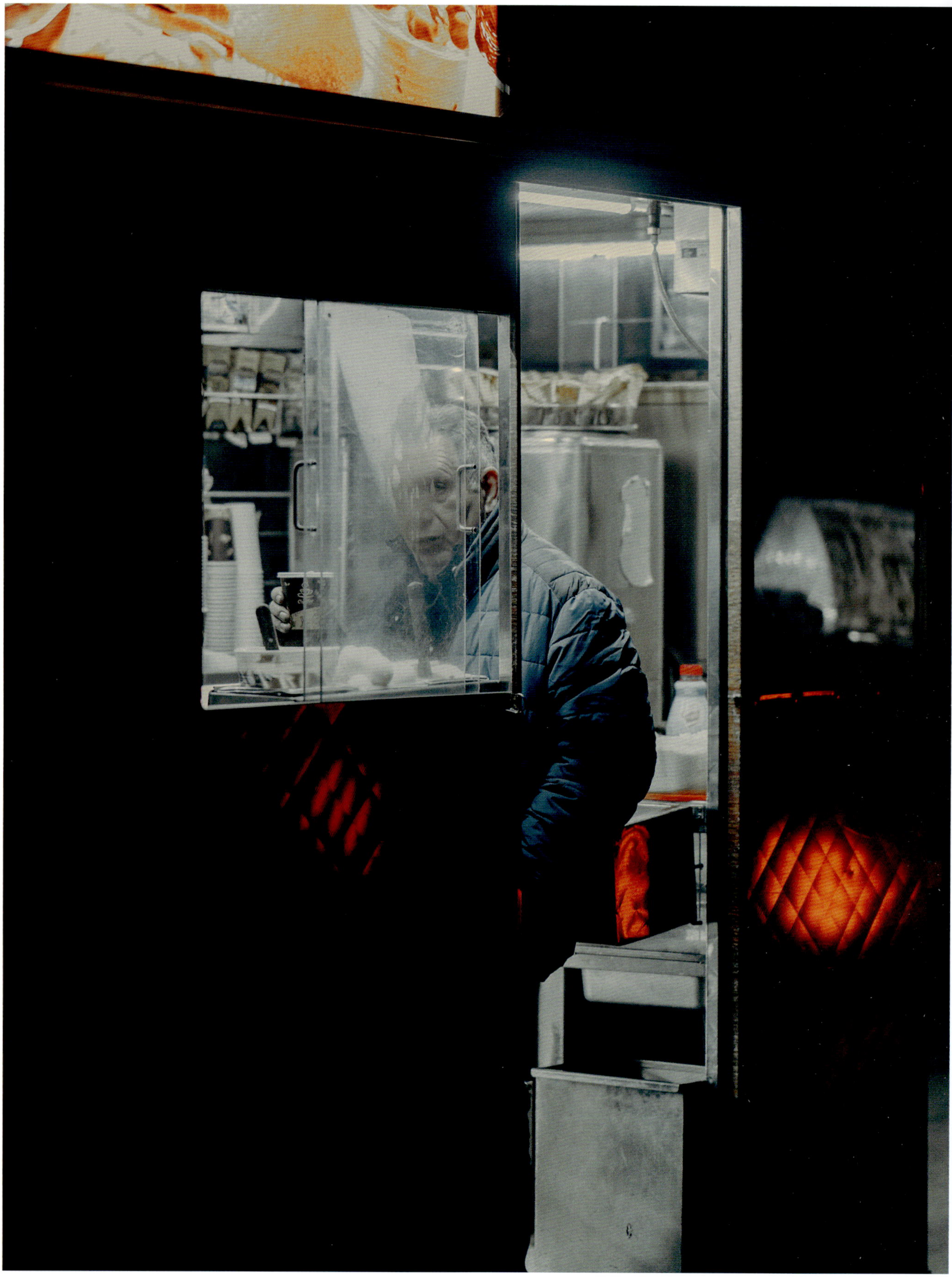

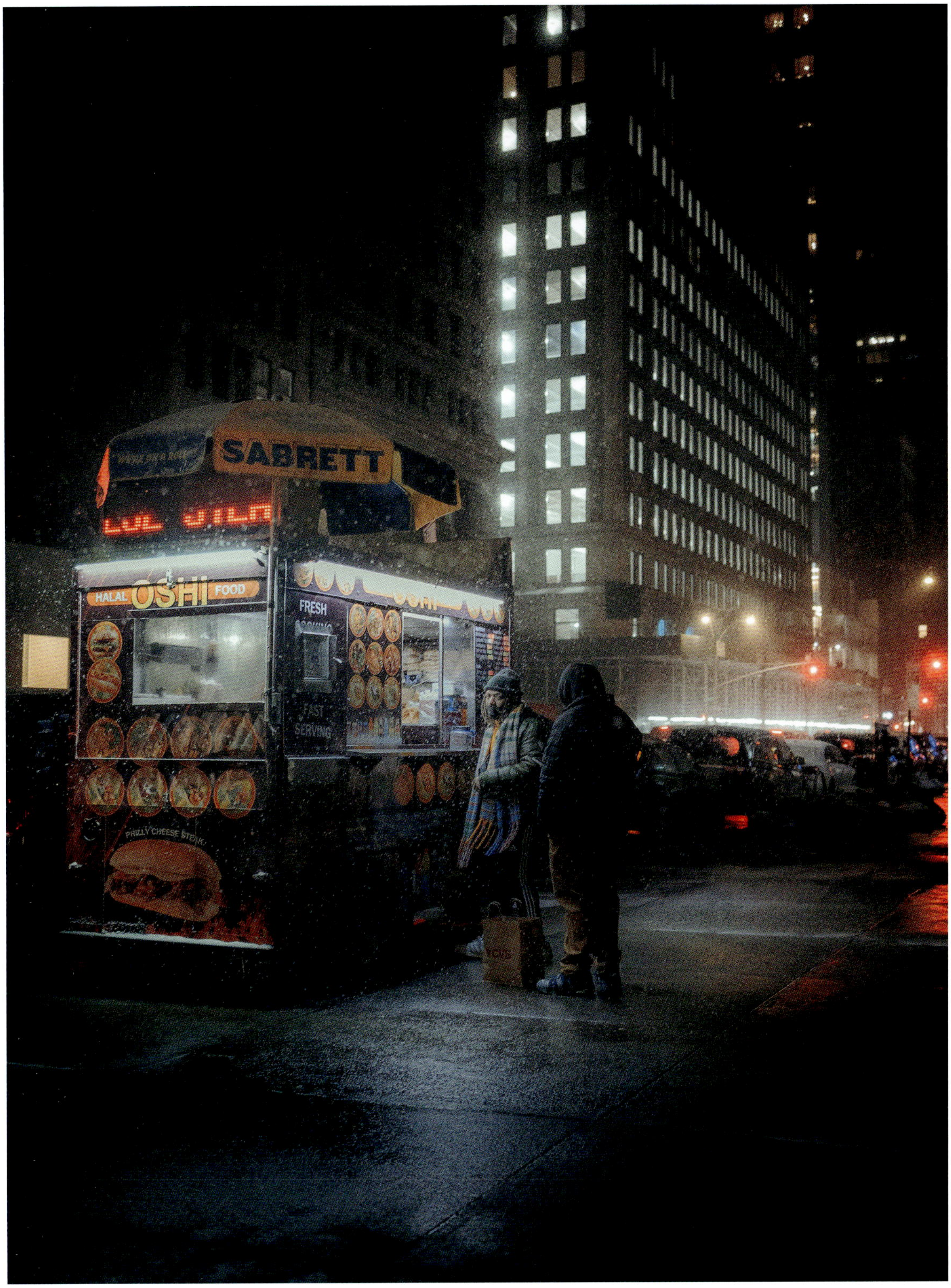
SABRETT
HALAL OSHI FOOD
FRESH
FAST SERVING

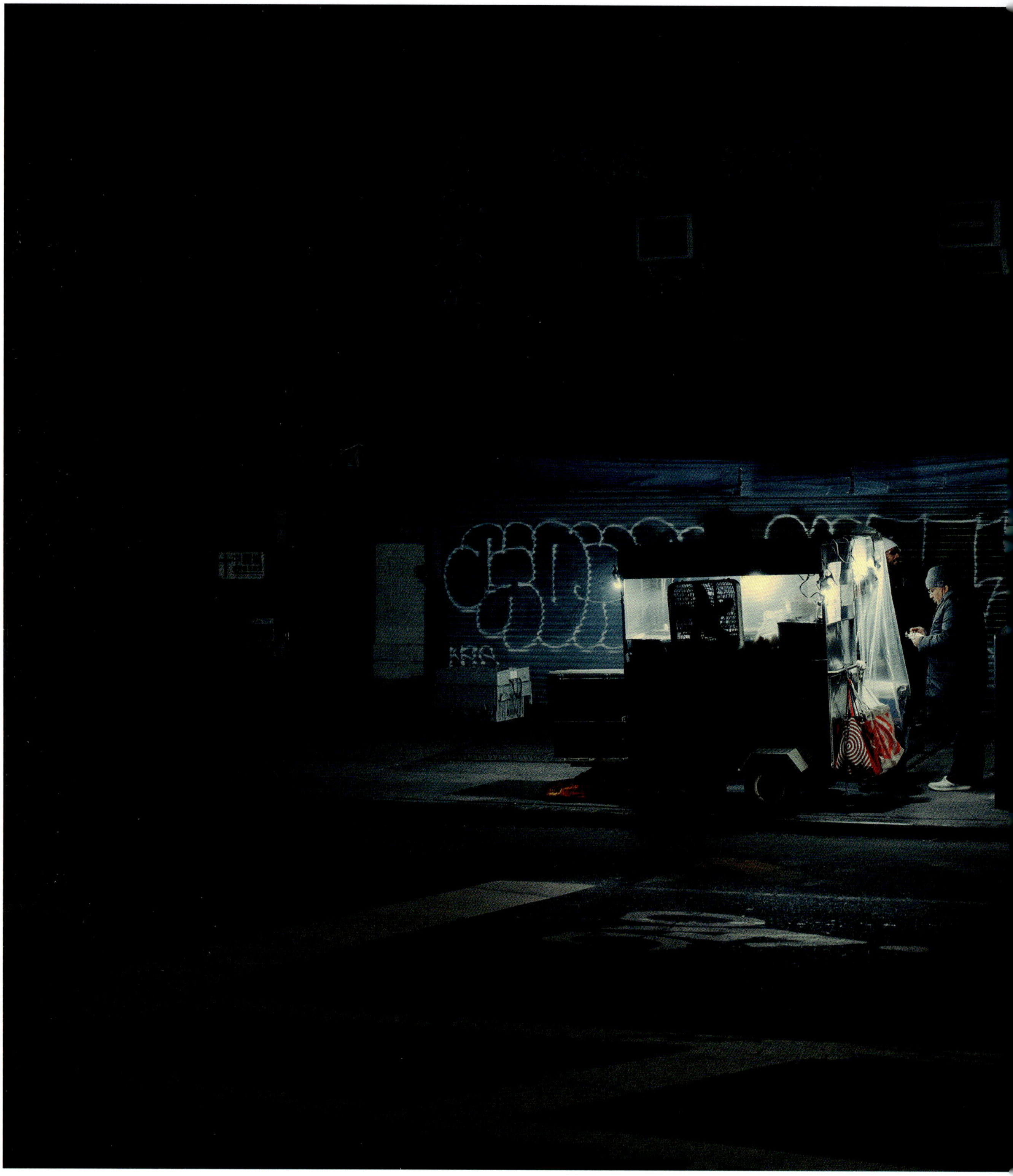

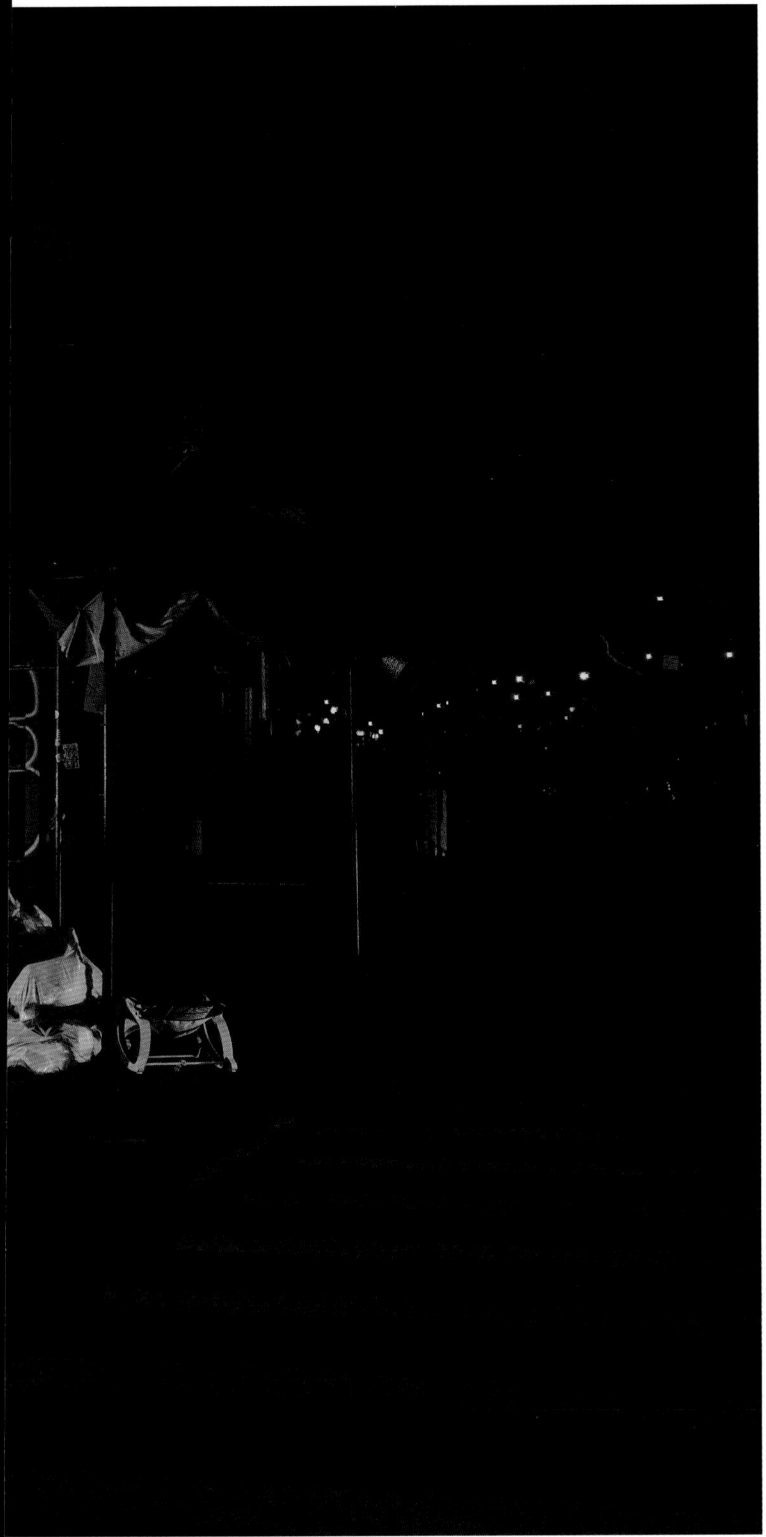

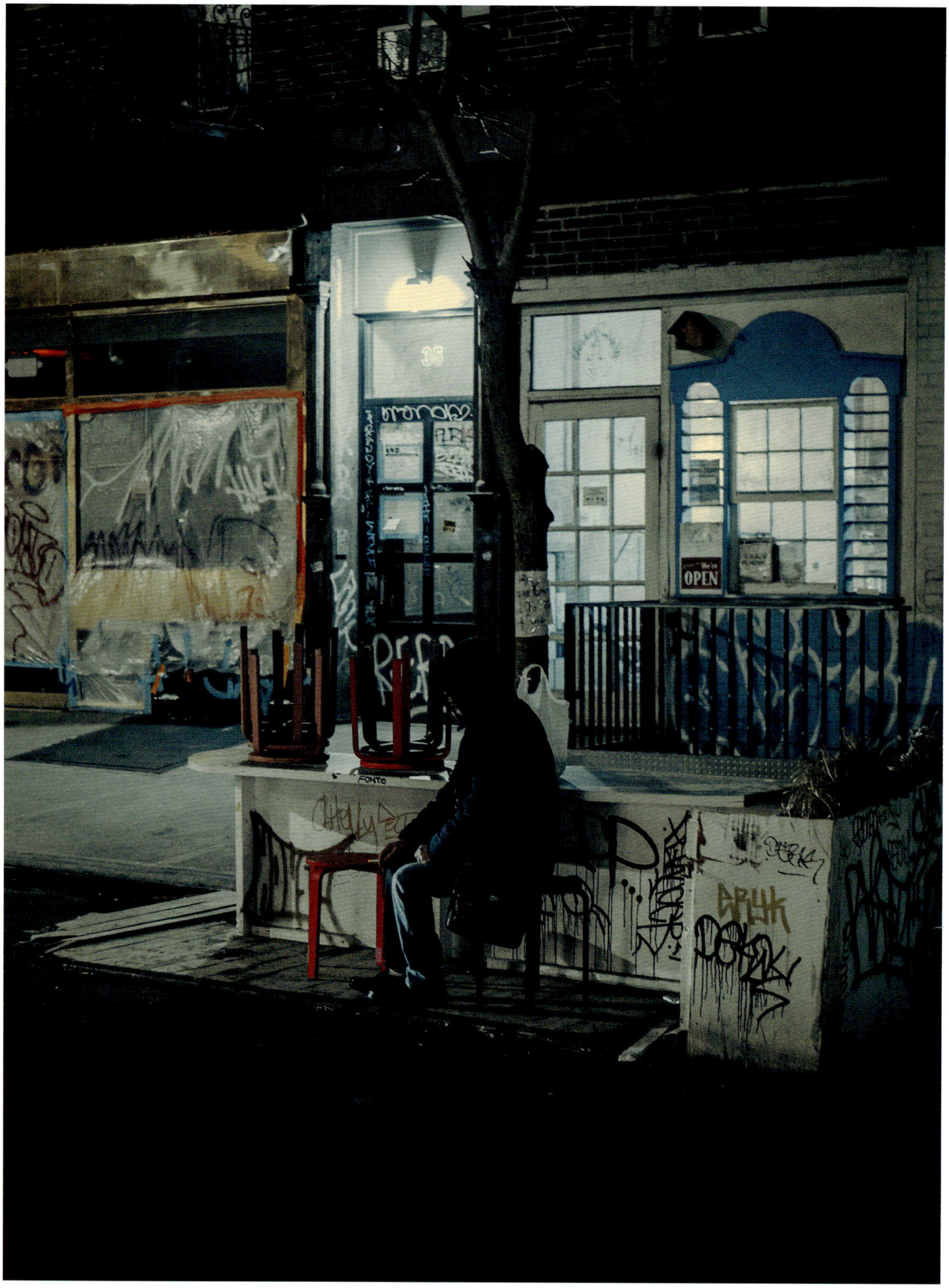
35
We're
OPEN

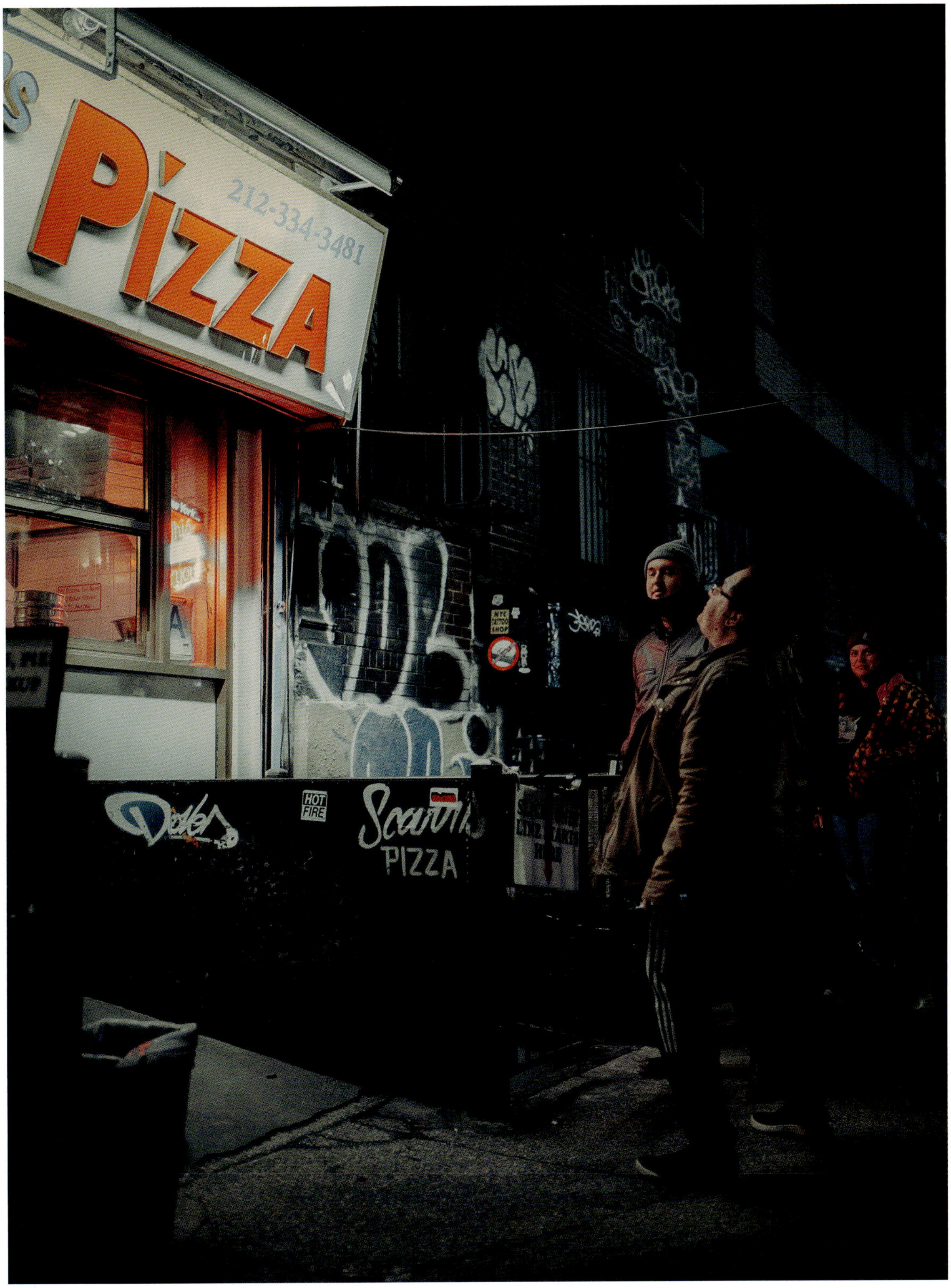
PIZZA
212-334-3481
HOT FIRE
PIZZA

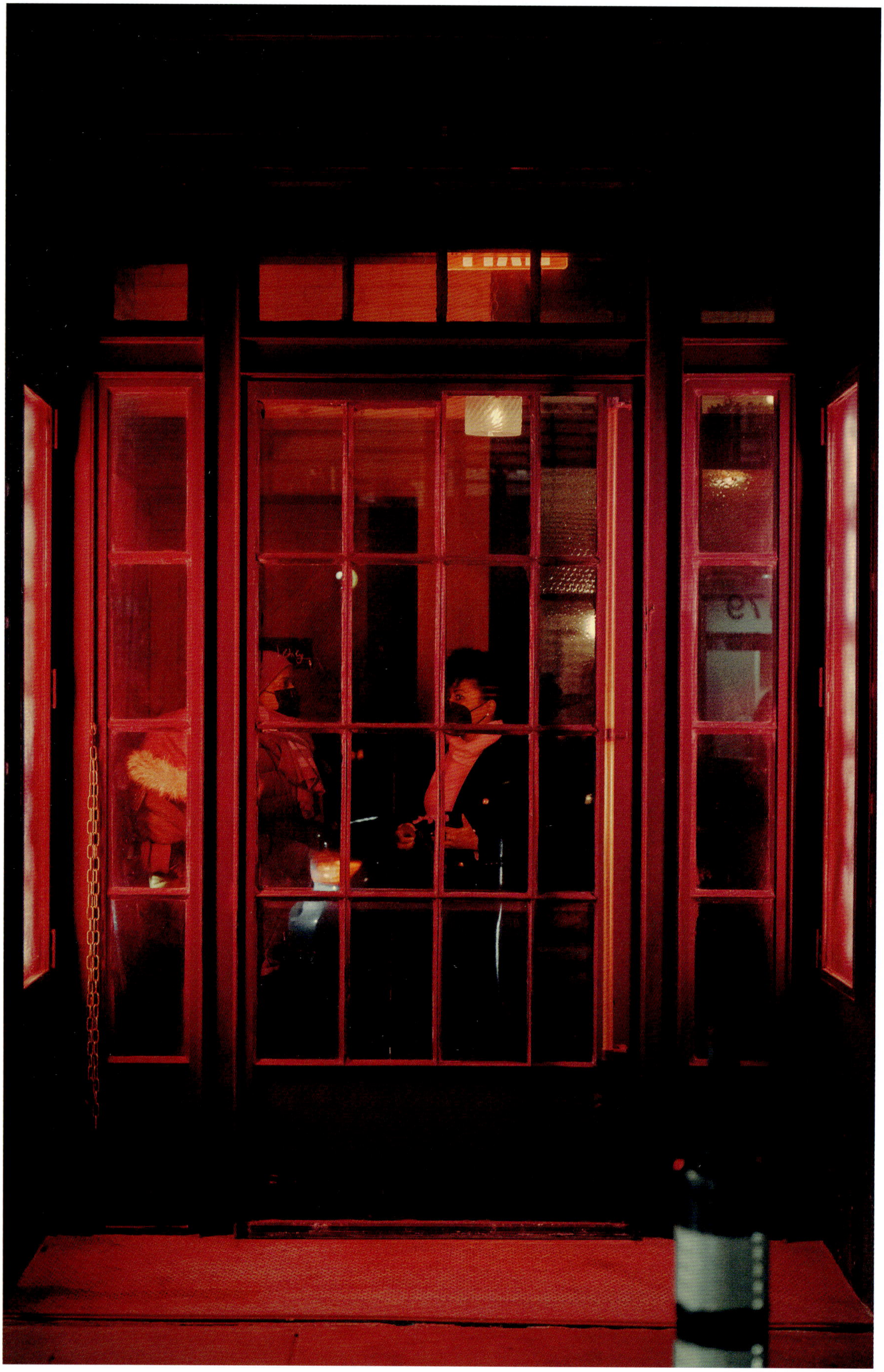

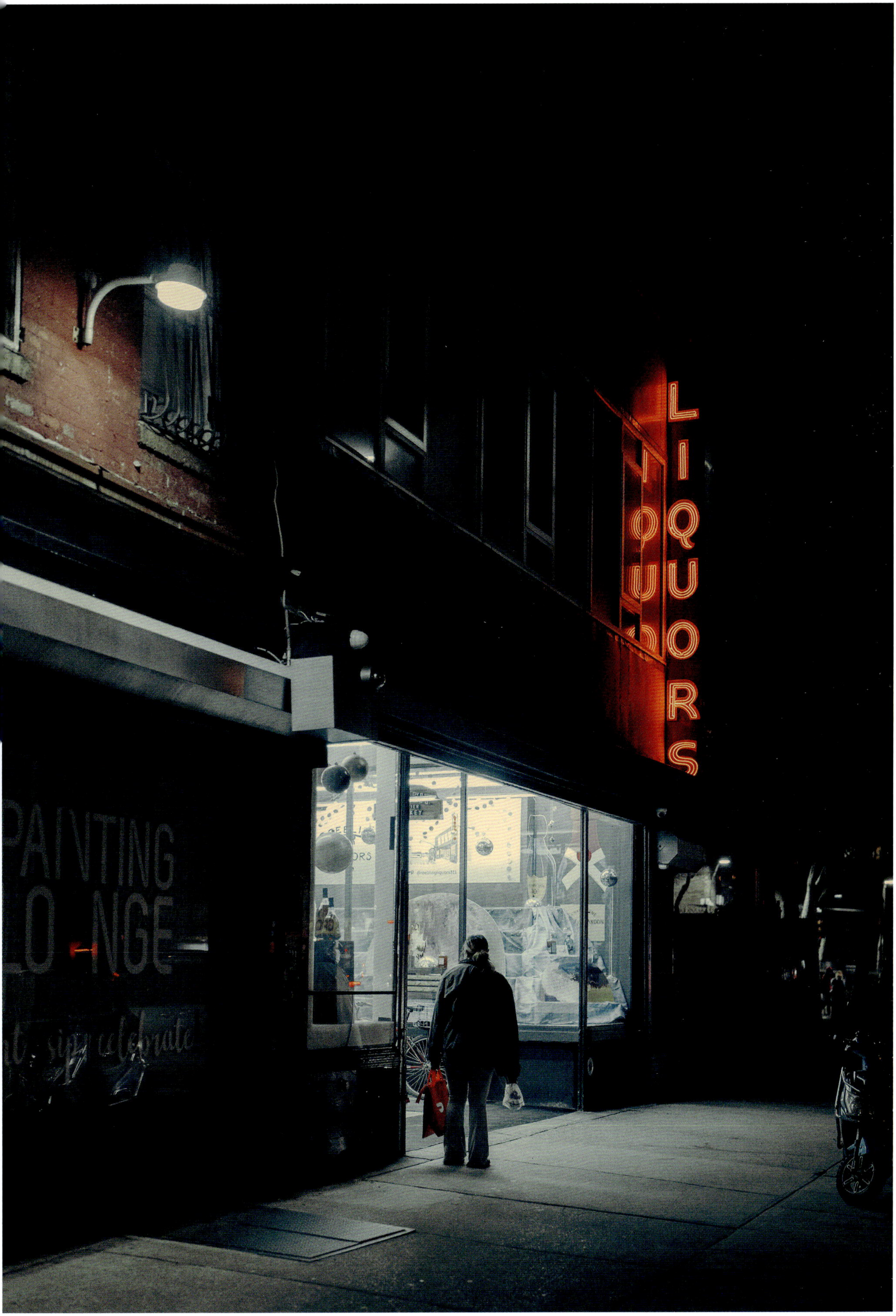
LIQUORS
PAINTING

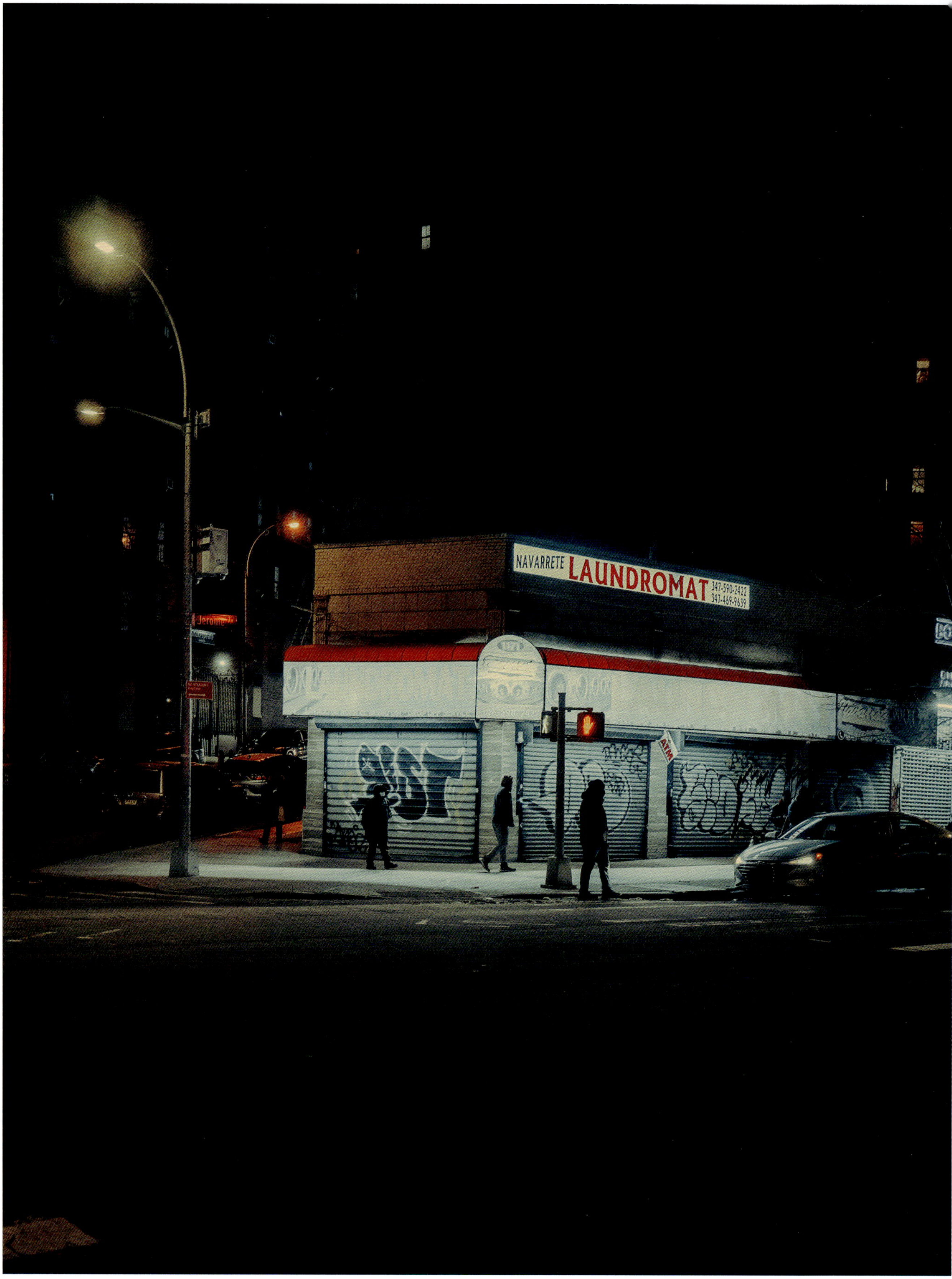
NAVARRETE LAUNDROMAT
347-590-2422
347-469-9639
Jerome
ATM

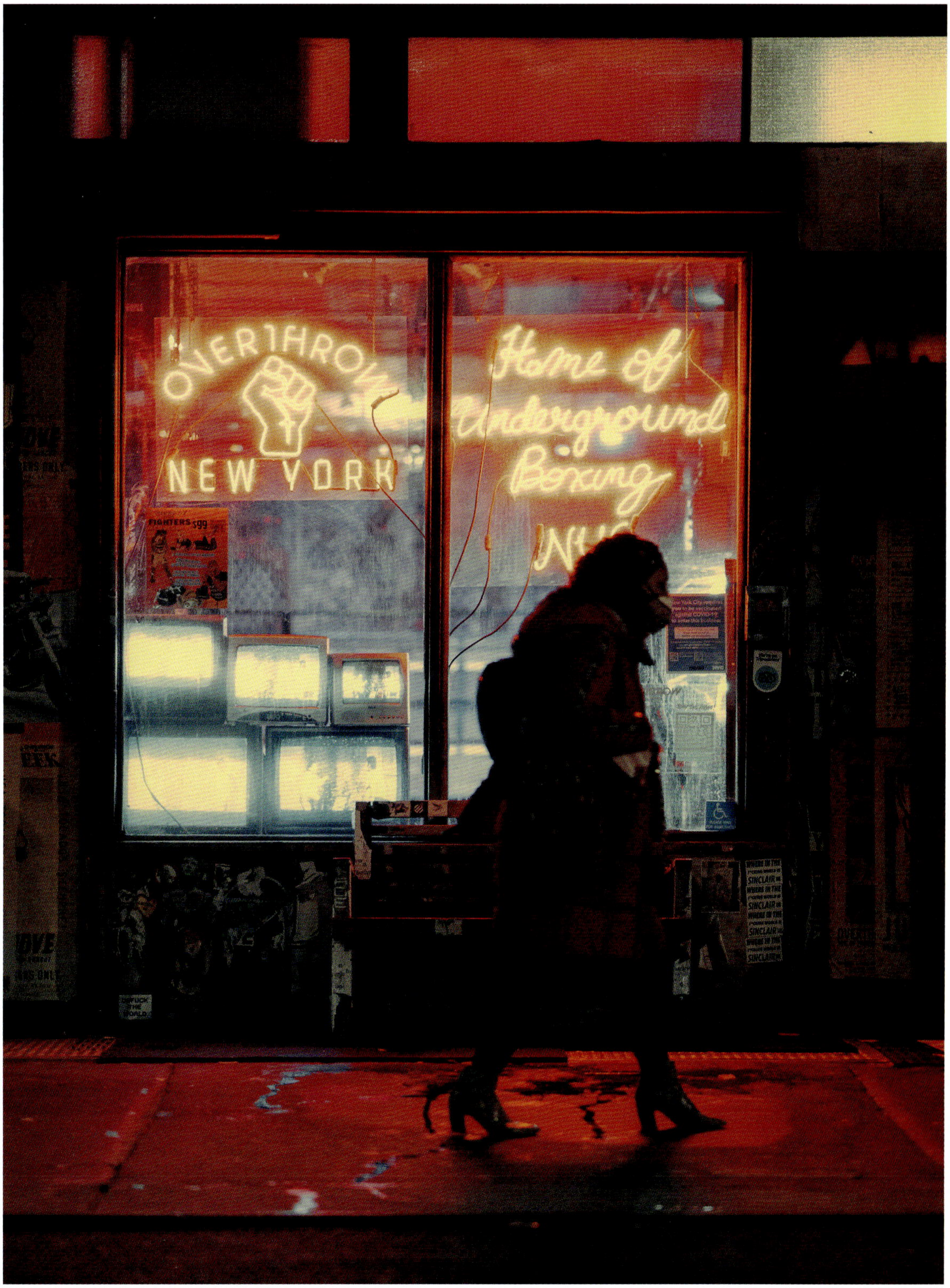
OVERTHROW
NEW YORK
Home of
Underground
Boxing

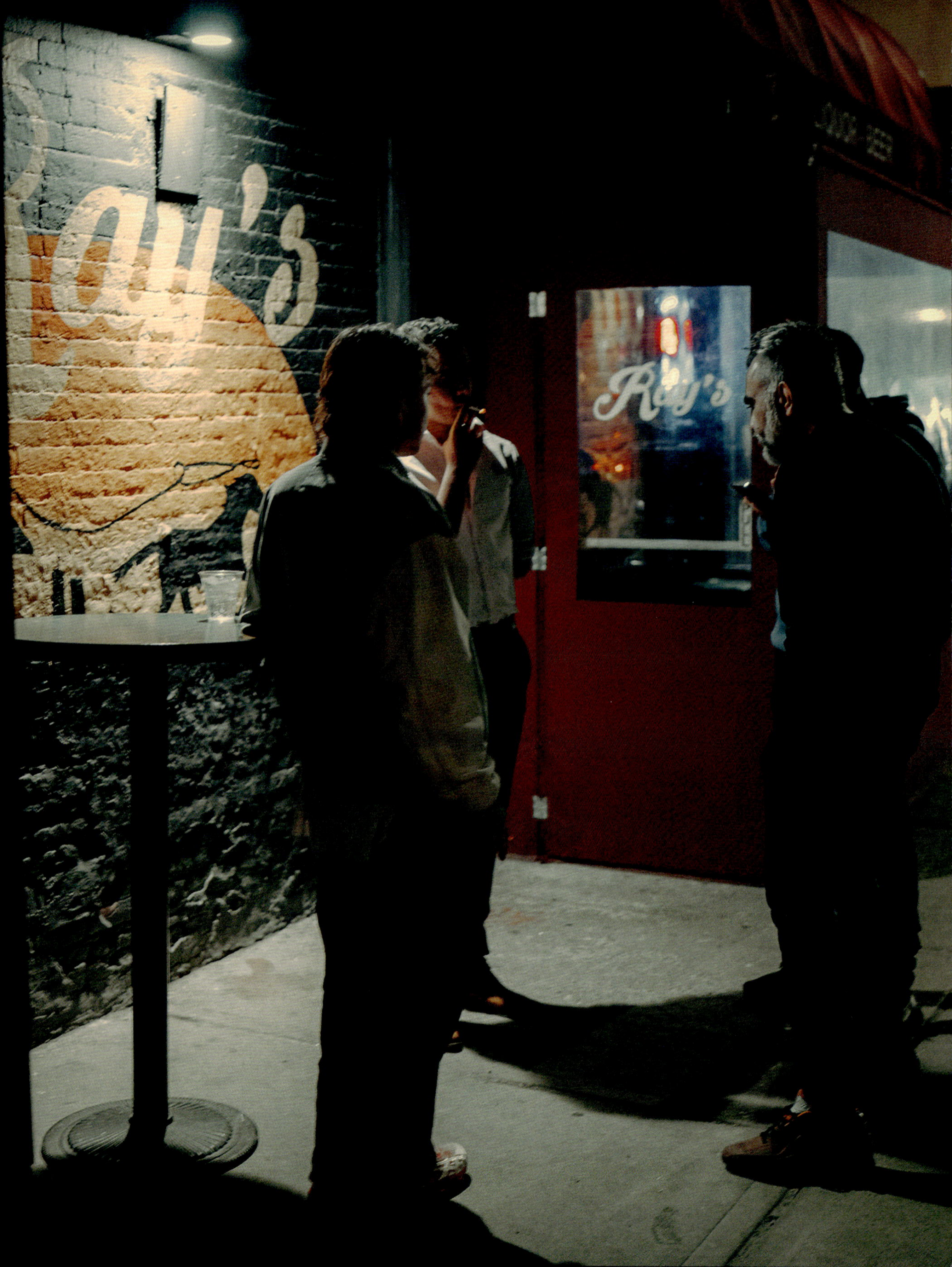
Ray's
Ray's

New York City has a reputation for constant movement, something that continues well after the sun goes down. Pedestrians walk New York's streets at all hours of the day; even late at night, it is uncommon to find yourself alone on the city's sidewalks. While overall volume may taper after midnight, the flow of pedestrians rarely stops.

Late dinners are often the norm in New York. In neighborhoods such as the West Village, the Lower East Side, Koreatown, and parts of Brooklyn, restaurants routinely seat guests at 9pm, 10pm, or later. It is common to see diners lingering over meals well past 11pm, particularly on Fridays and Saturdays. Some establishments operate until midnight or later, while 24-hour diners and some casual eateries continue serving throughout the night. Sidewalks outside restaurants remain active, with patrons waiting for tables, lingering over conversations, or walking between venues.

Bars and nightlife venues extend activity further into the early morning. New York State law permits alcohol service until 4am, and many bars, clubs, and lounges operate until that time. In areas with high concentrations of nightlife—such as the East Village, Williamsburg, Bushwick, and parts of Midtown—groups move steadily between locations late into the night. Lines form outside popular venues, security staff manage entry points, and rideshare vehicles queue along curbs. Food vendors frequently position carts near clusters of late-night patrons, providing quick service

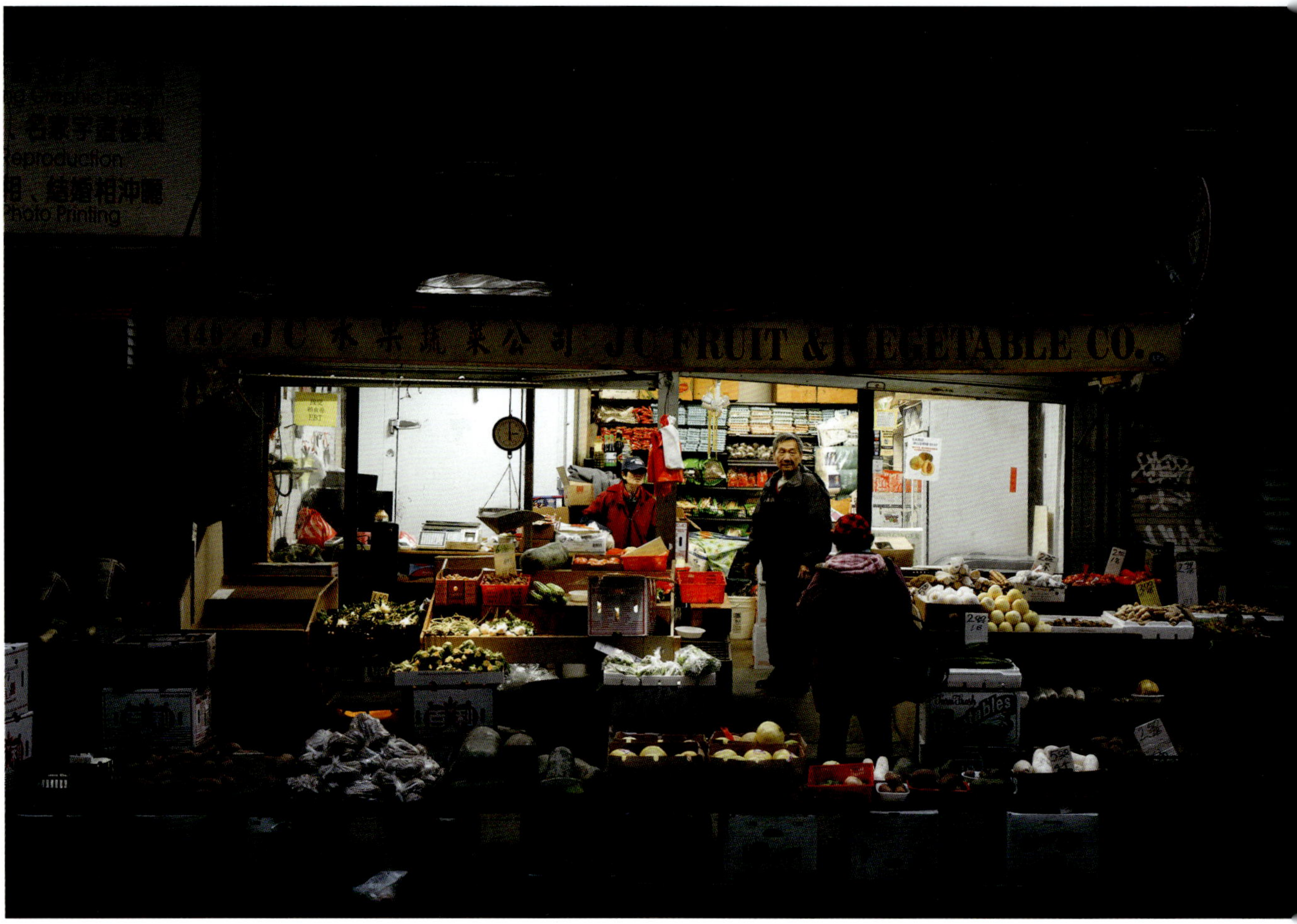
Reproduction
Photo Printing
FRUIT &

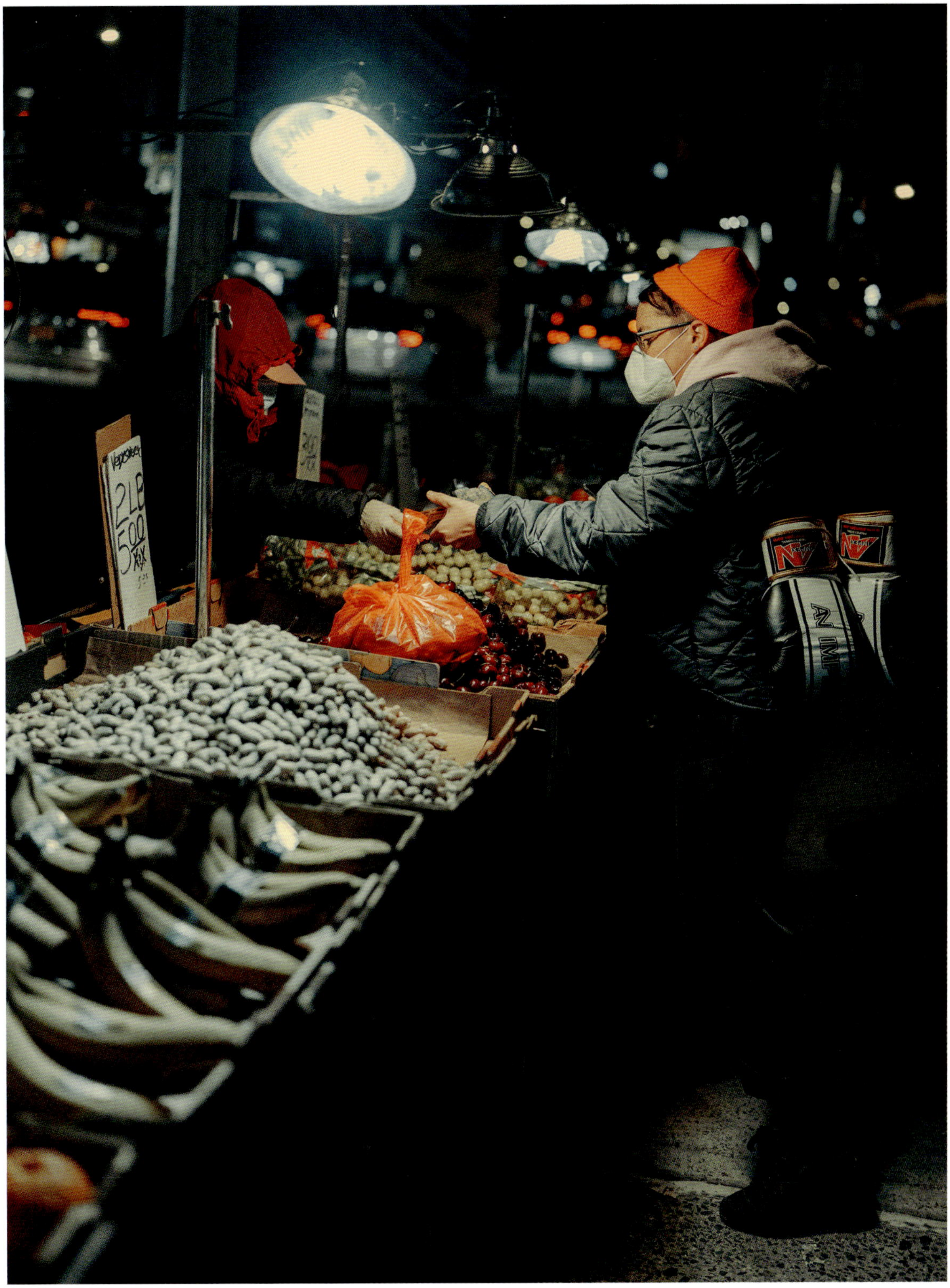
2LB
500

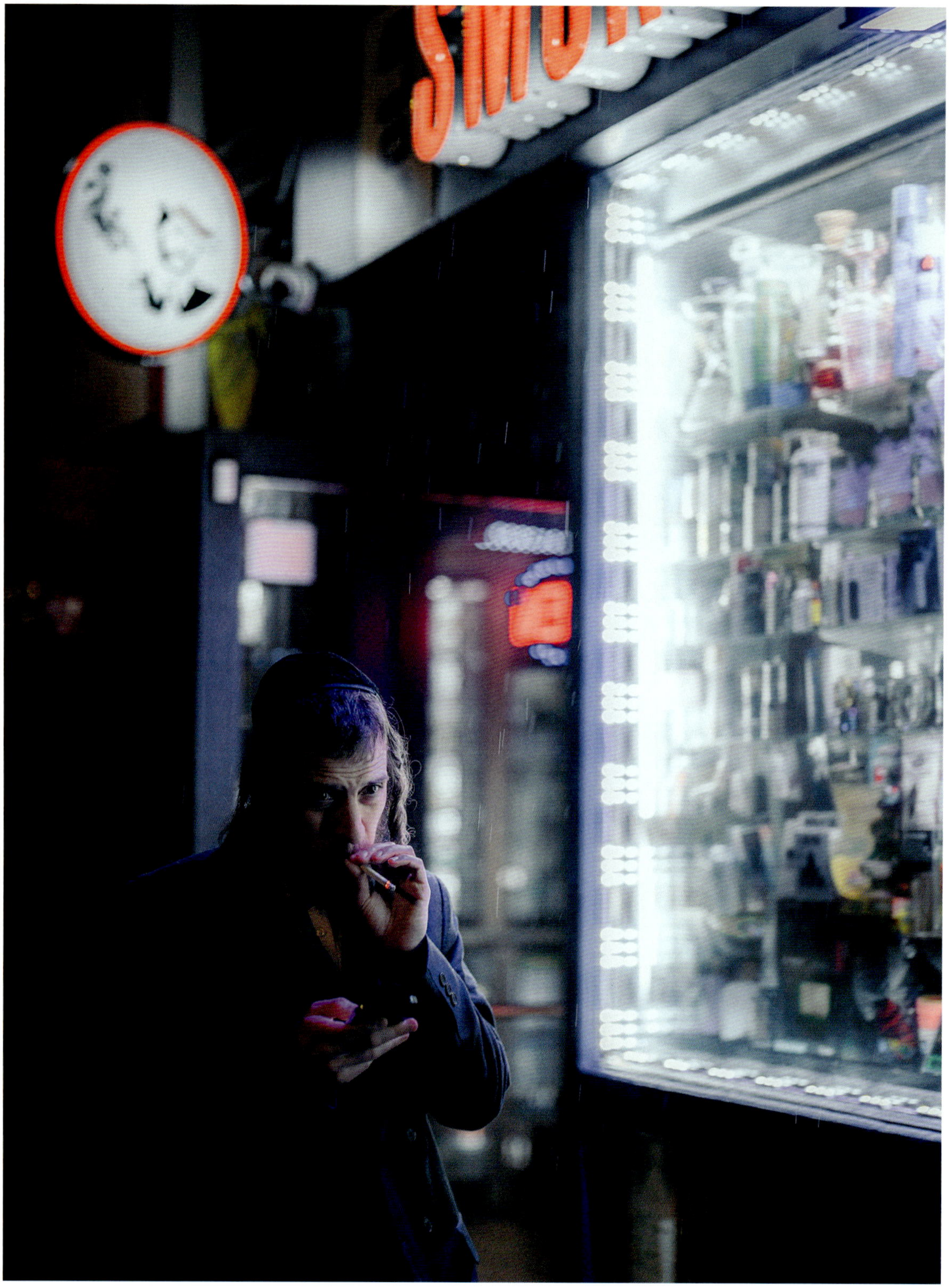

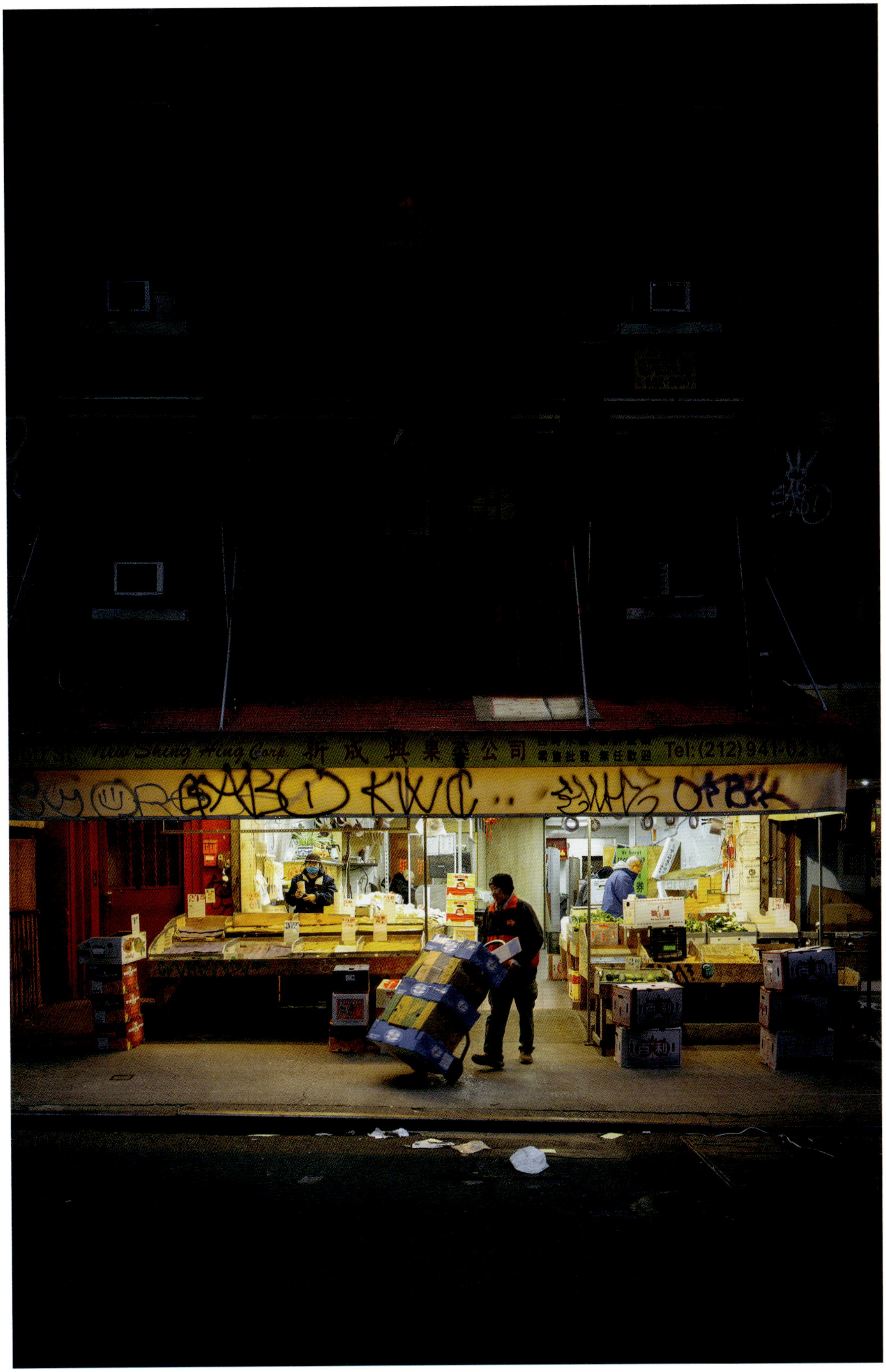

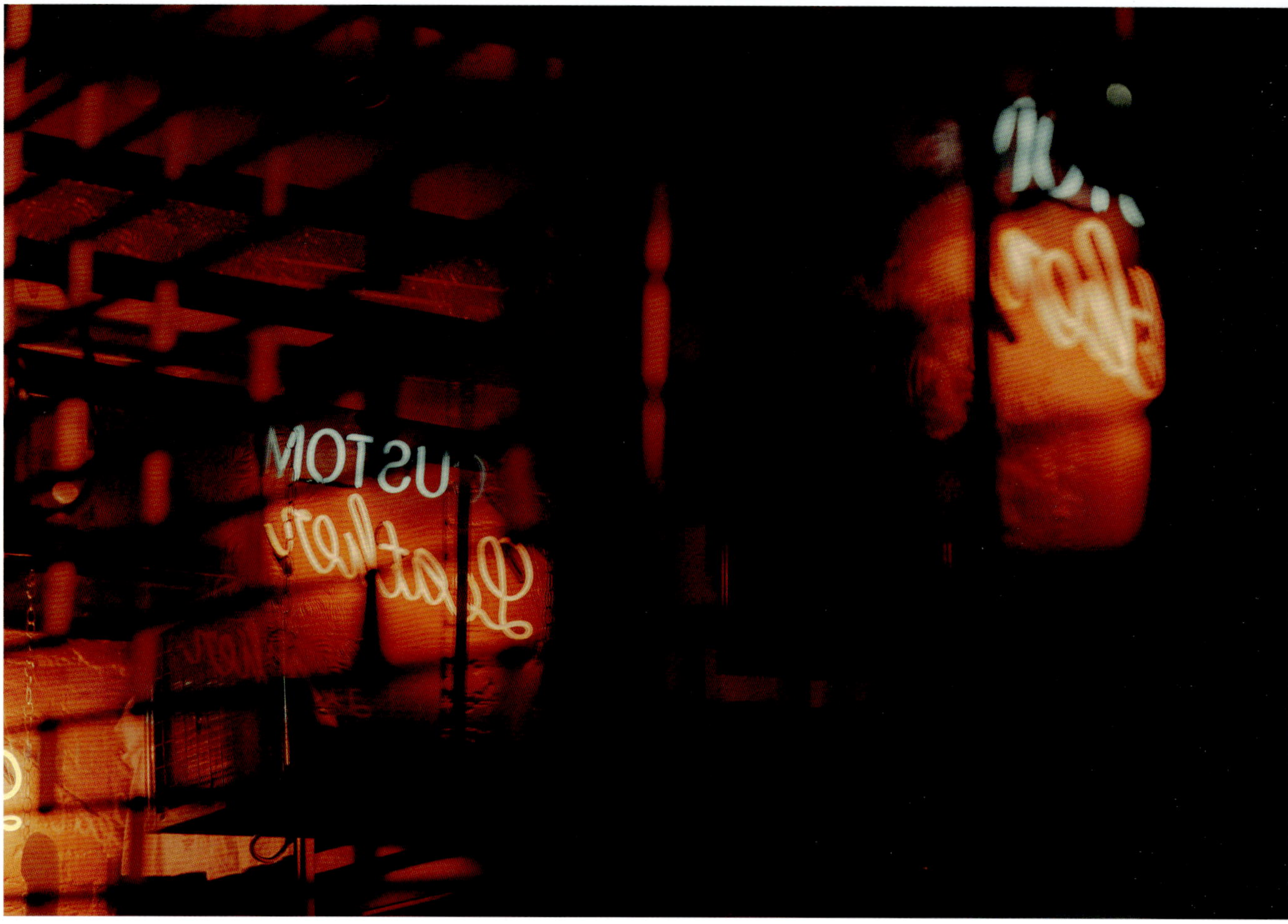

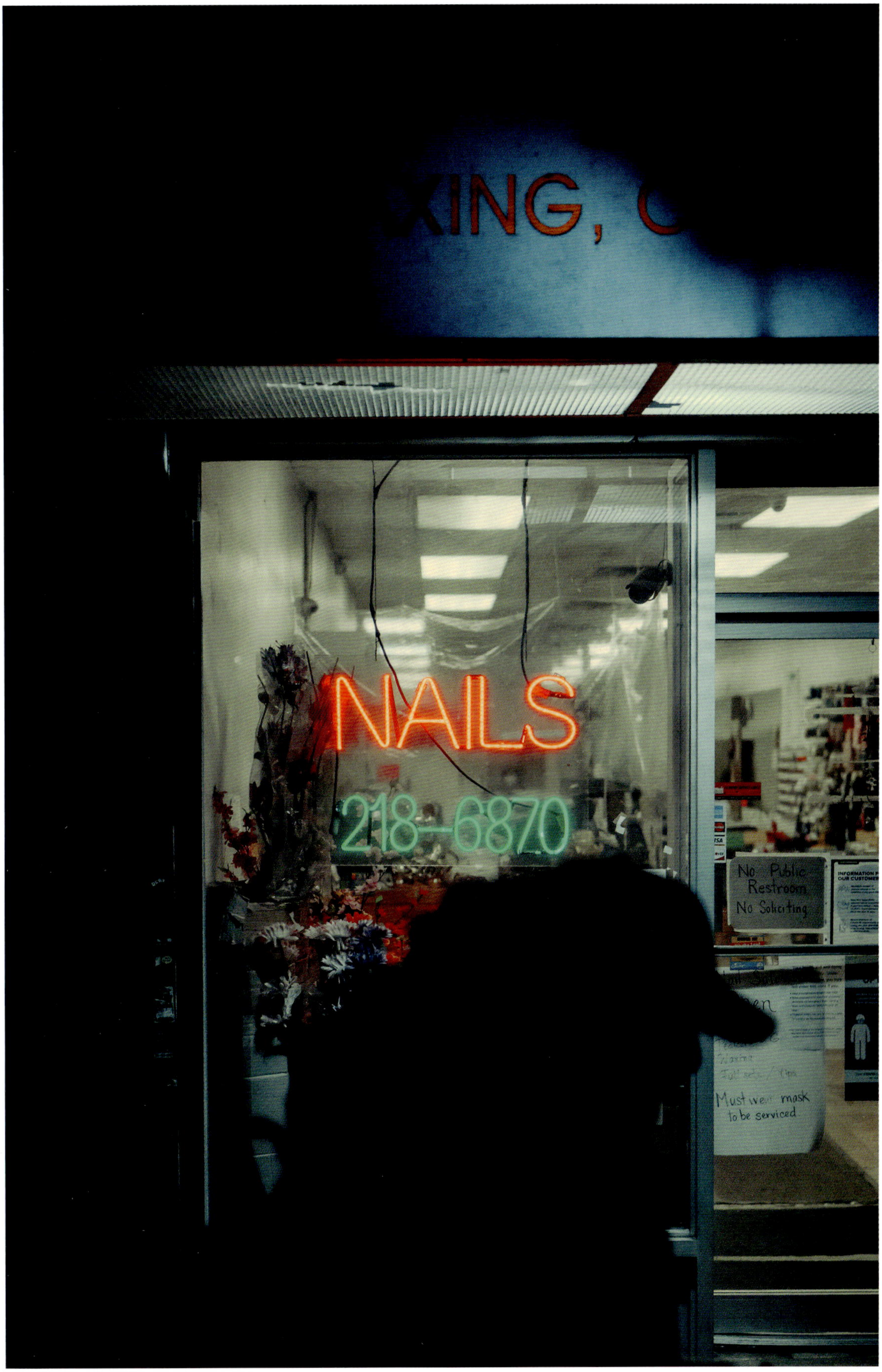
XING,
NAILS
218-6870
No Public
Restroom
No Soliciting
Must wear mask
to be serviced

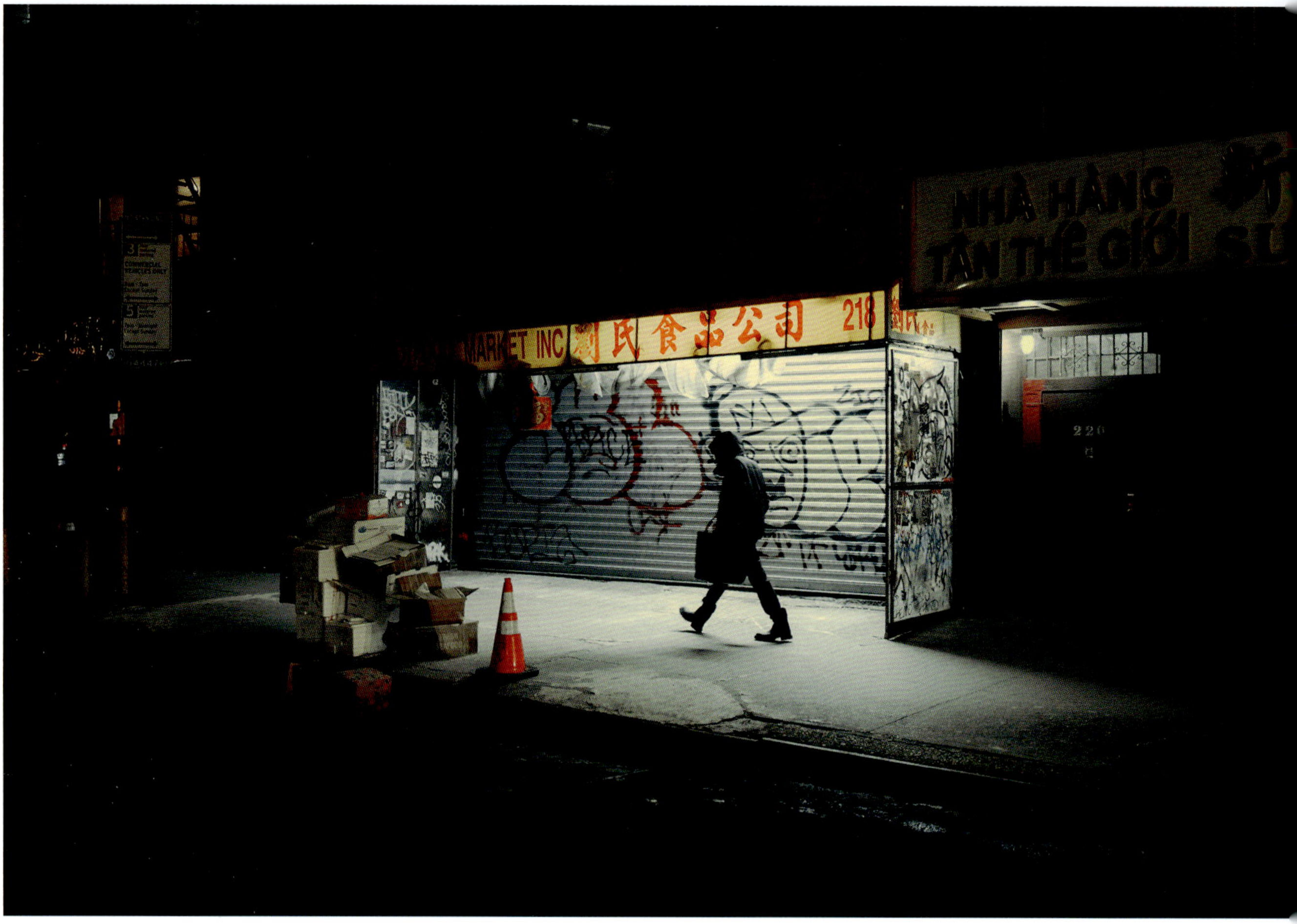
NHÀ HÀNG
TÂN THẾ GIỚI
MARKET INC 劉氏食品公司 218

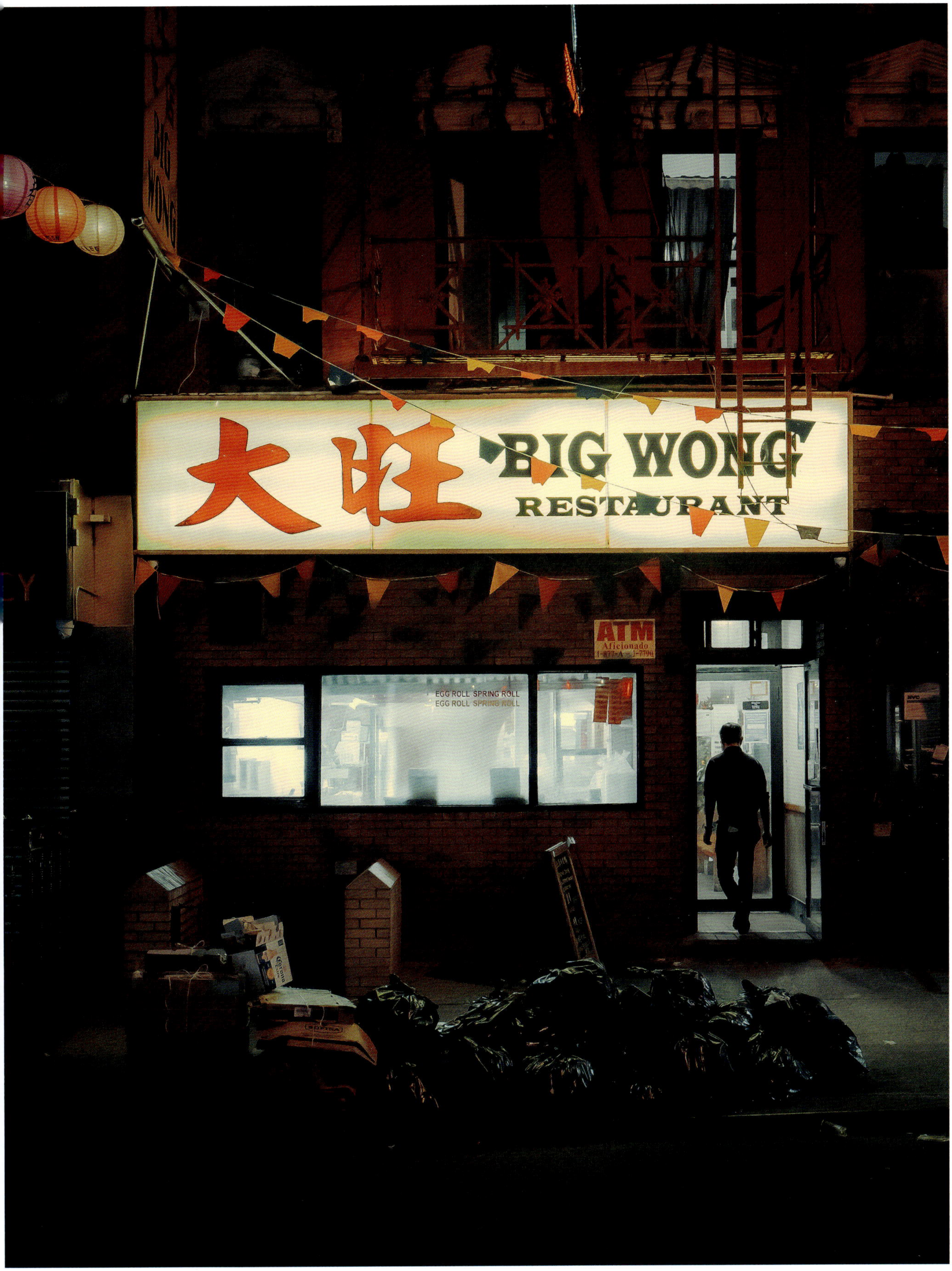
BIG WONG
大旺
BIG WONG
RESTAURANT
ATM
Aficionado
EGG ROLL SPRING ROLL
EGG ROLL SPRING ROLL

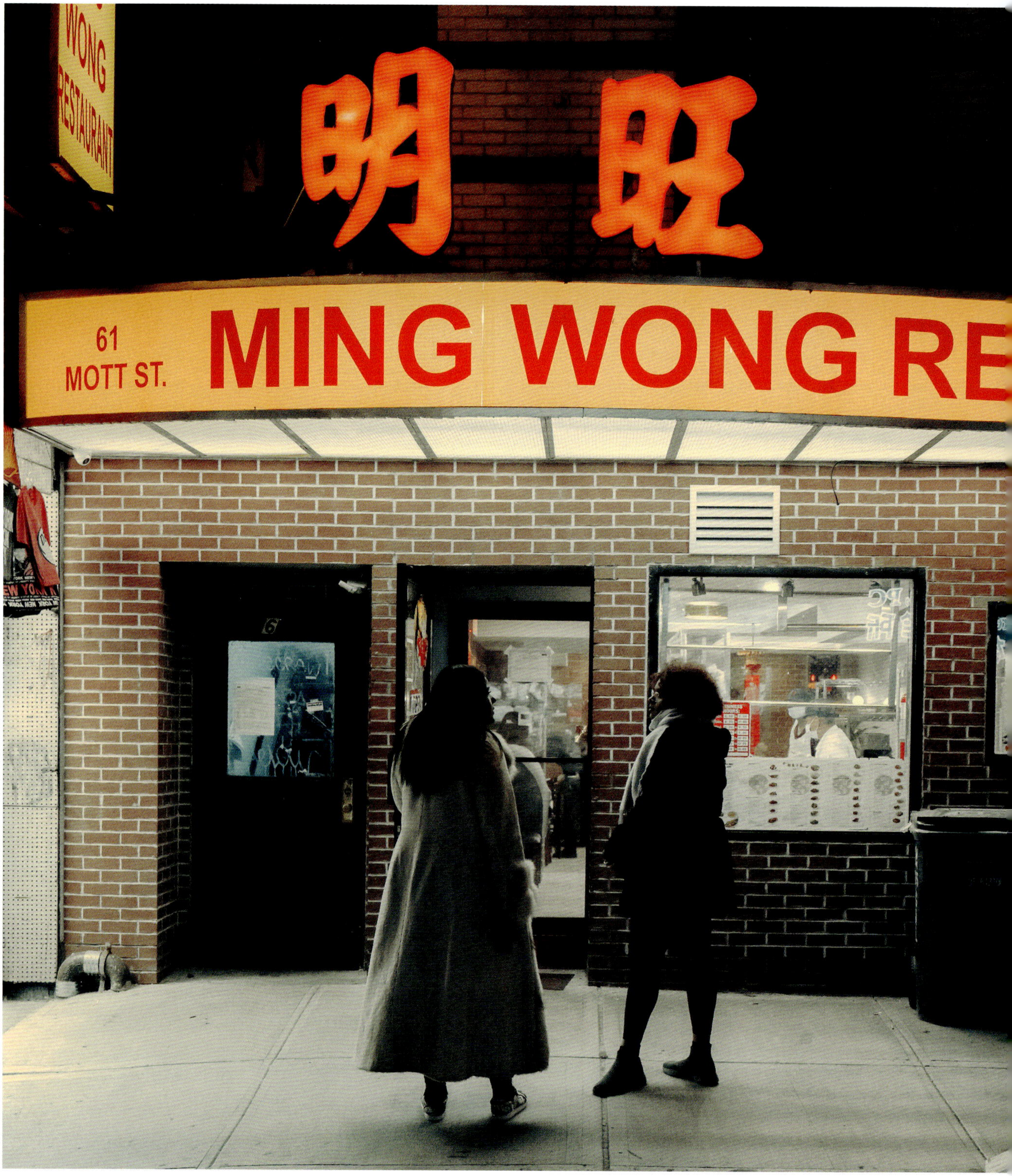
WONG
RESTAURANT
明旺
61
MOTT ST.
MING WONG RE

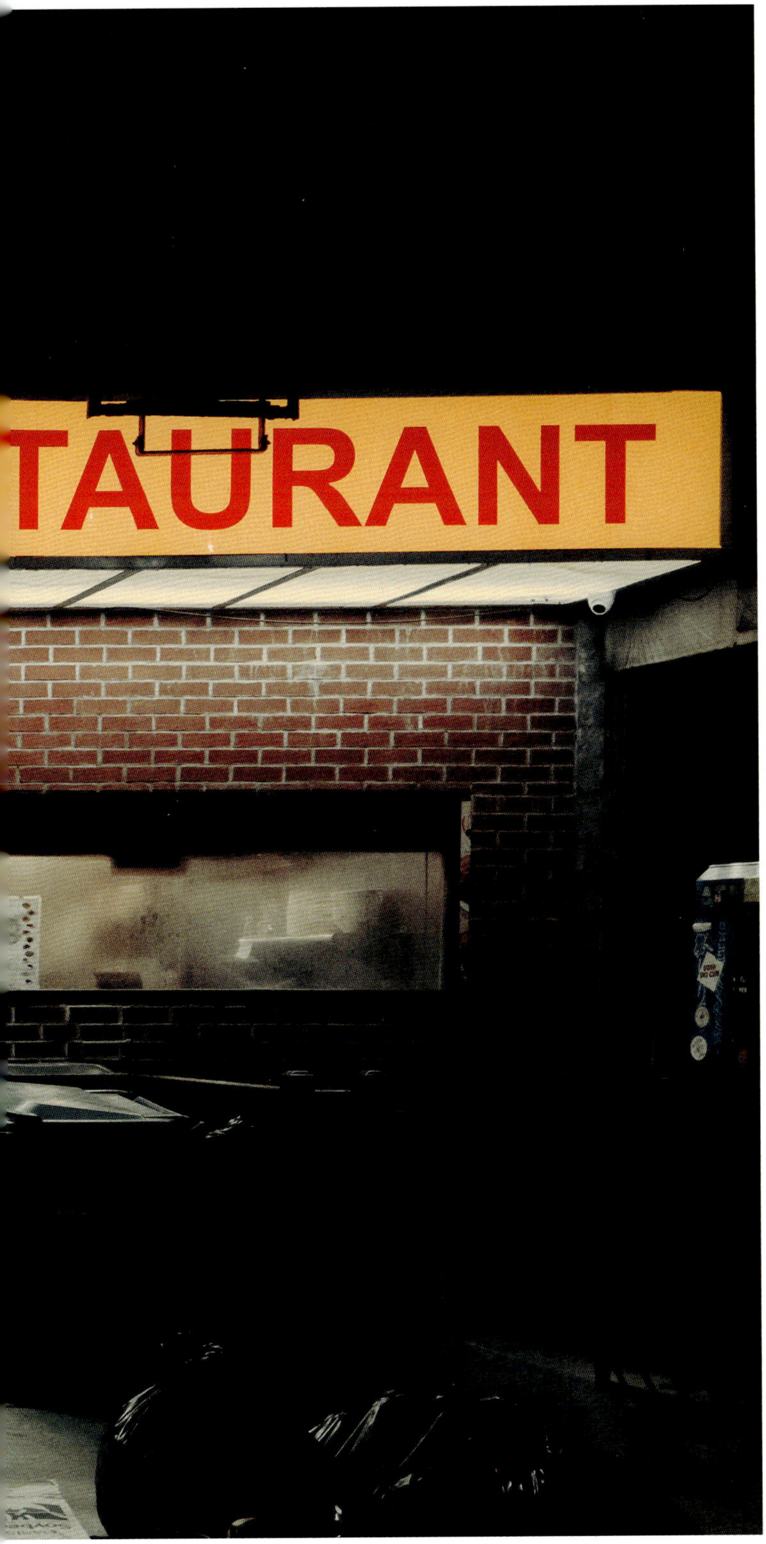
TAURANT

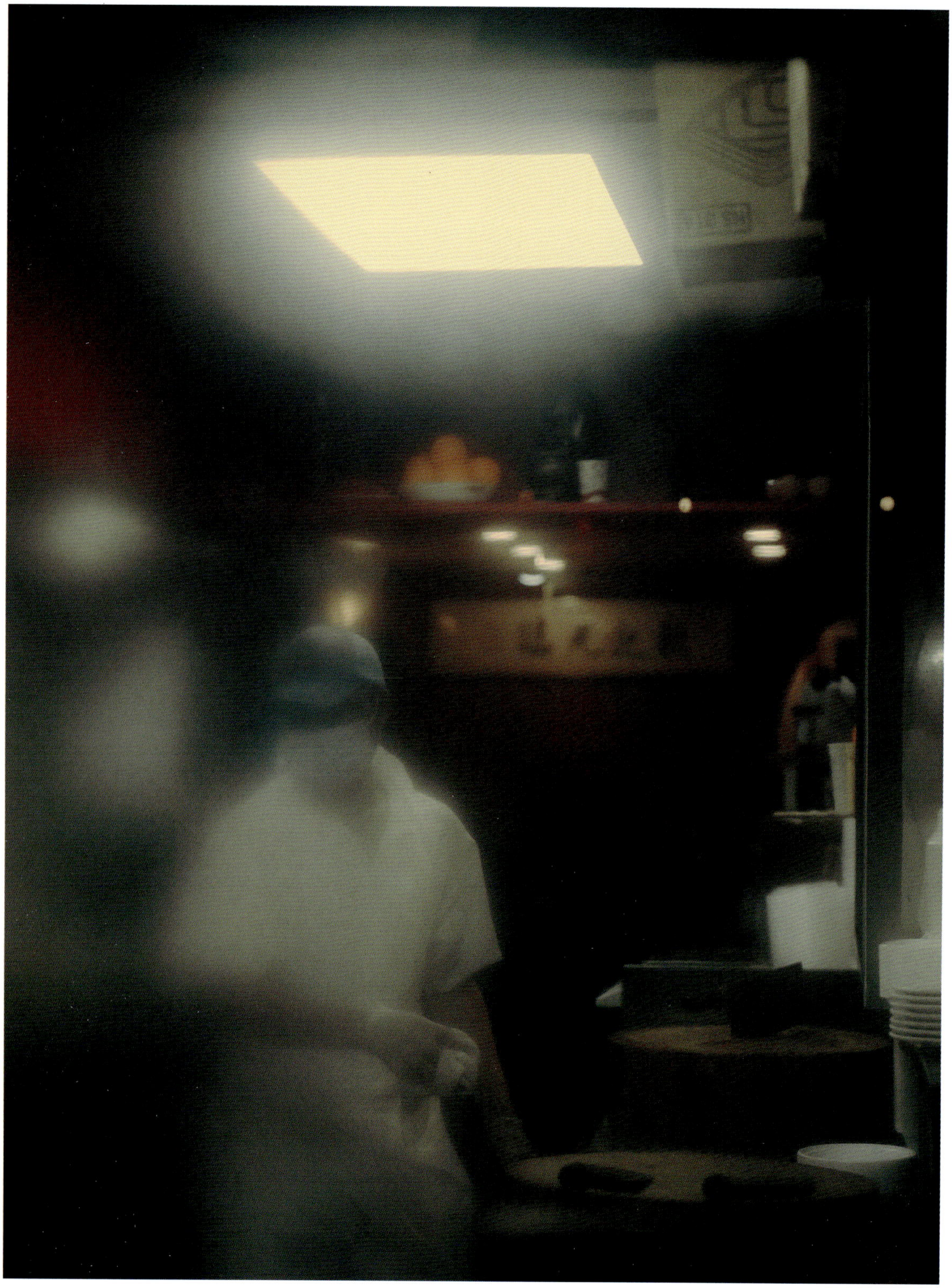

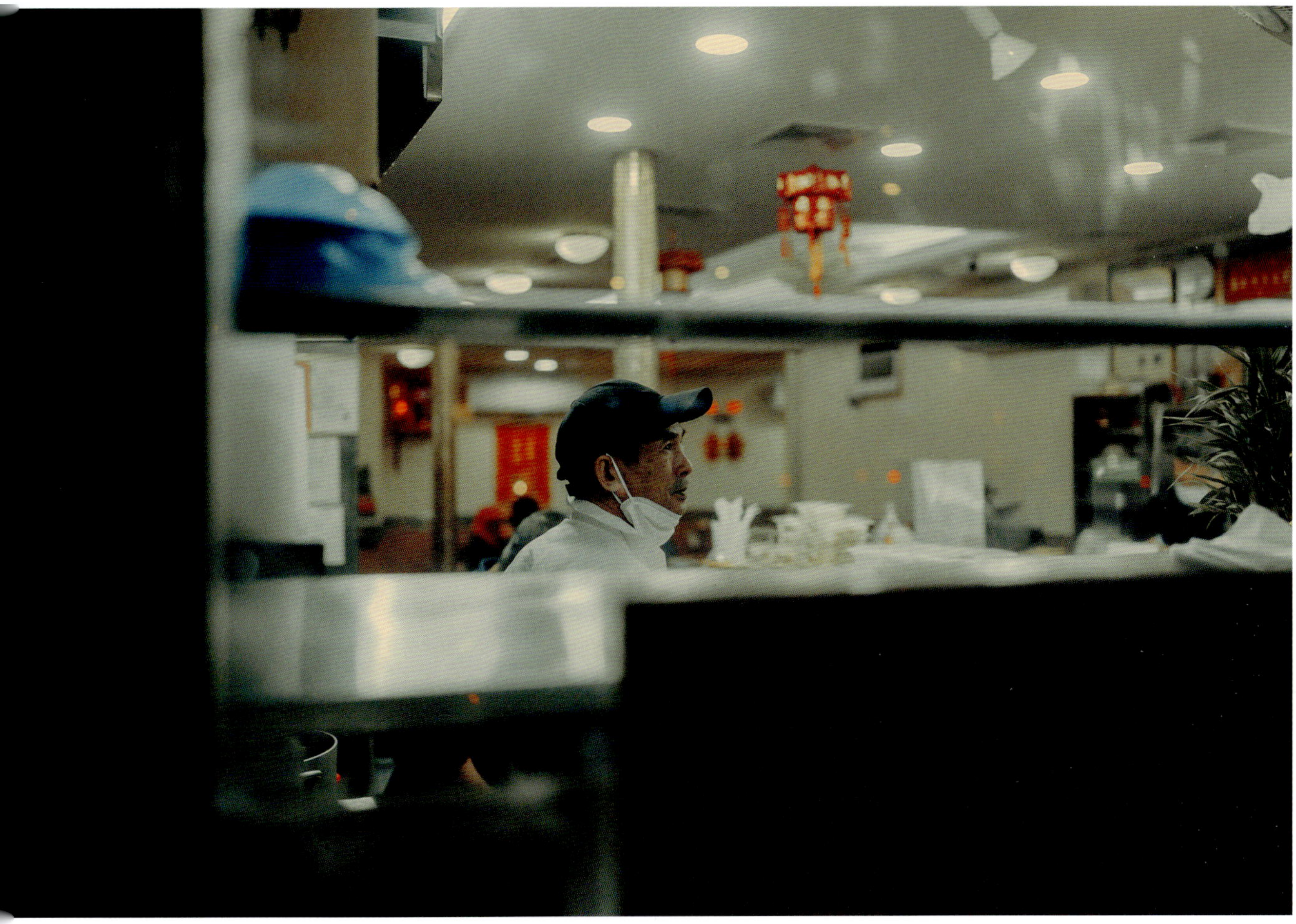

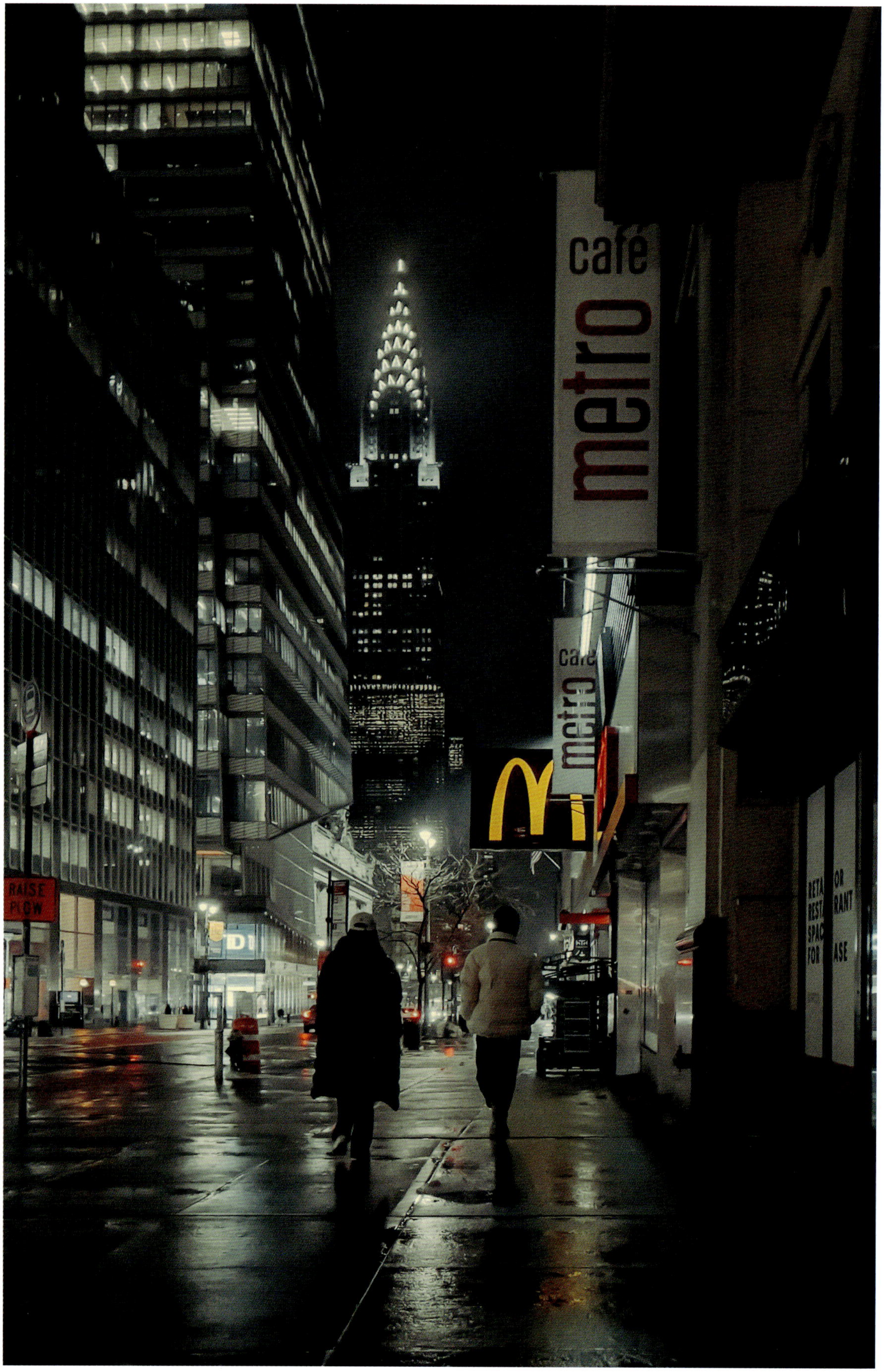
café
metro
RAISE
PLOW

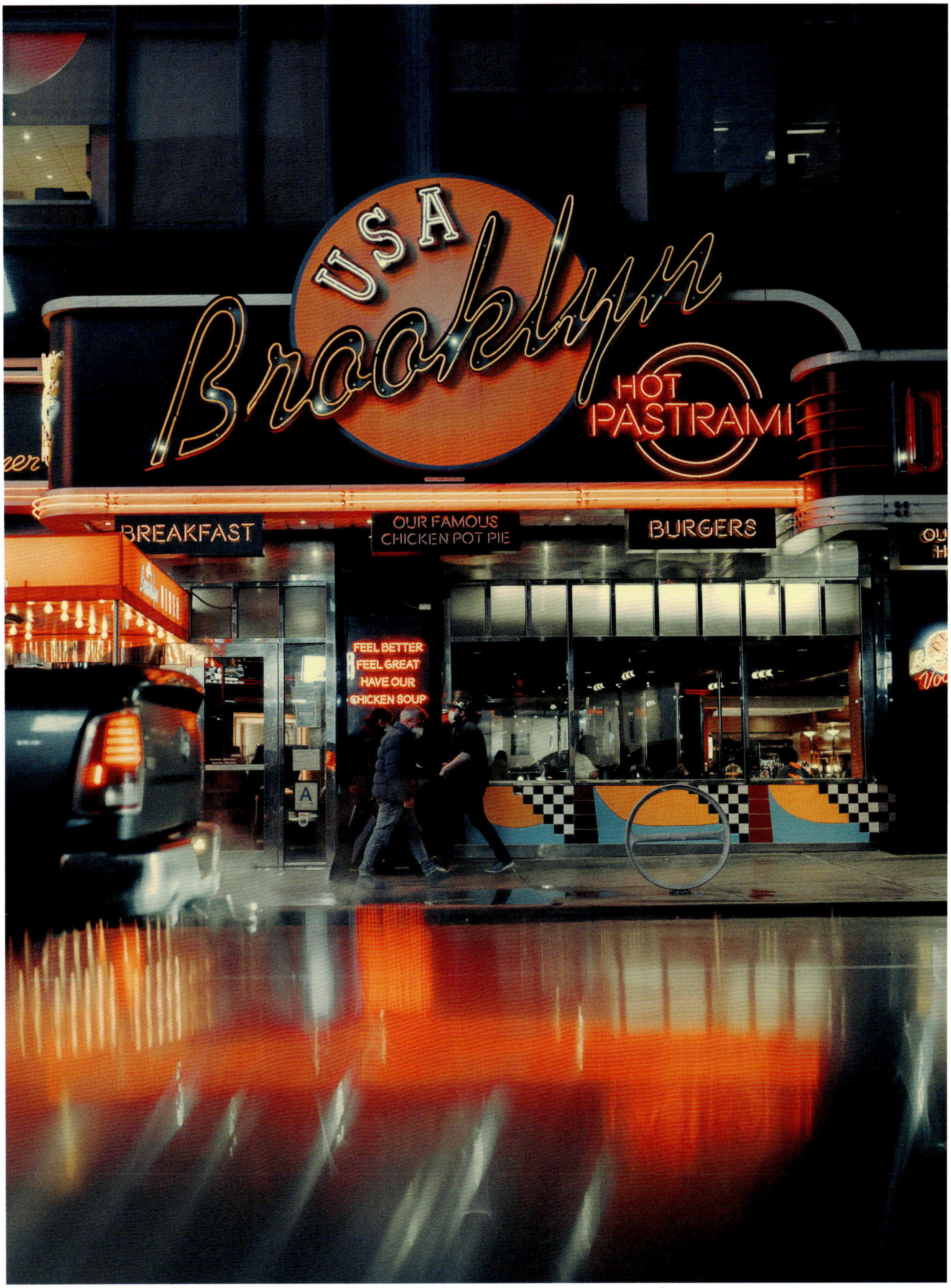
USA
Brooklyn
HOT PASTRAMI
BREAKFAST
OUR FAMOUS CHICKEN POT PIE
BURGERS
FEEL BETTER
FEEL GREAT
HAVE OUR
CHICKEN SOUP

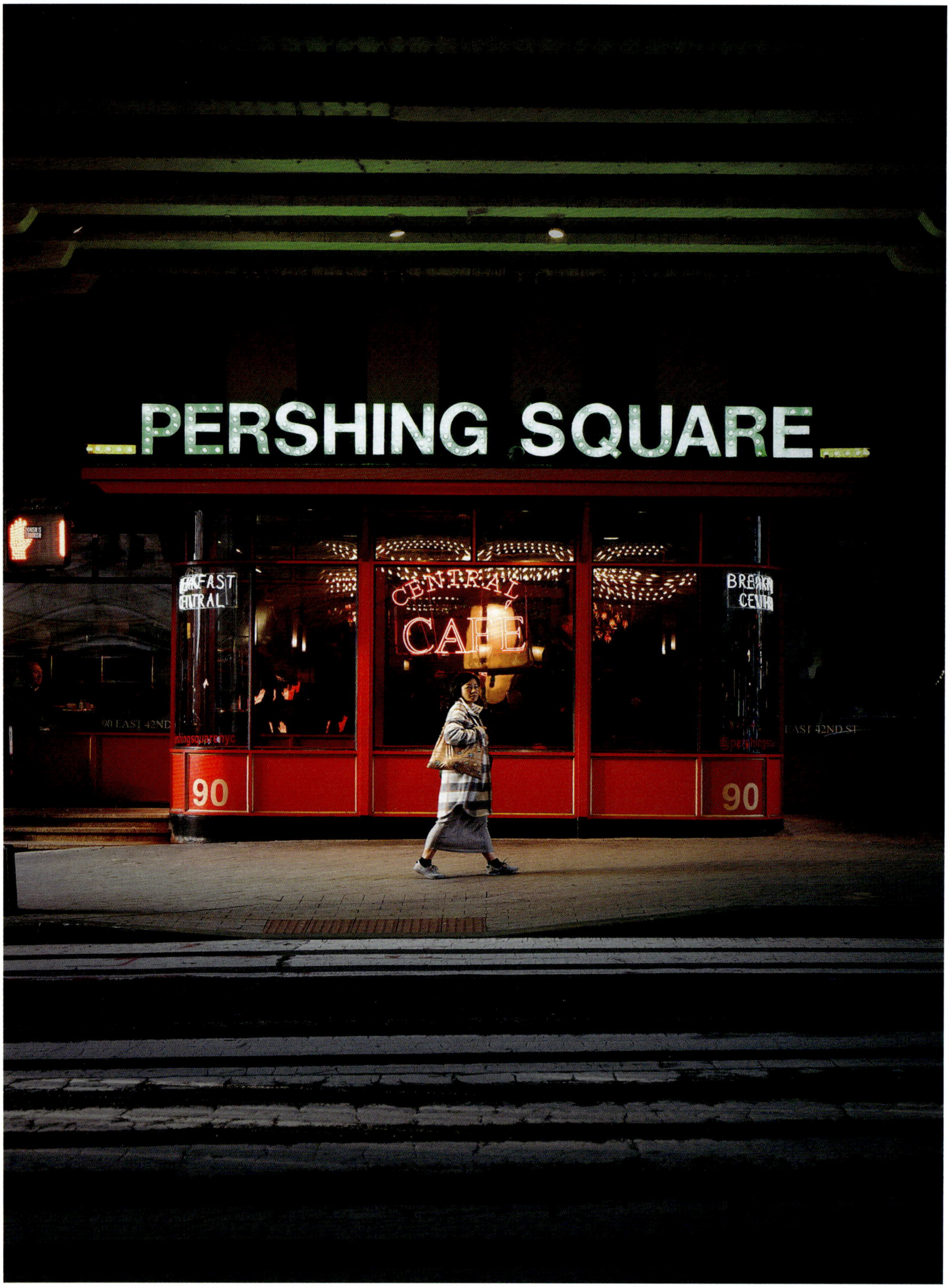
PERSHING SQUARE
CENTRAL
CAFÉ
90
90

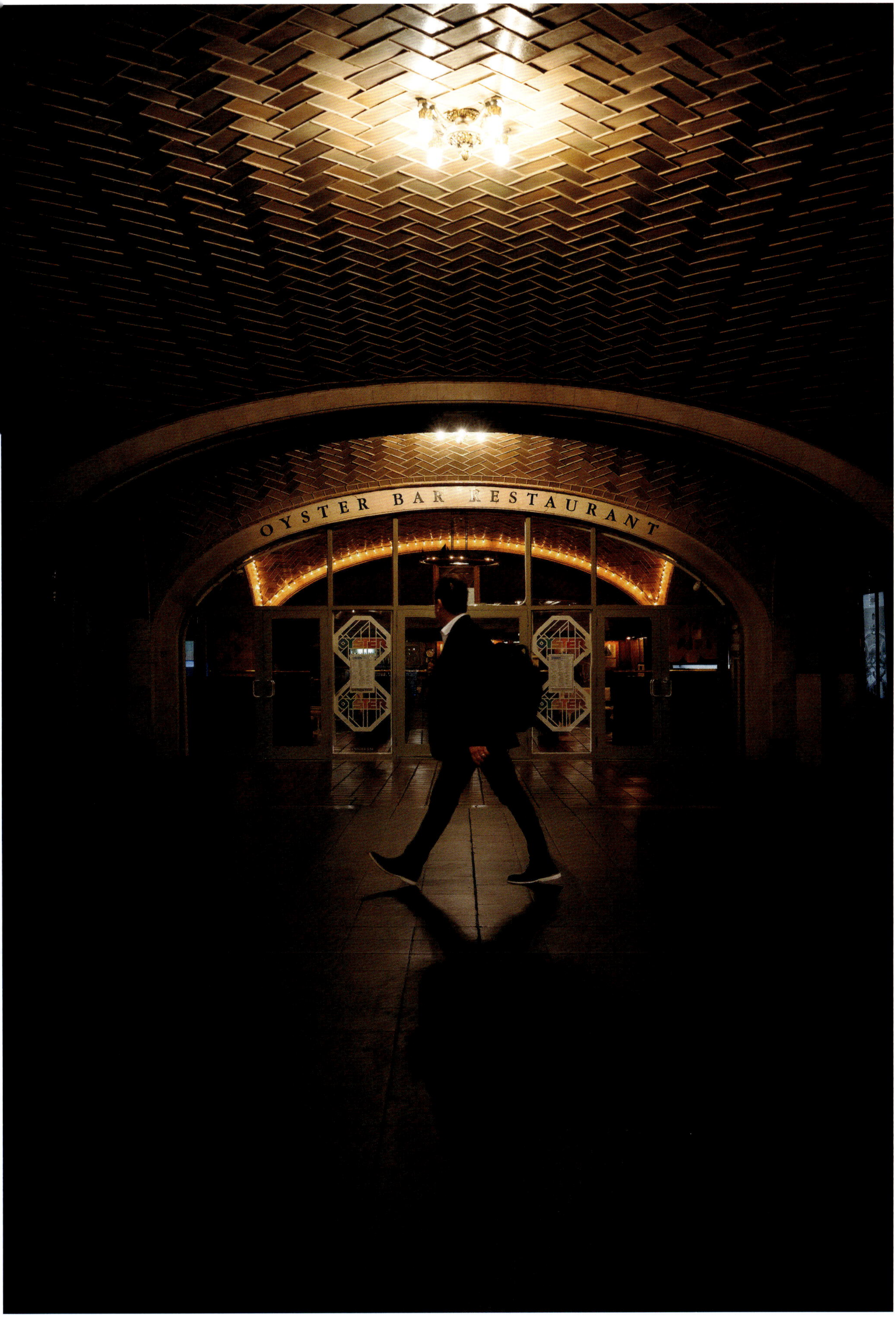
OYSTER BAR RESTAURANT

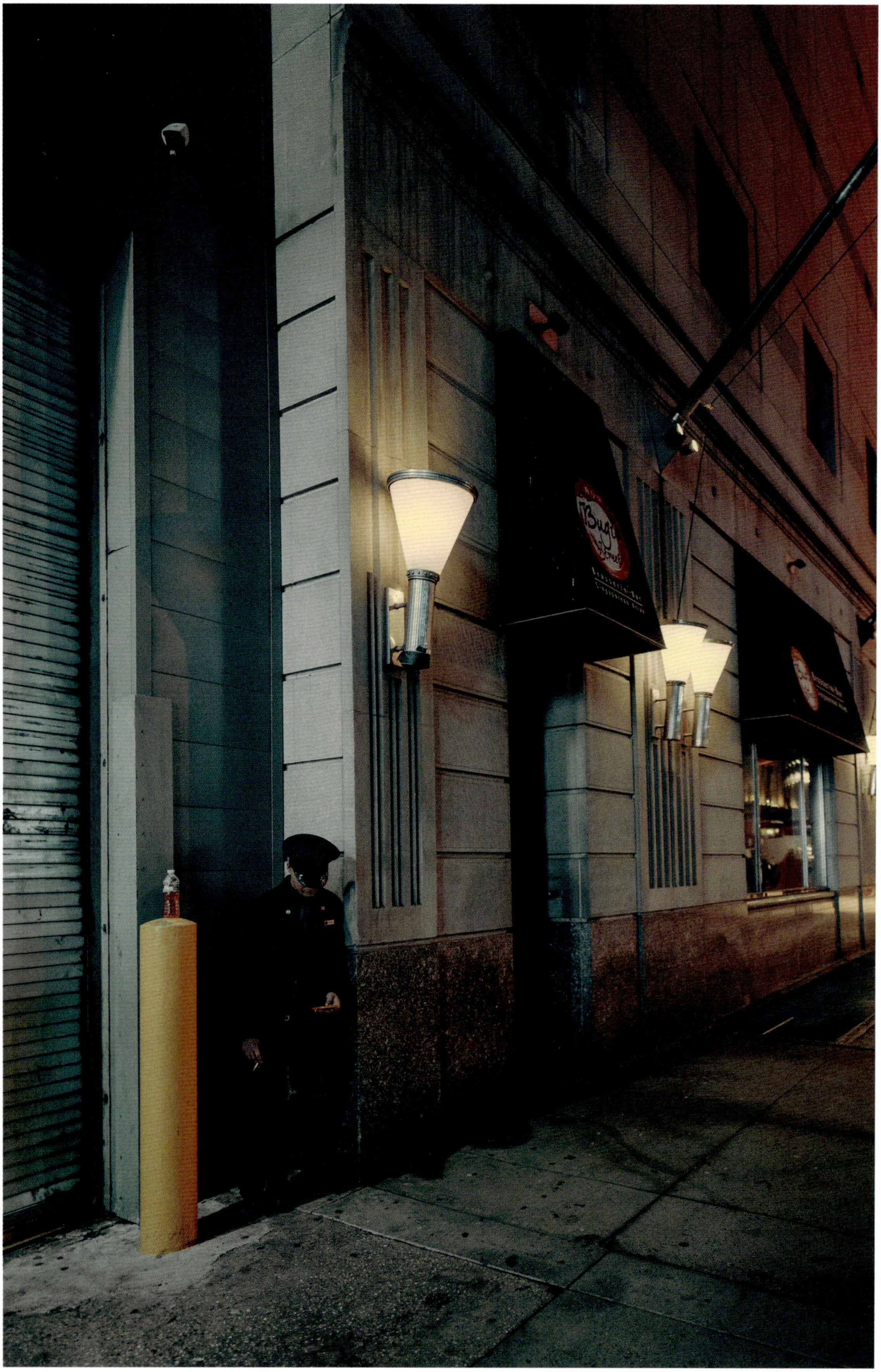

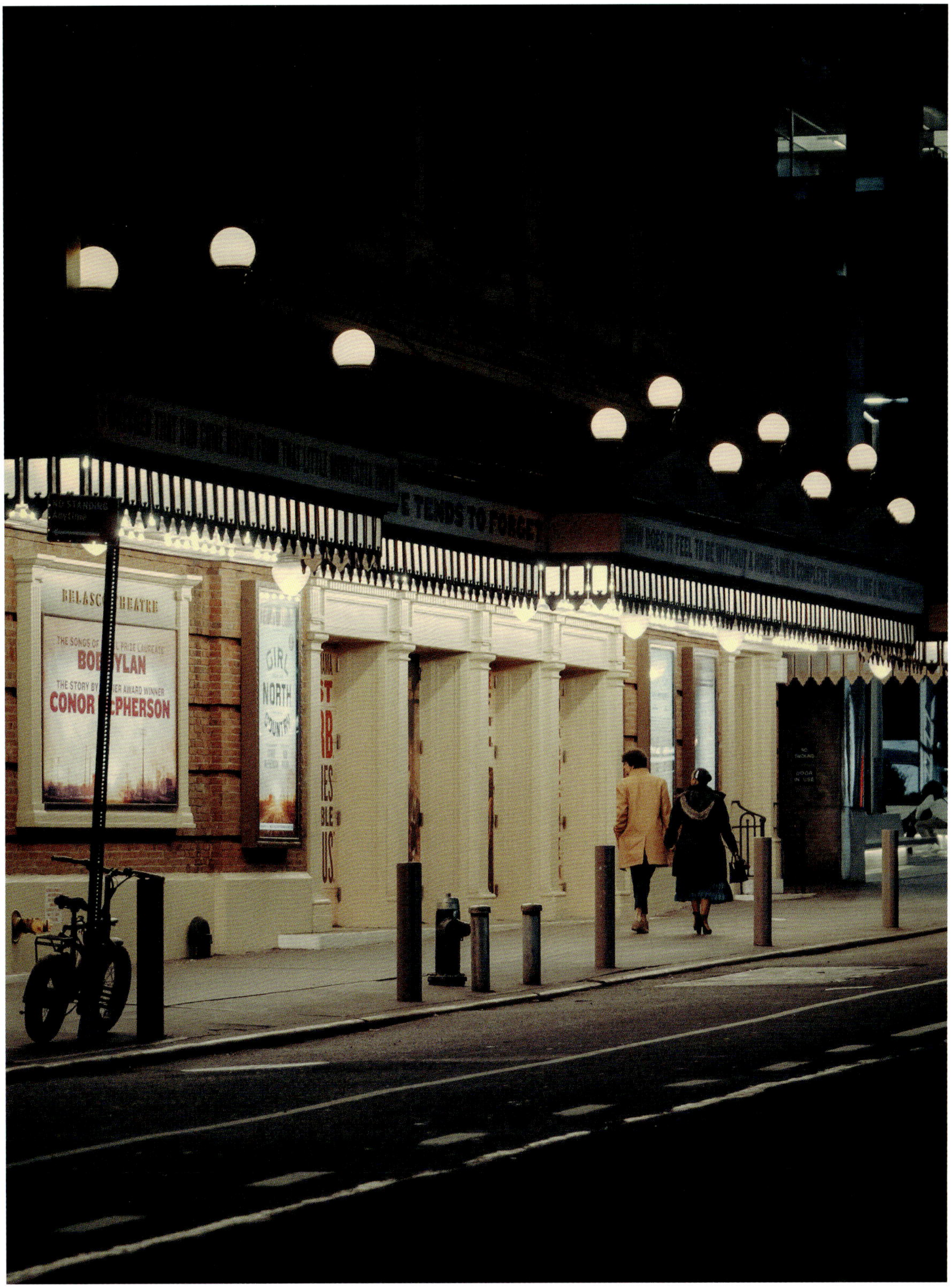
GIRL
NORTH
COUNTRY

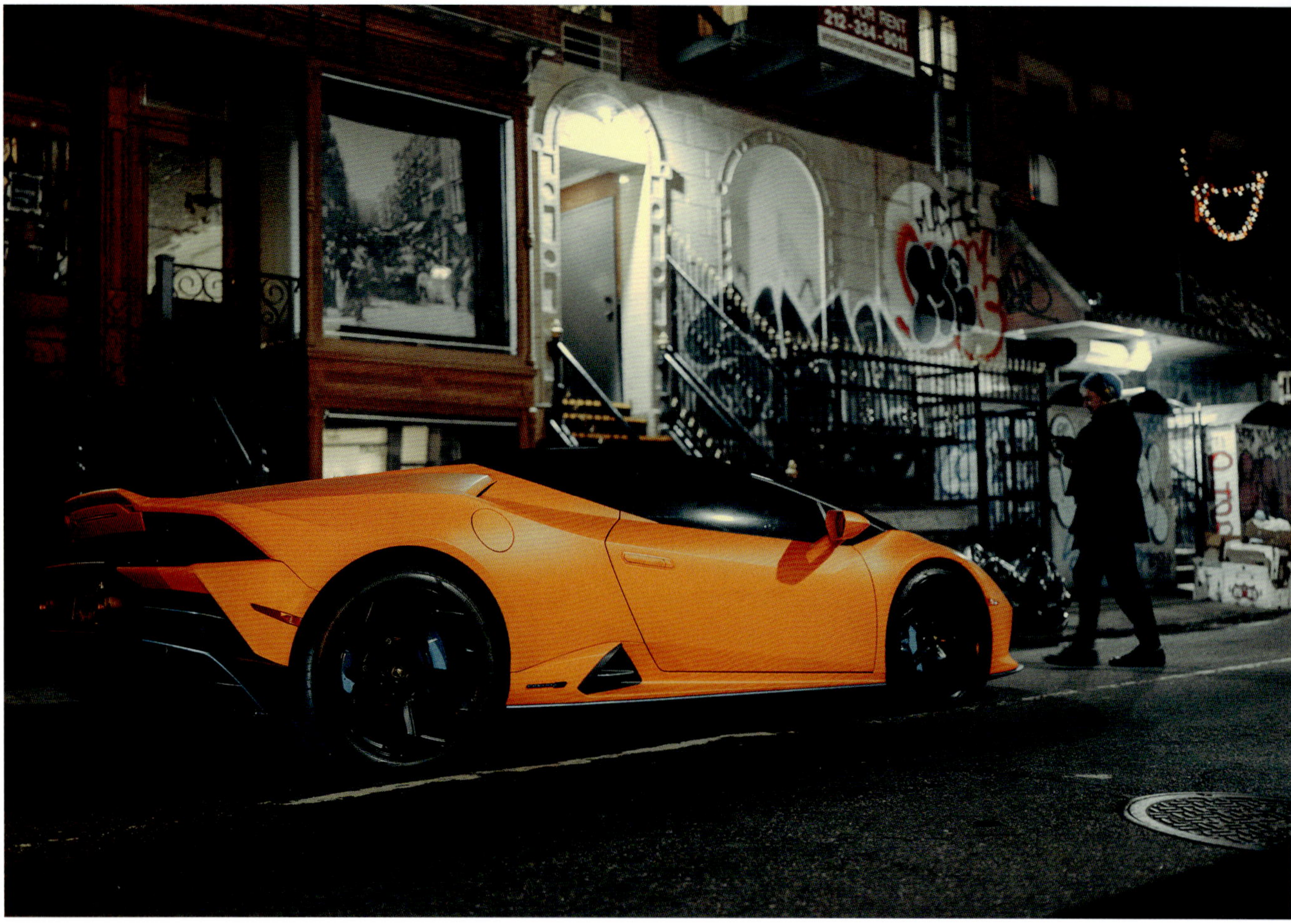
FOR RENT
212-334-9011

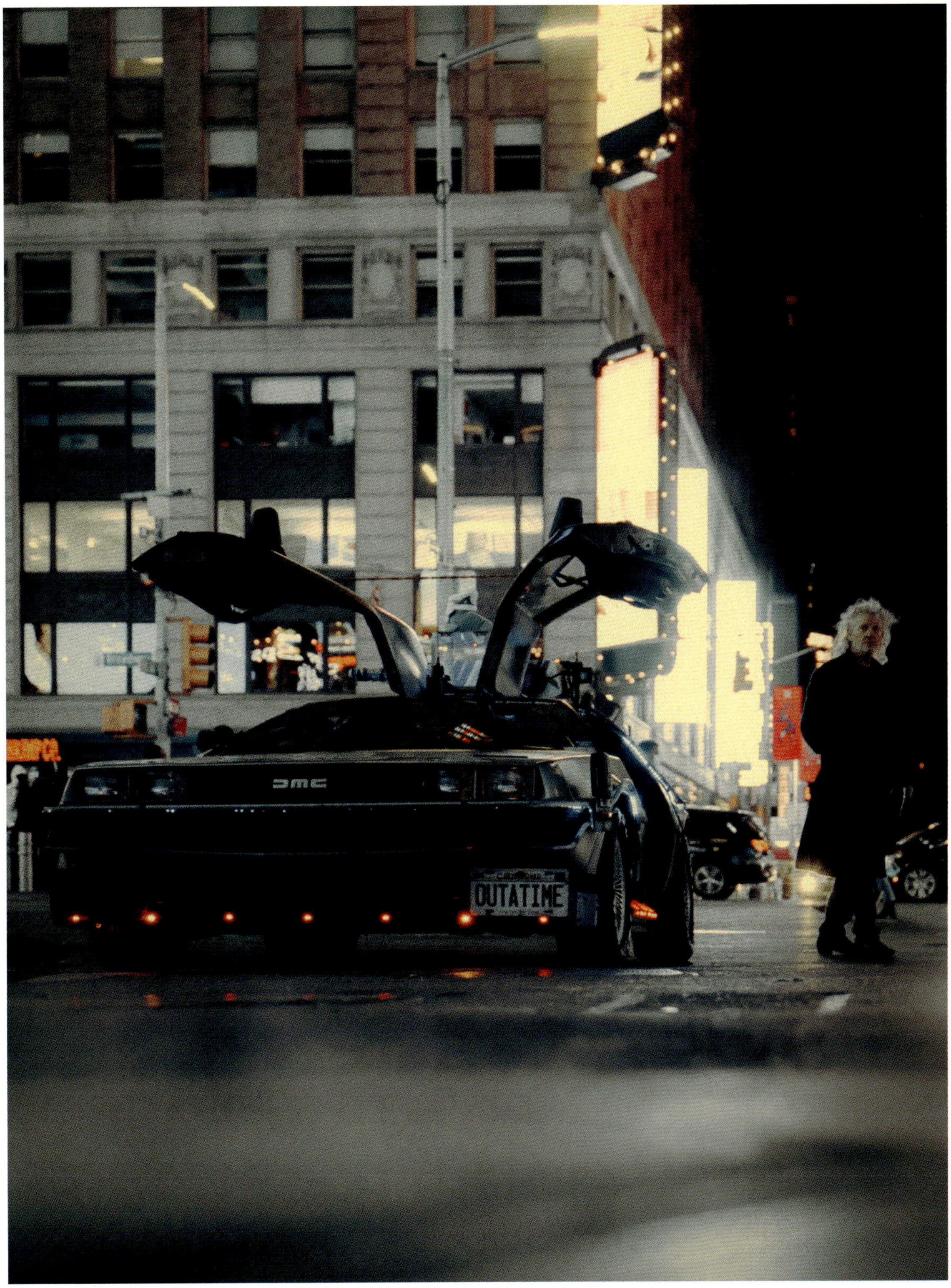
DMC
OUTATIME

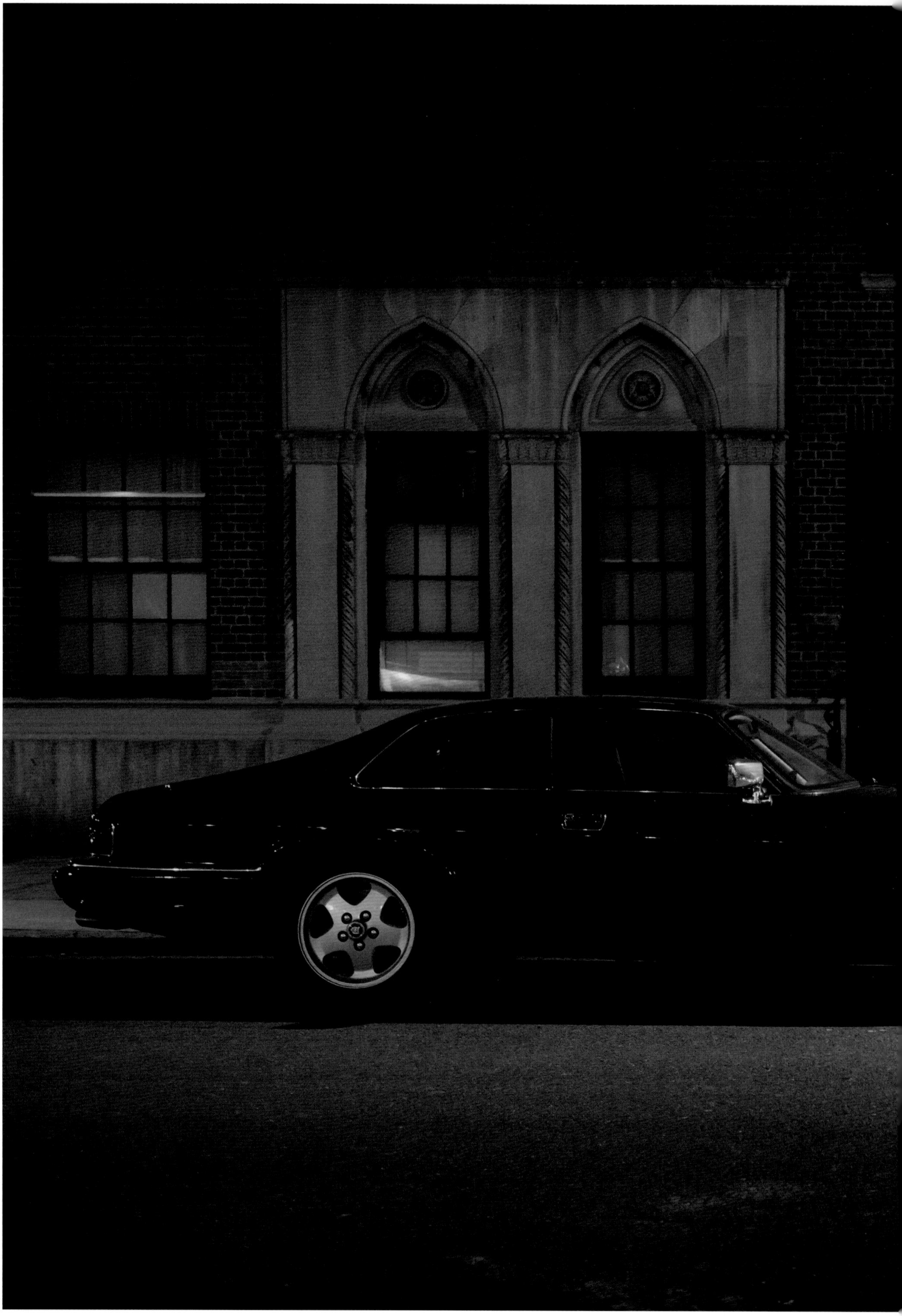

GREENWICH VILLAGE

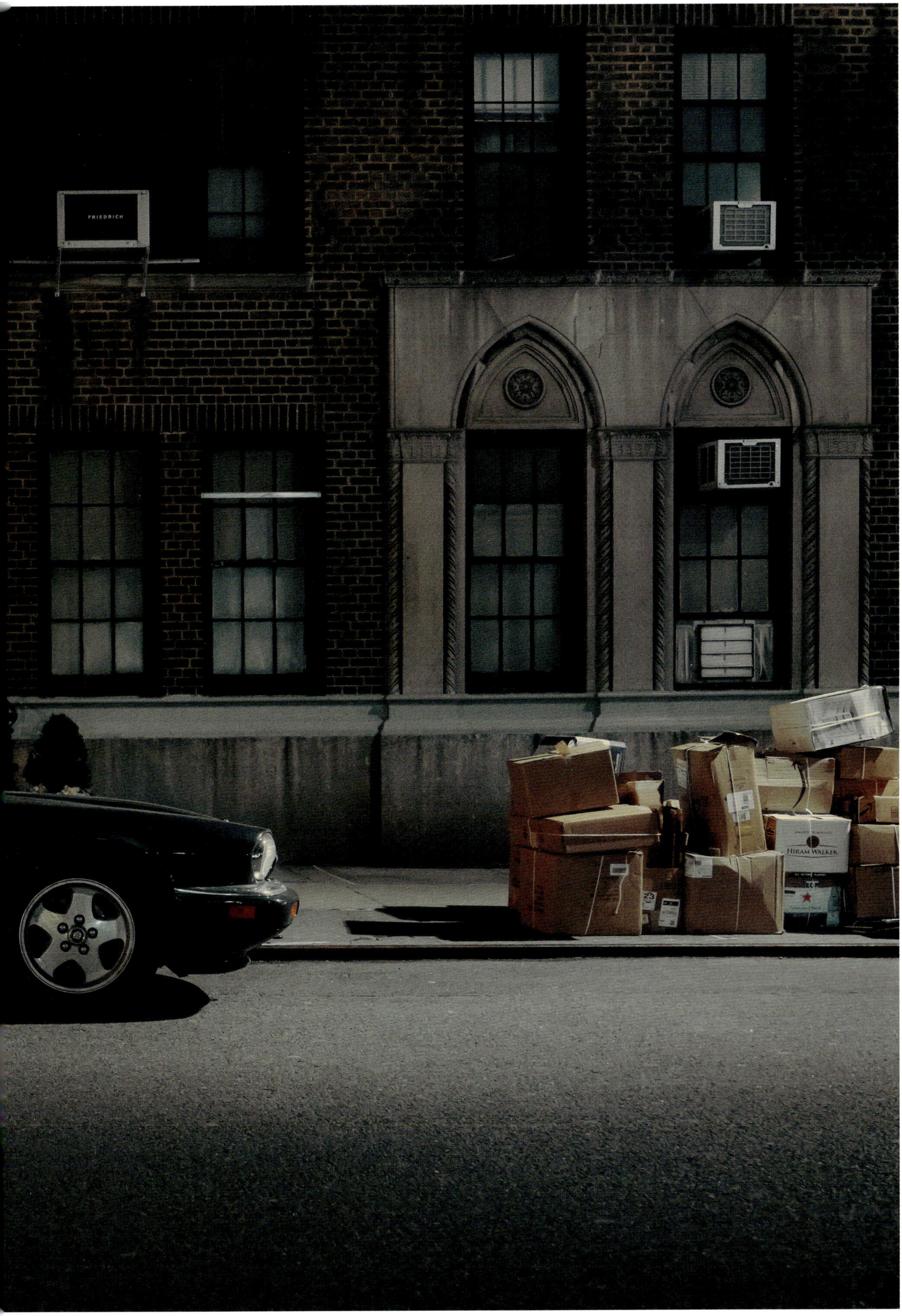
FRIEDRICH
HIRAM WALKER

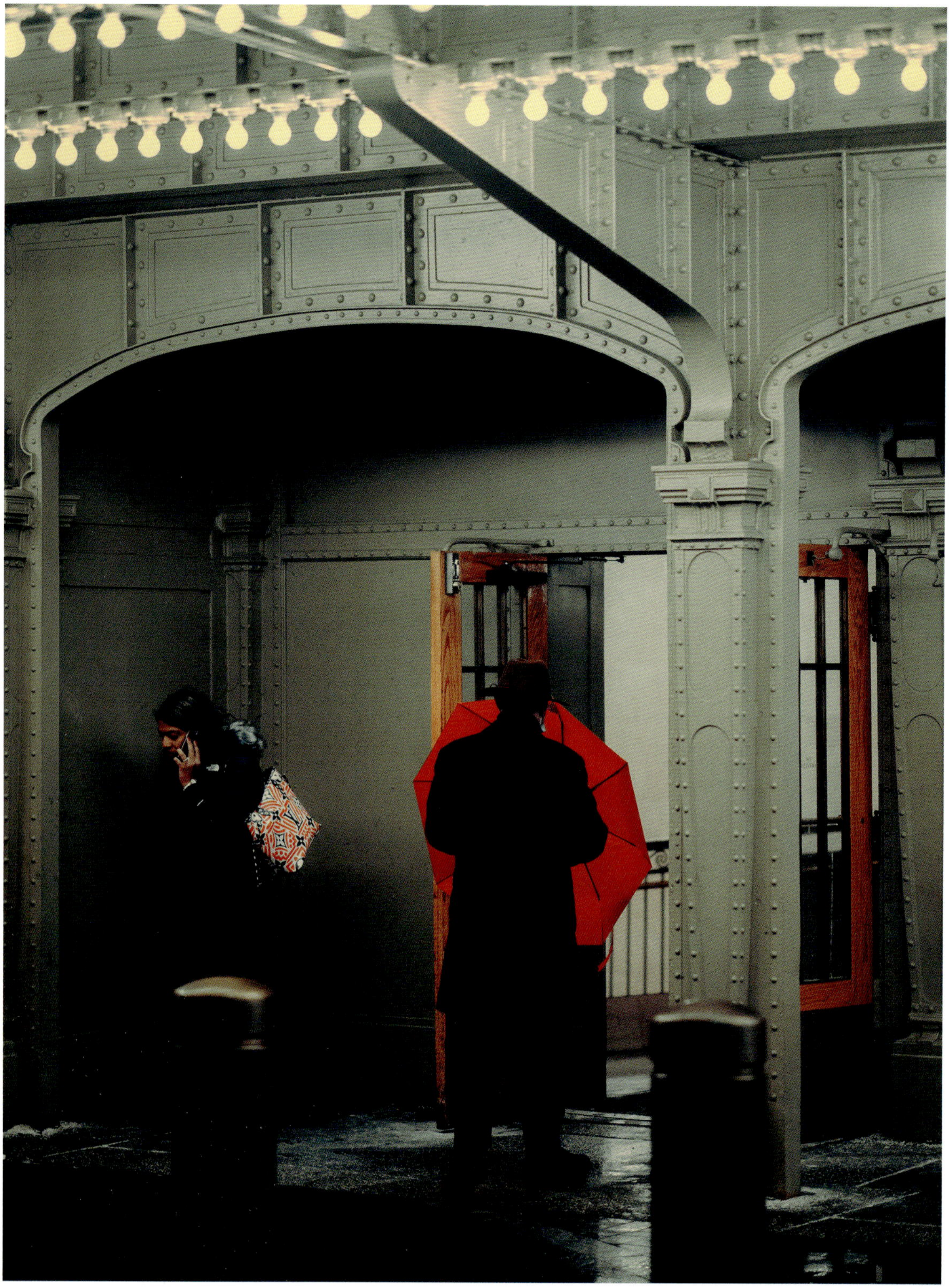

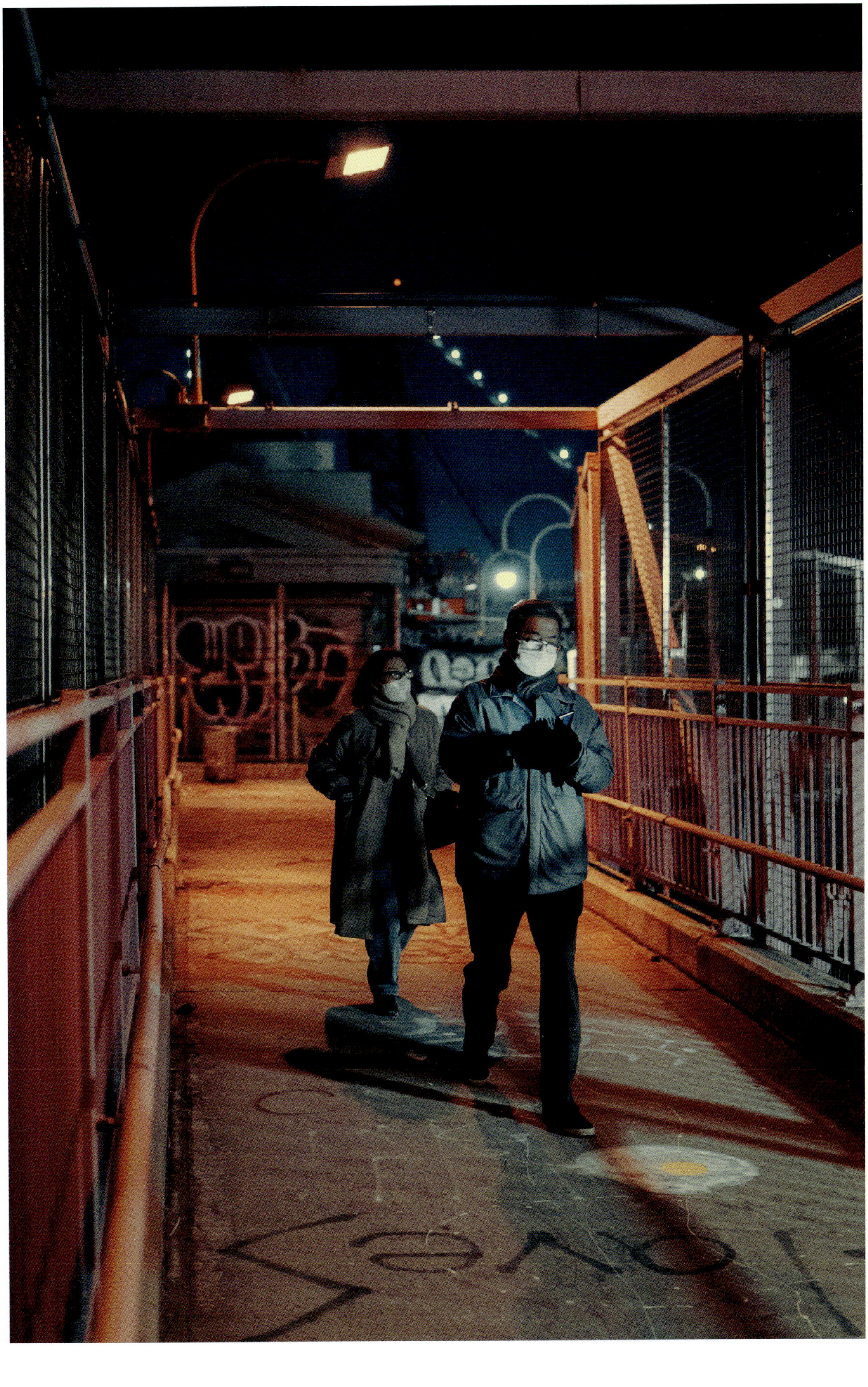

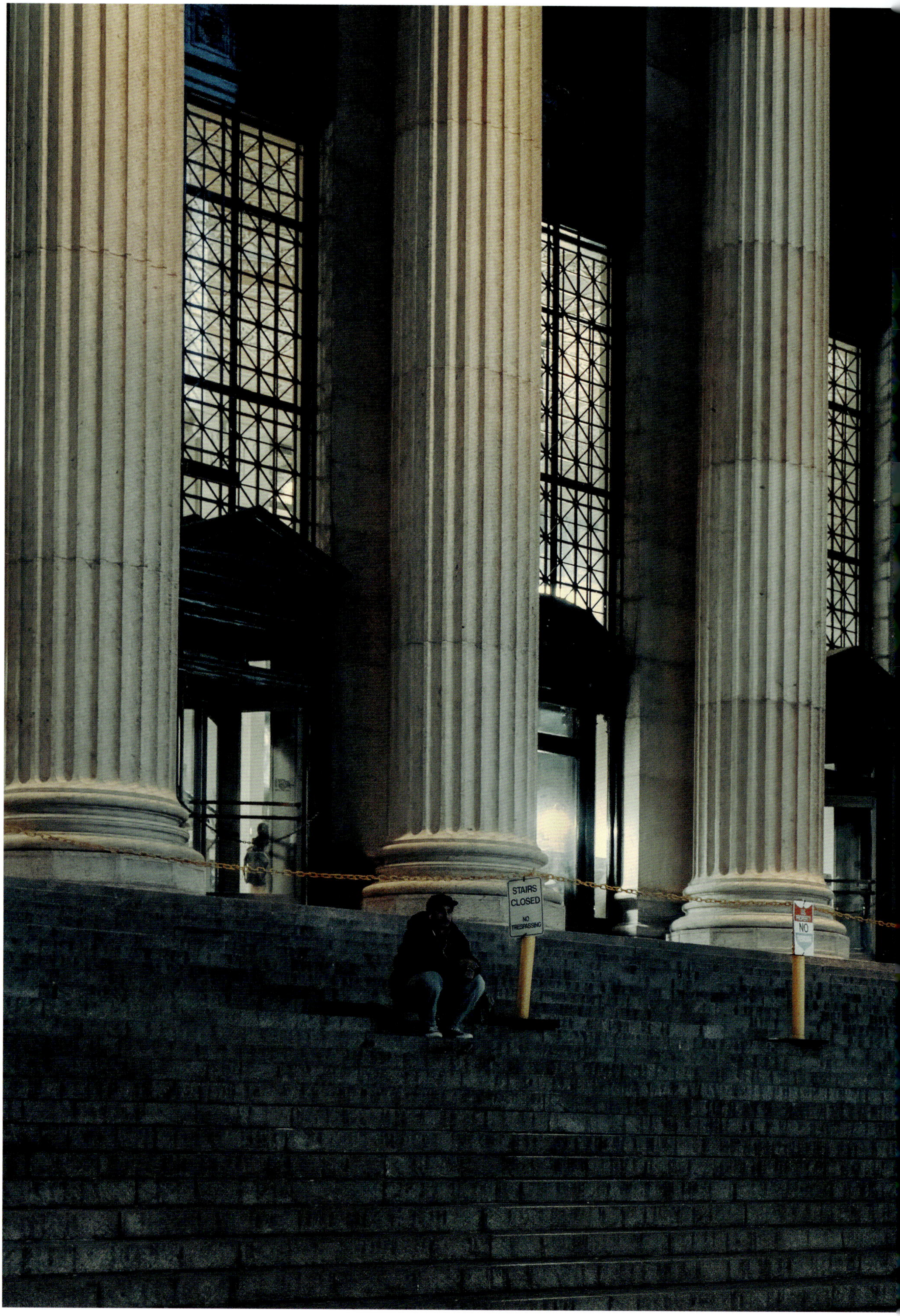

JAMES A. FARLEY BUILDING

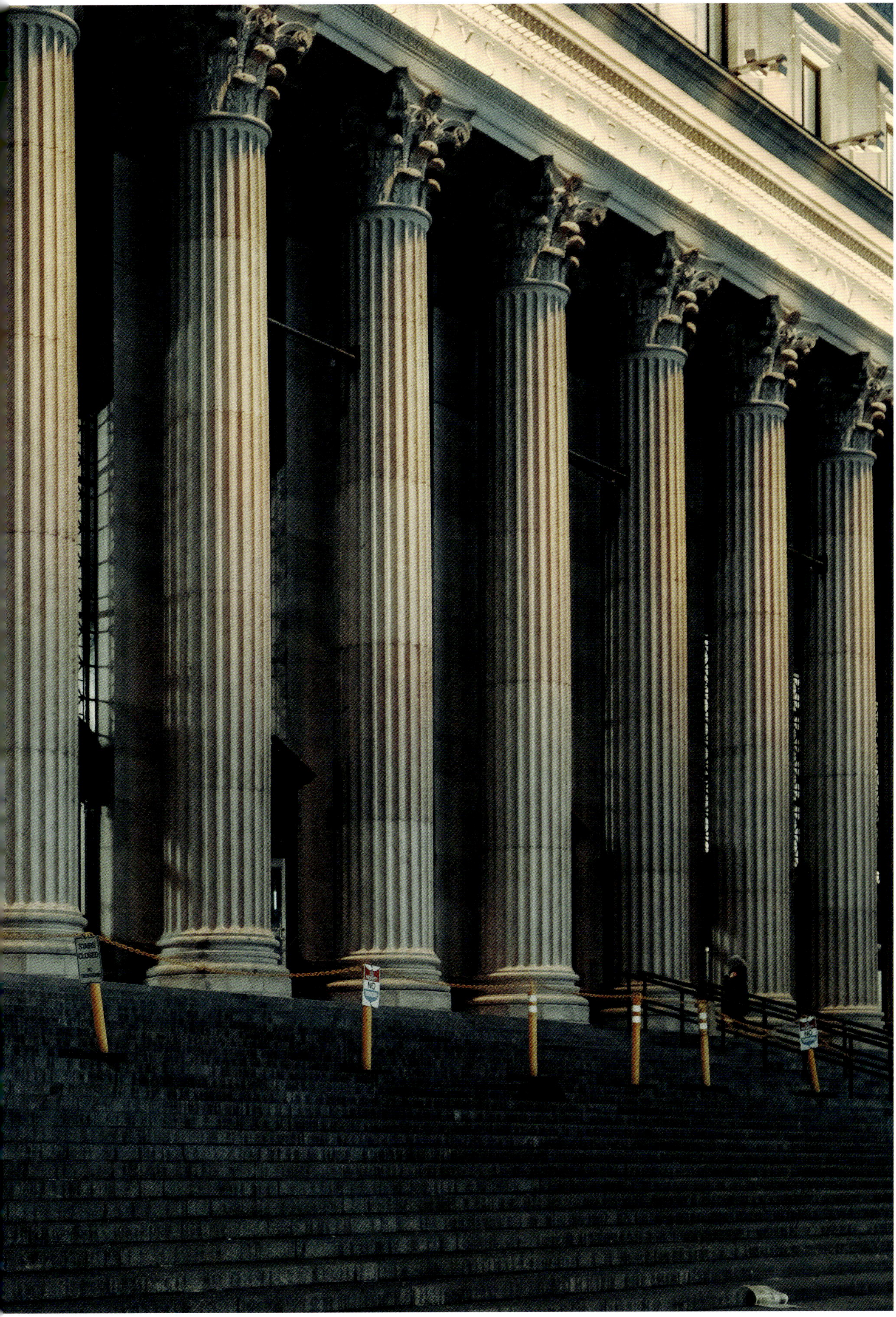

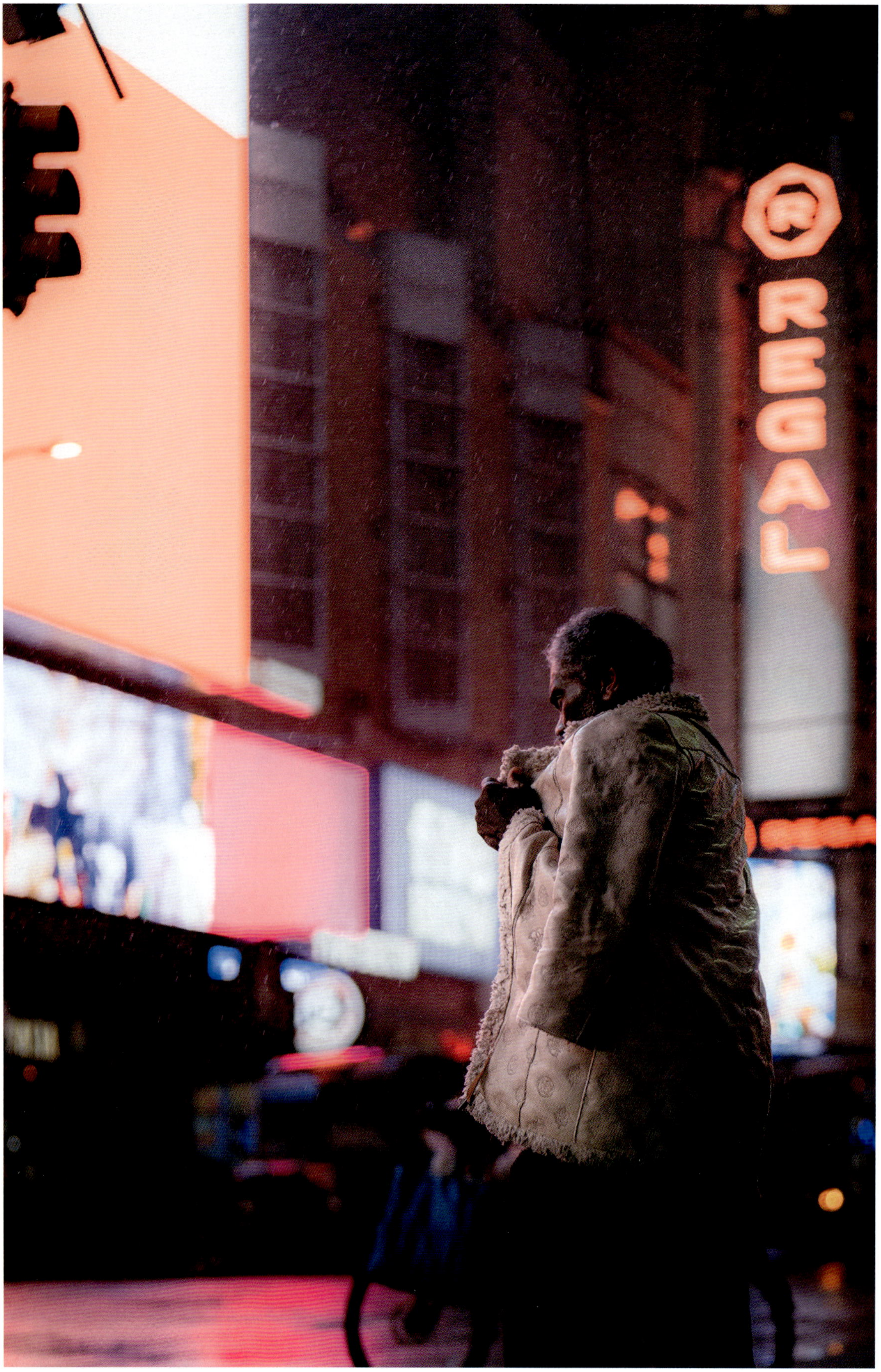
REGAL

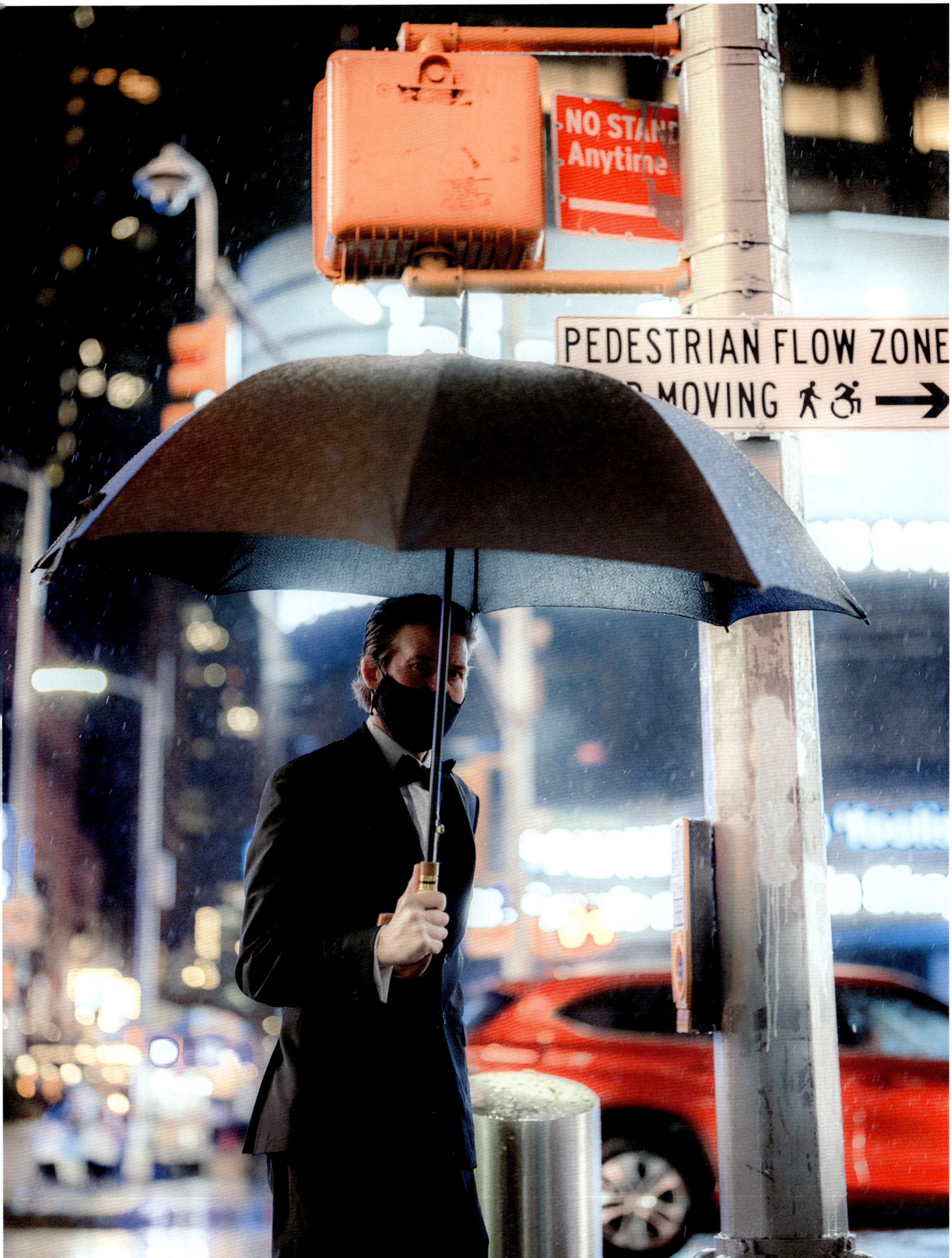
Anytime
PEDESTRIAN FLOW ZONE
MOVING

At night, Broadway and the Theater District transform into one of the brightest corridors in New York City. The area, generally extending from West 40th to West 54th Streets between Sixth and Eighth Avenues, is defined by concentrated exterior lighting from marquees, digital billboards, and illuminated signage. Once the sun goes down, lighting becomes the dominant visual element of the streetscape.

The district's brightness is closely associated with Times Square, where large-format LED displays operate continuously. While modern signage relies heavily on digital technology, the tradition of lighted theater advertising dates to the late 19th and early 20th centuries. Broadway was among the first major thoroughfares in the country to adopt widespread electric lighting, leading to the nickname "The Great White Way." Early incandescent bulbs and neon tubing were used to attract attention to theatrical productions and commercial venues.

Individual theaters contribute to the nighttime glow through vertical blade signs and overhead marquees. Marquees commonly incorporate rows of exposed bulbs or LED strips outlining their edges, producing consistent bands of light along the sidewalks. Vertical signs extend upward from façades, increasing visibility from a distance.

The area remains one of the busiest in Manhattan, particularly between the hours of 6pm and 11pm, with peak pedestrian volumes just before curtain times and immediately after performances end. During these windows, the sidewalks fill with theatergoers lining up beneath marquees or gathering for photos.

Times Square alone draws hundreds of thousands of visitors daily, and evening hours are among the busiest, particularly on weekends and during peak tourist seasons. Even people not attending performances are drawn to the area to specifically experience the illuminated billboards and nighttime atmosphere.

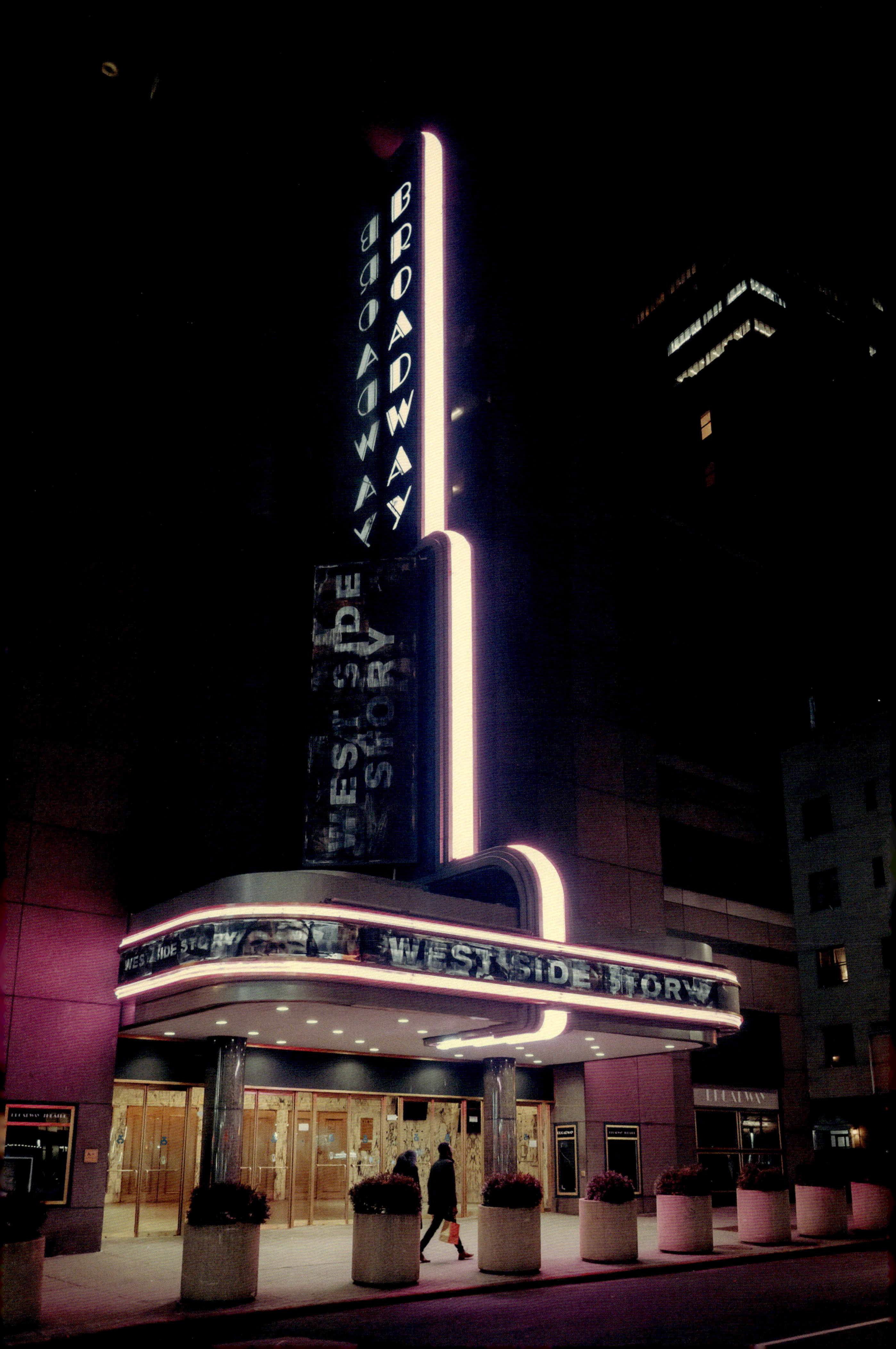
BROADWAY
WEST SIDE STORY
WEST SIDE STORY

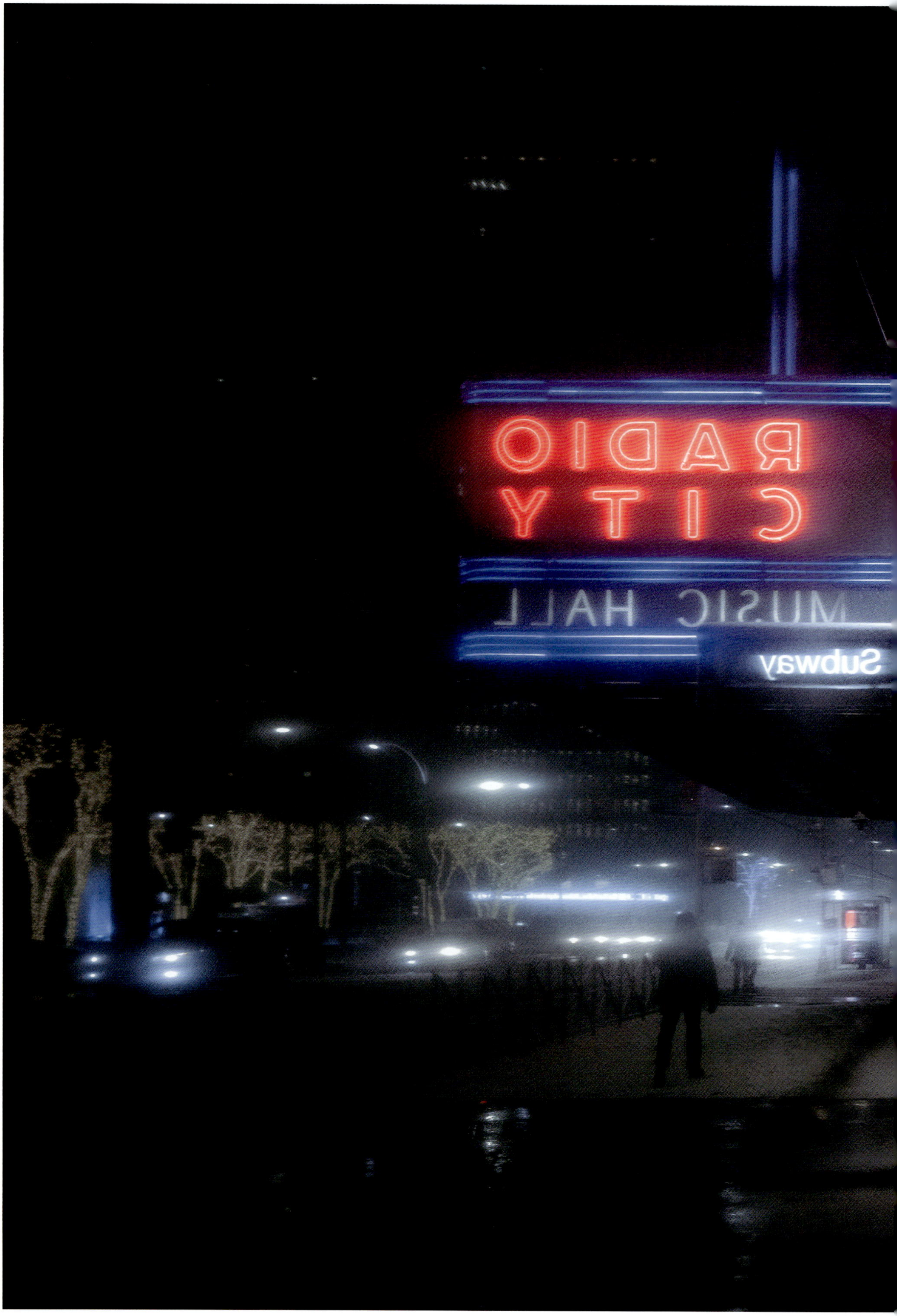

RADIO CITY MUSIC HALL

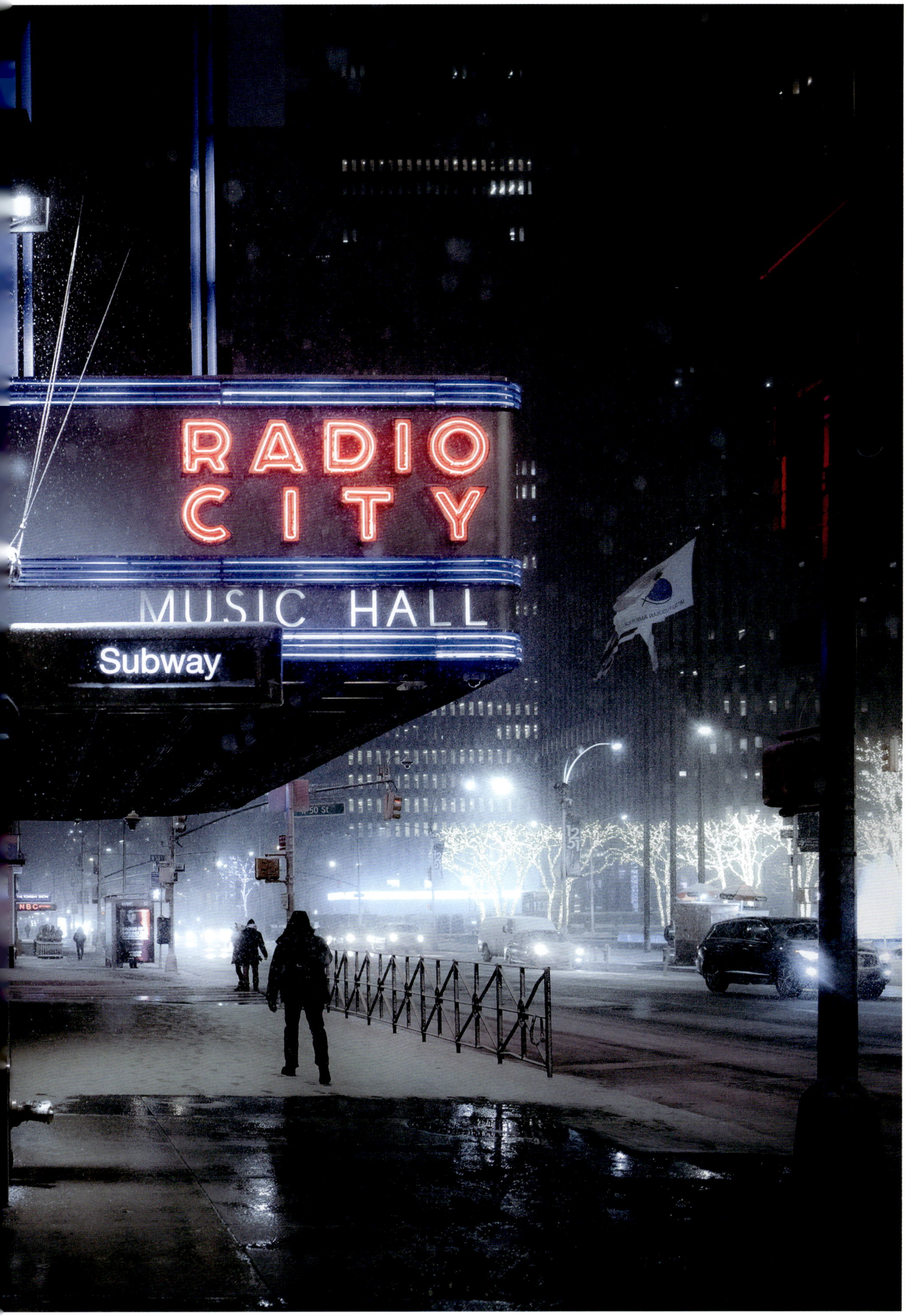
RADIO
CITY
MUSIC HALL
Subway

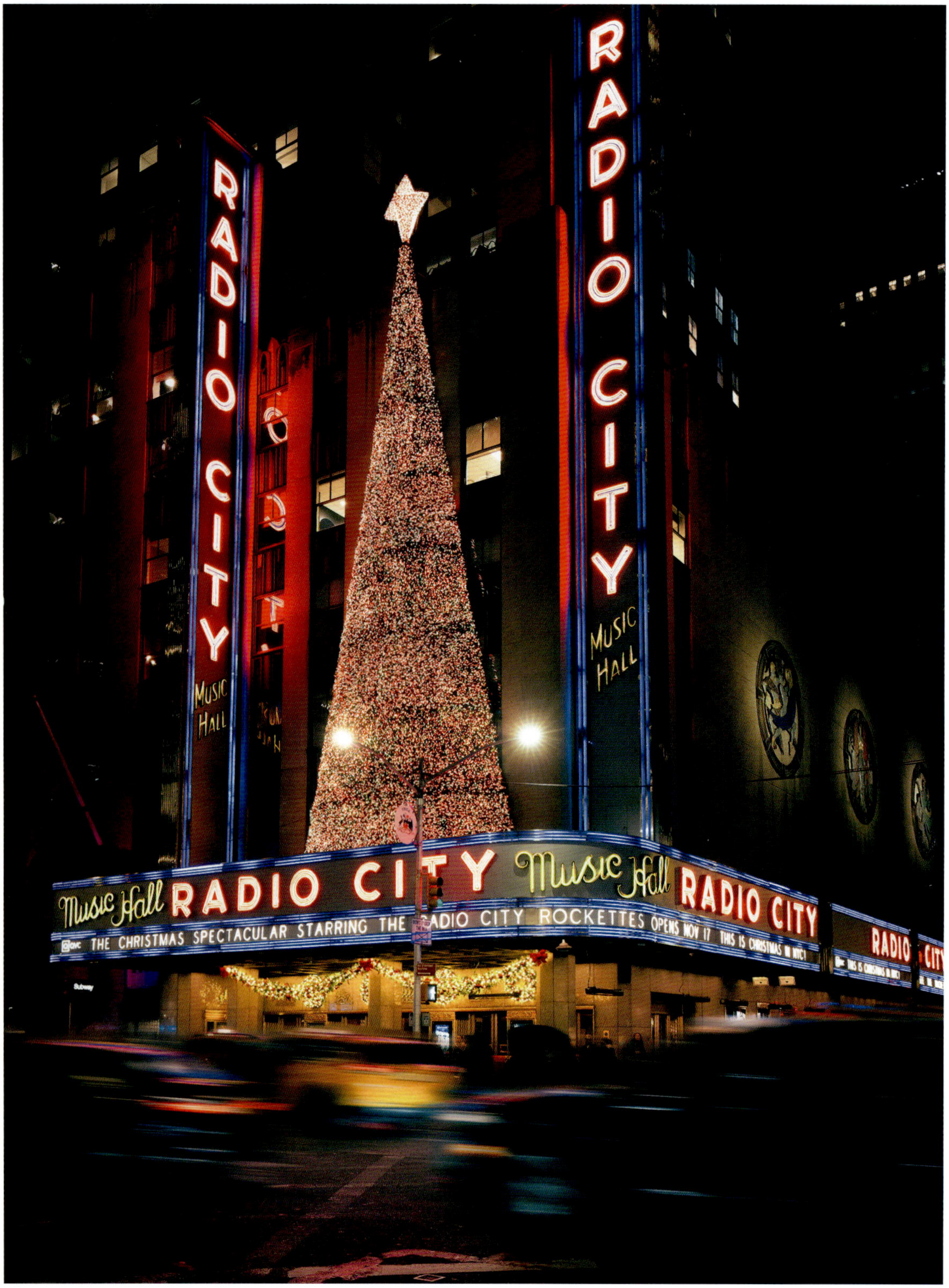
RADIO CITY
RADIO CITY
MUSIC HALL
Music Hall RADIO CITY Music Hall RADIO CITY
THE CHRISTMAS SPECTACULAR STARRING THE RADIO CITY ROCKETTES OPENS NOV 17 THIS IS CHRISTMAS IN NYC!

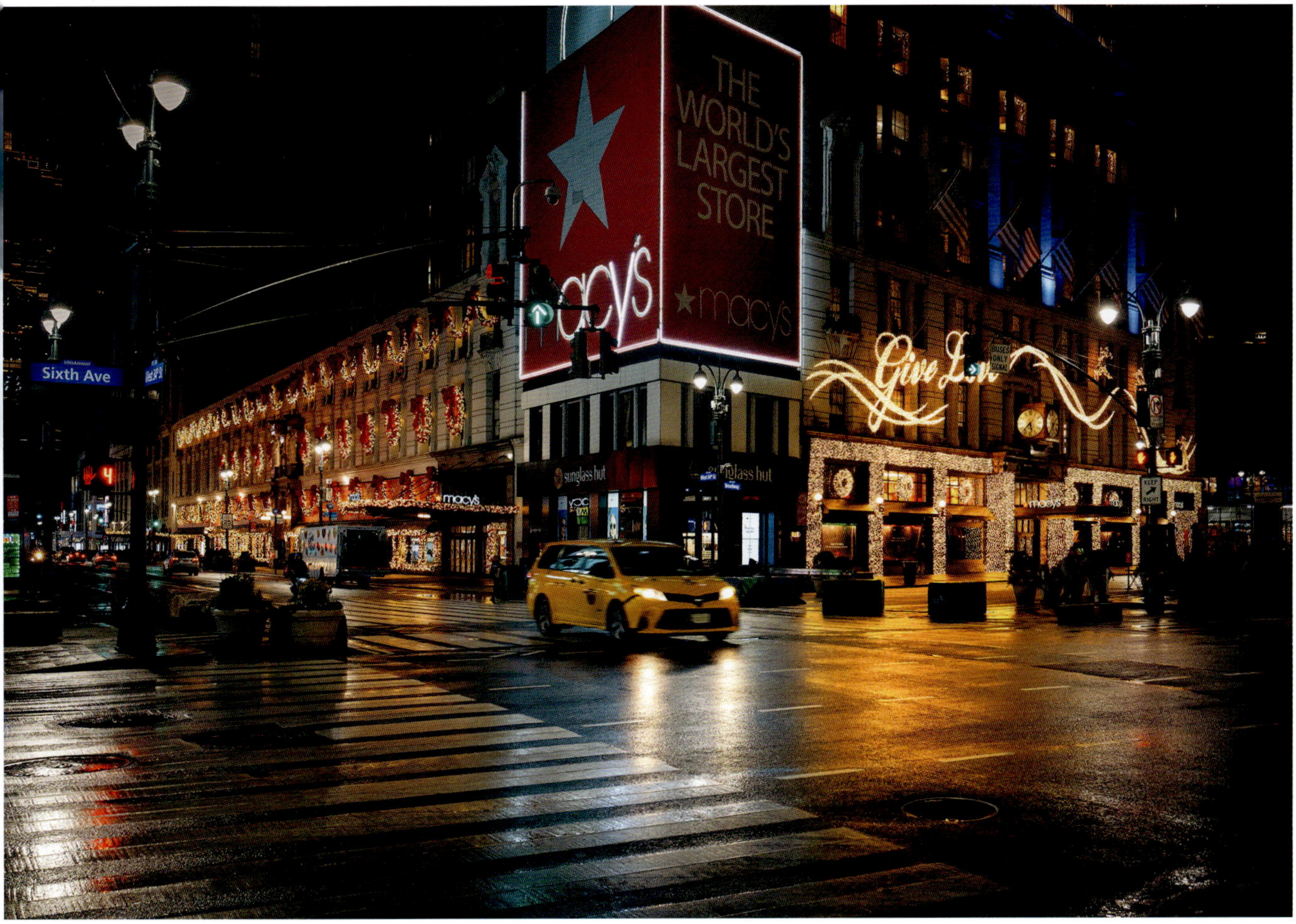
THE WORLD'S LARGEST STORE
macy's
★macy's
Sixth Ave
sunglass hut

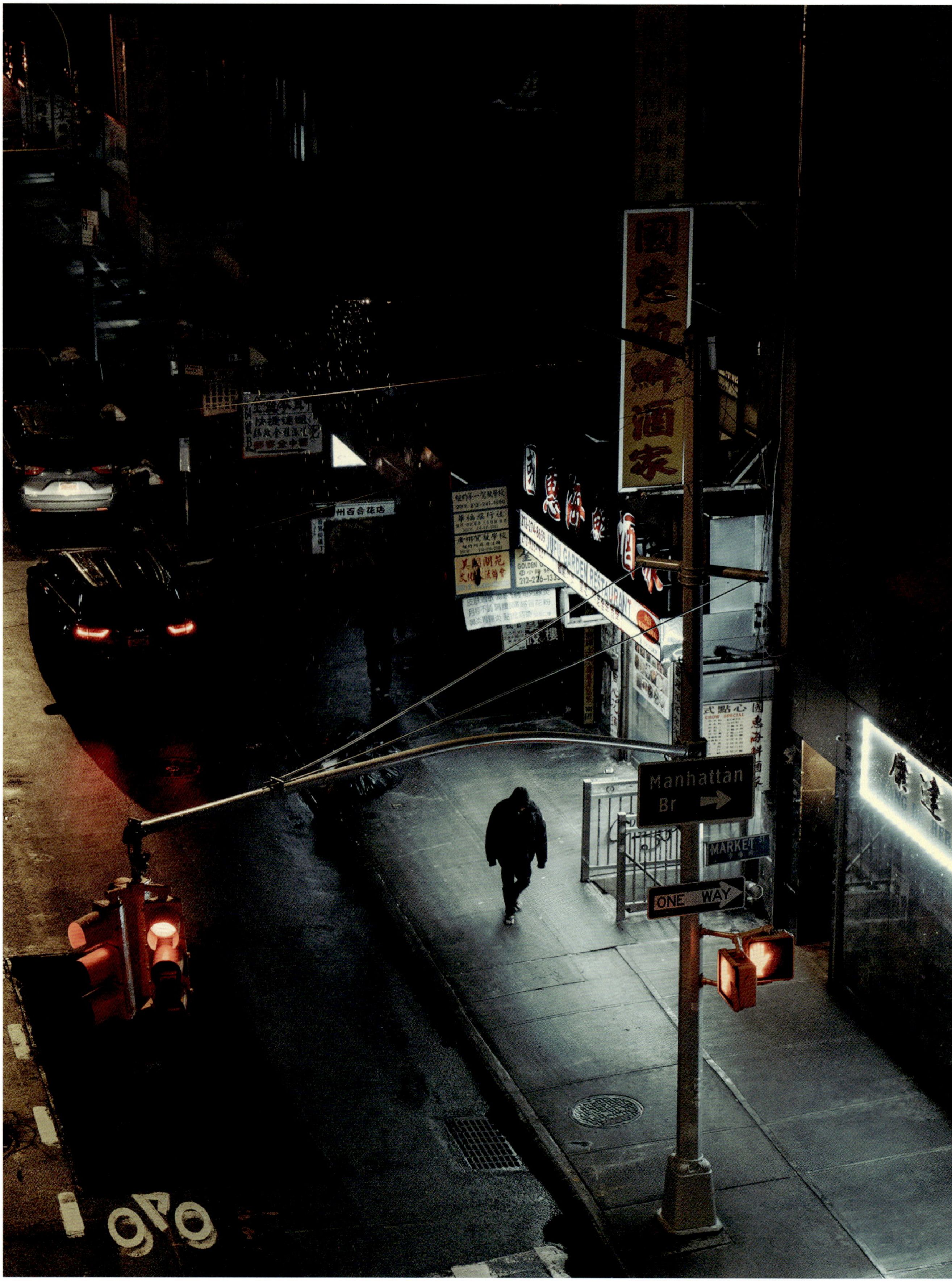
國惠海鮮酒家
Manhattan
Br
MARKET
ONE WAY

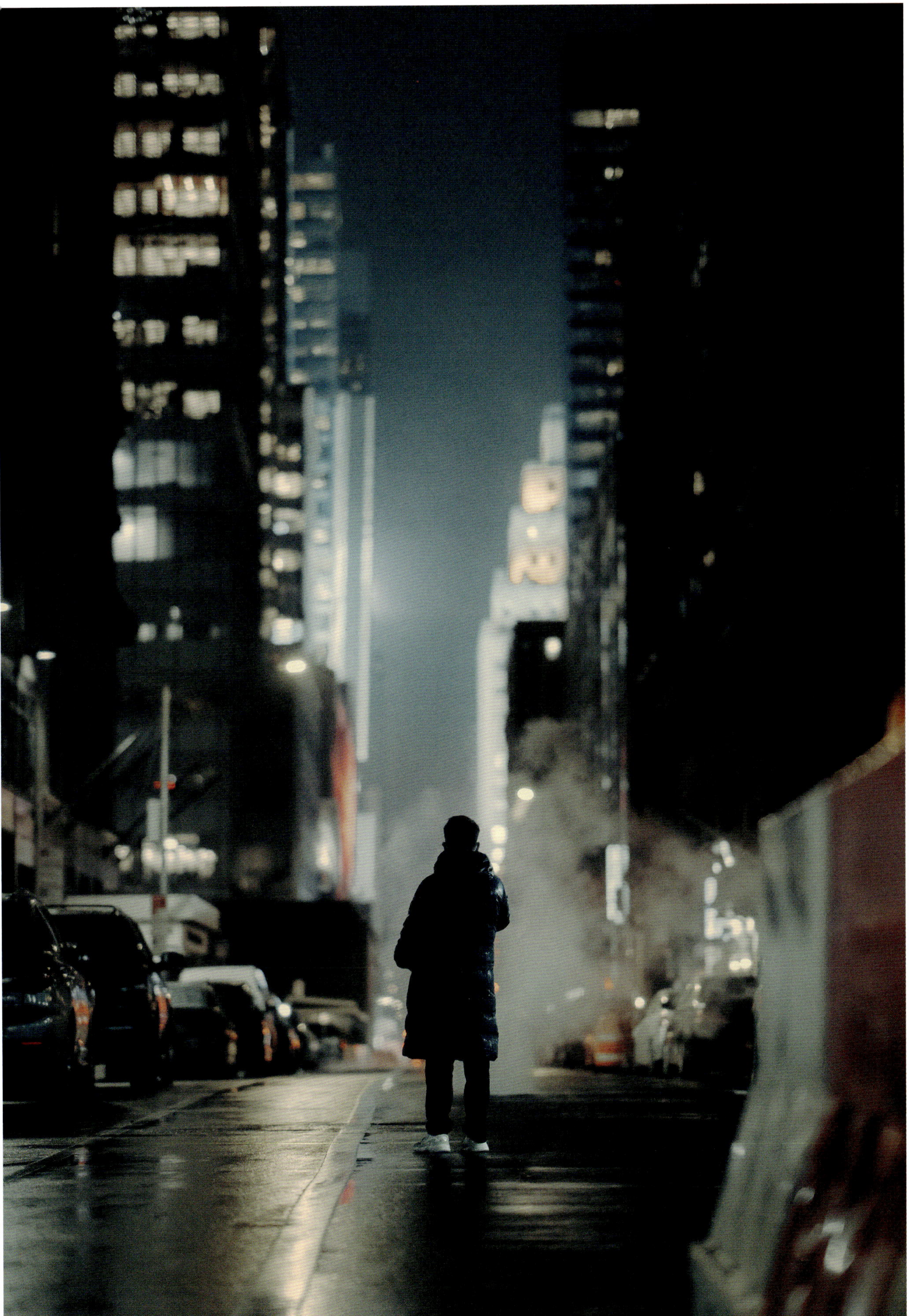

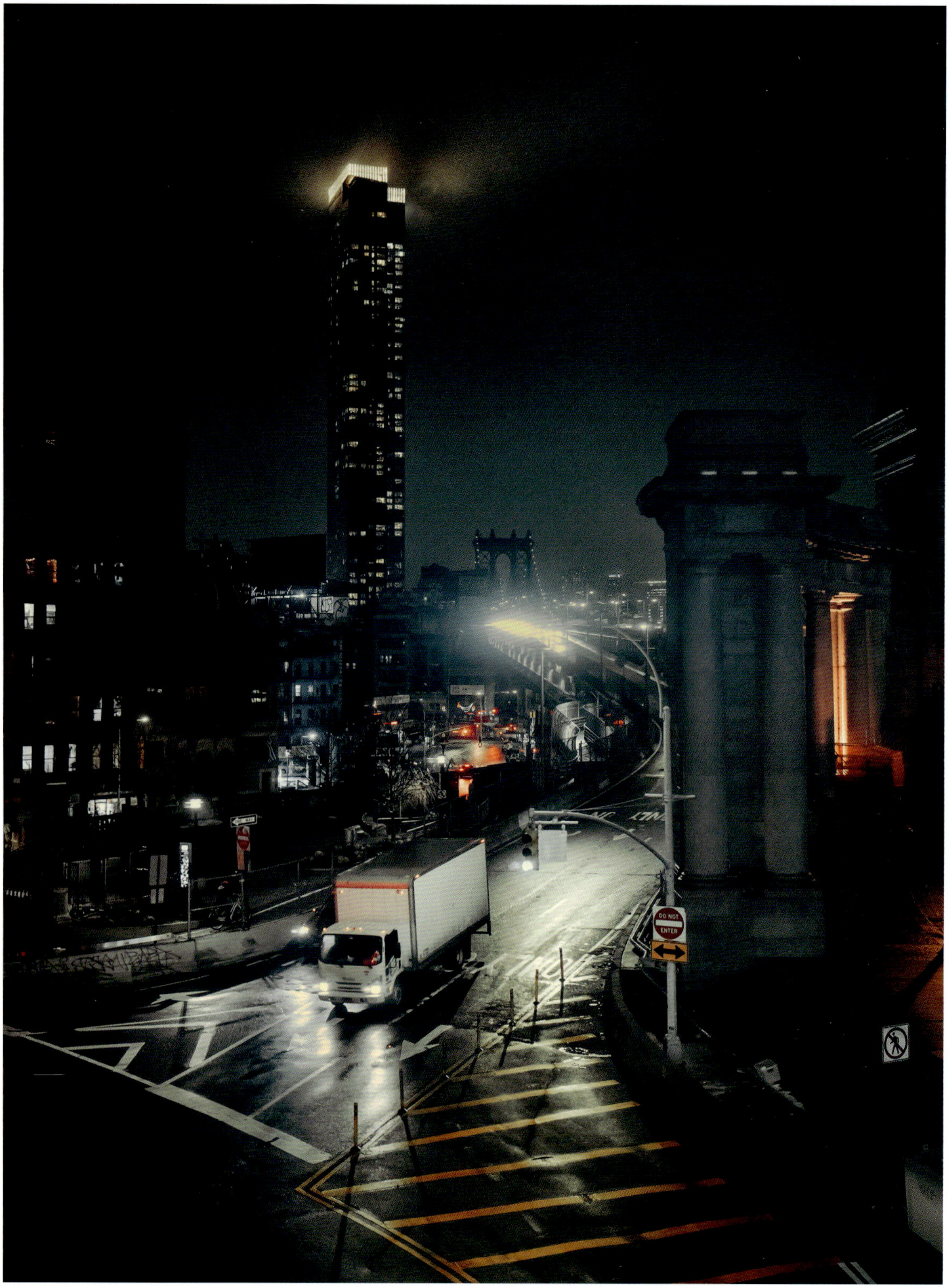
DO NOT
ENTER

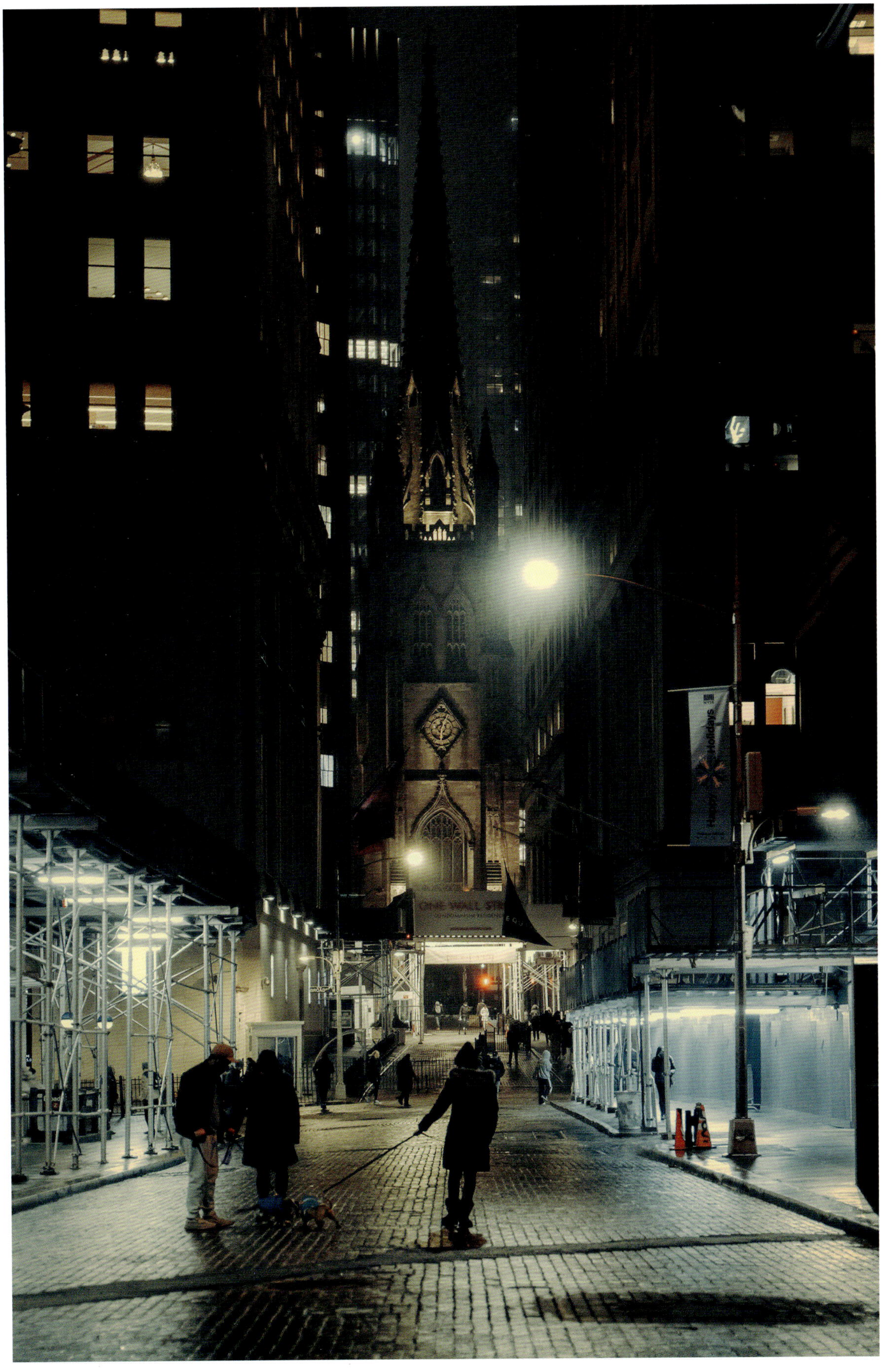
ONE WALL STREET

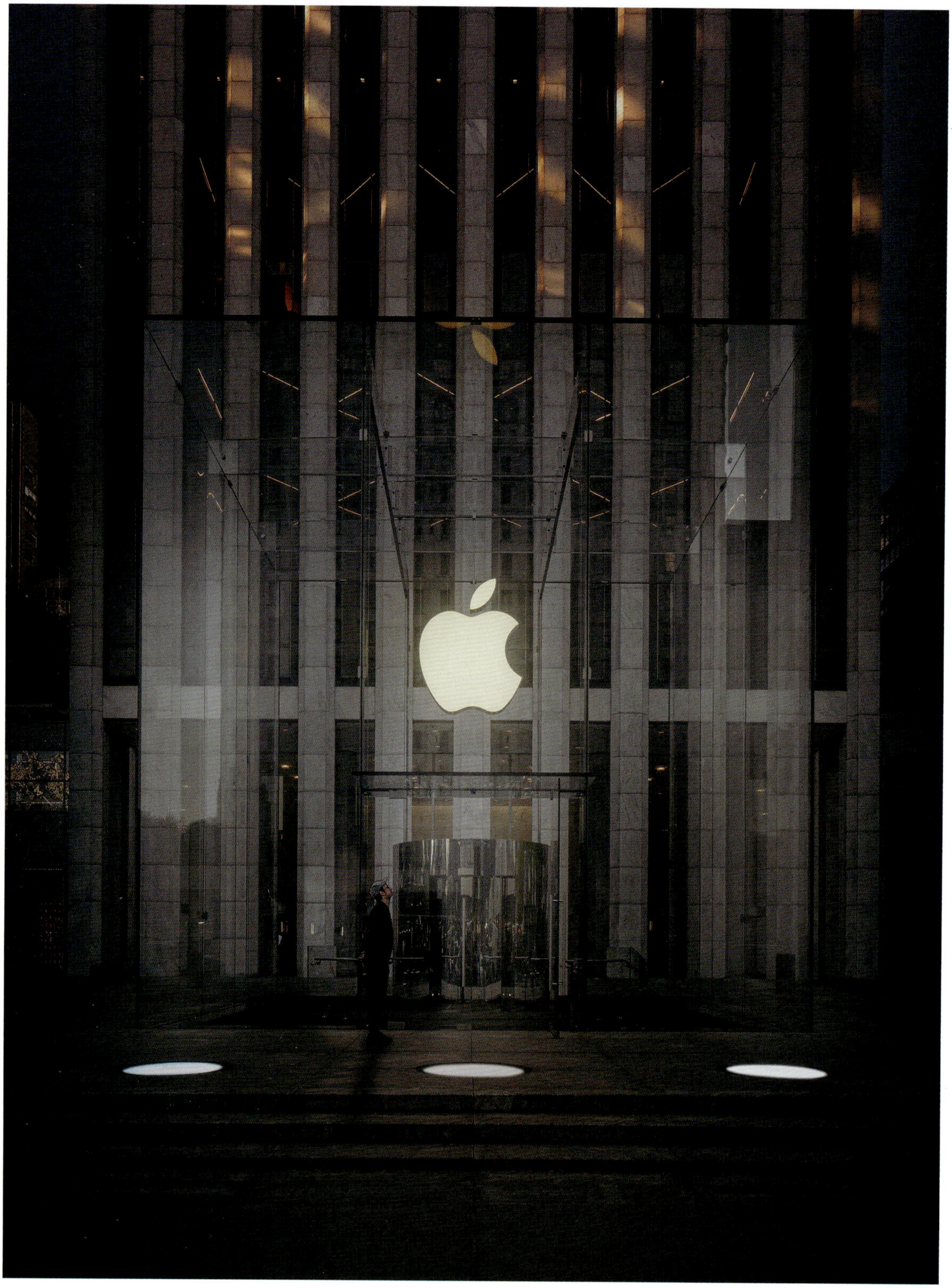

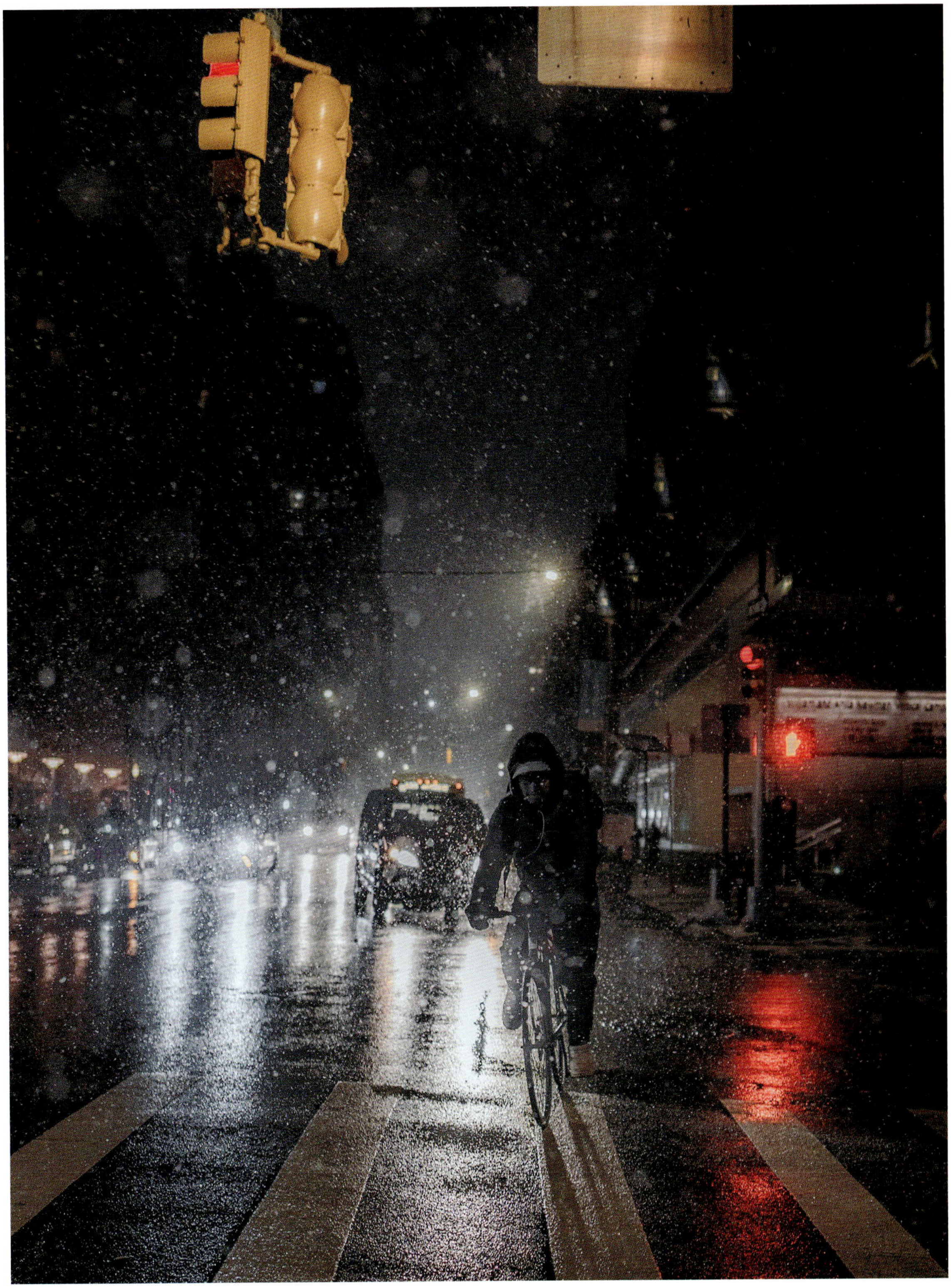

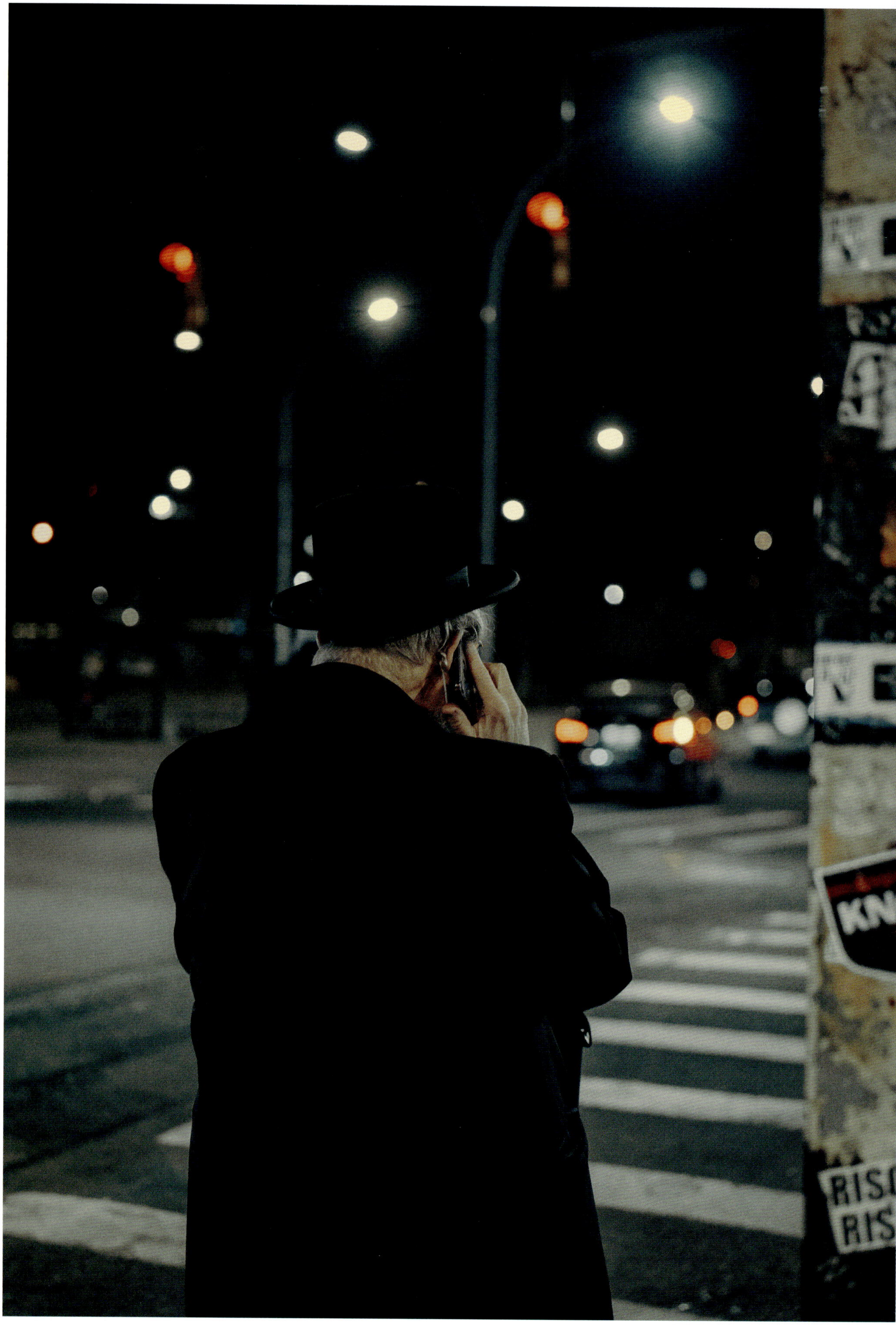

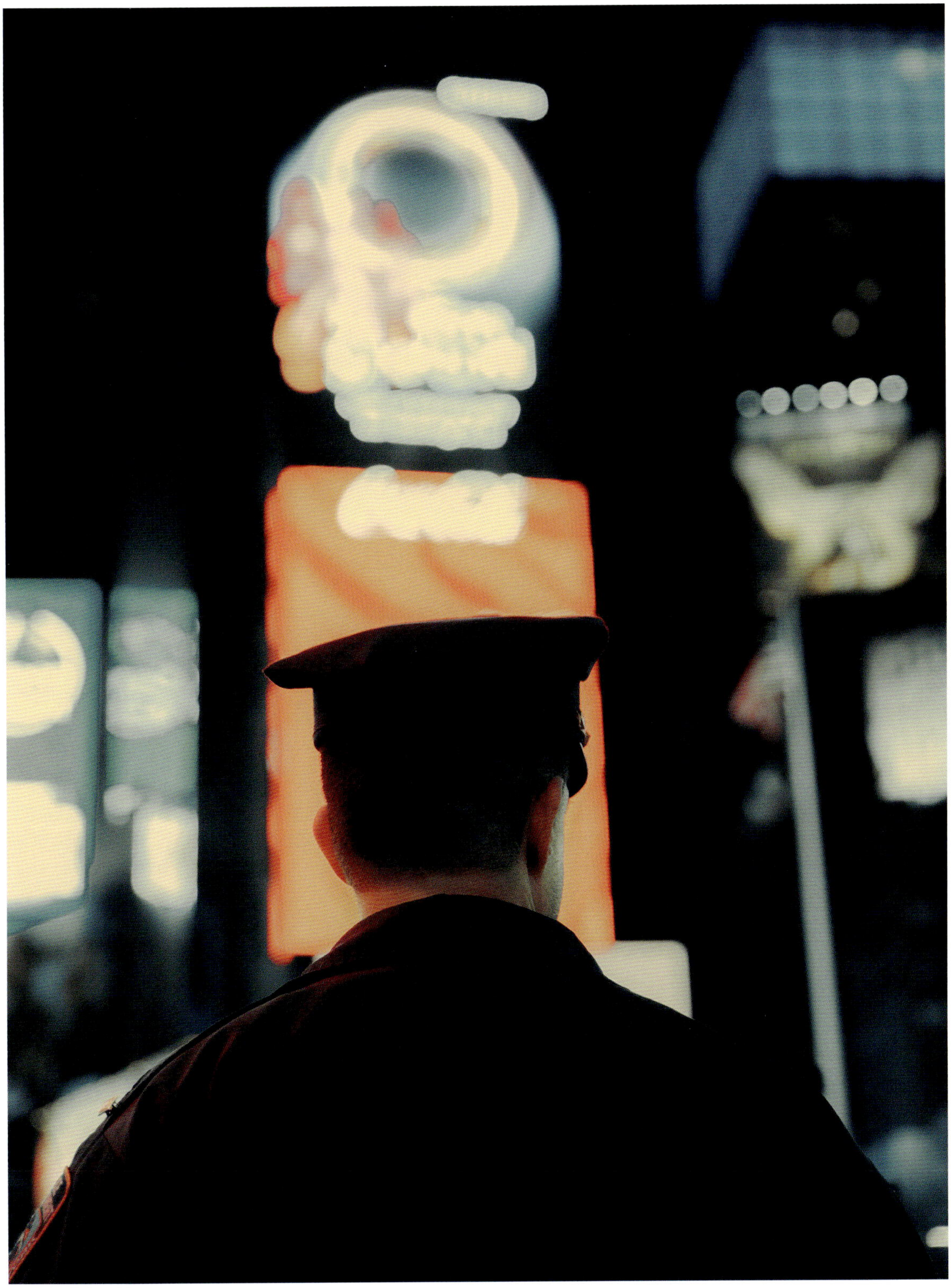

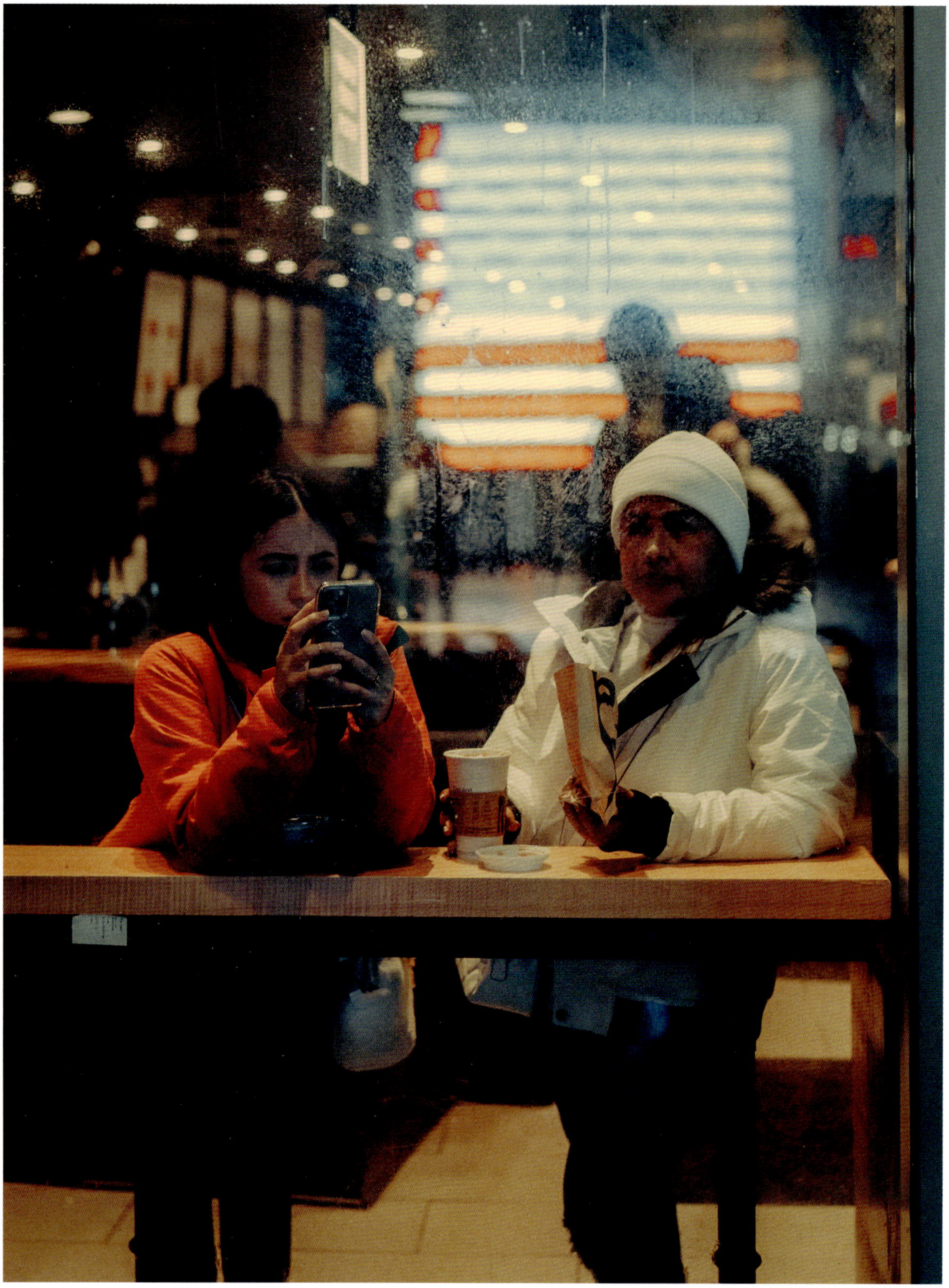

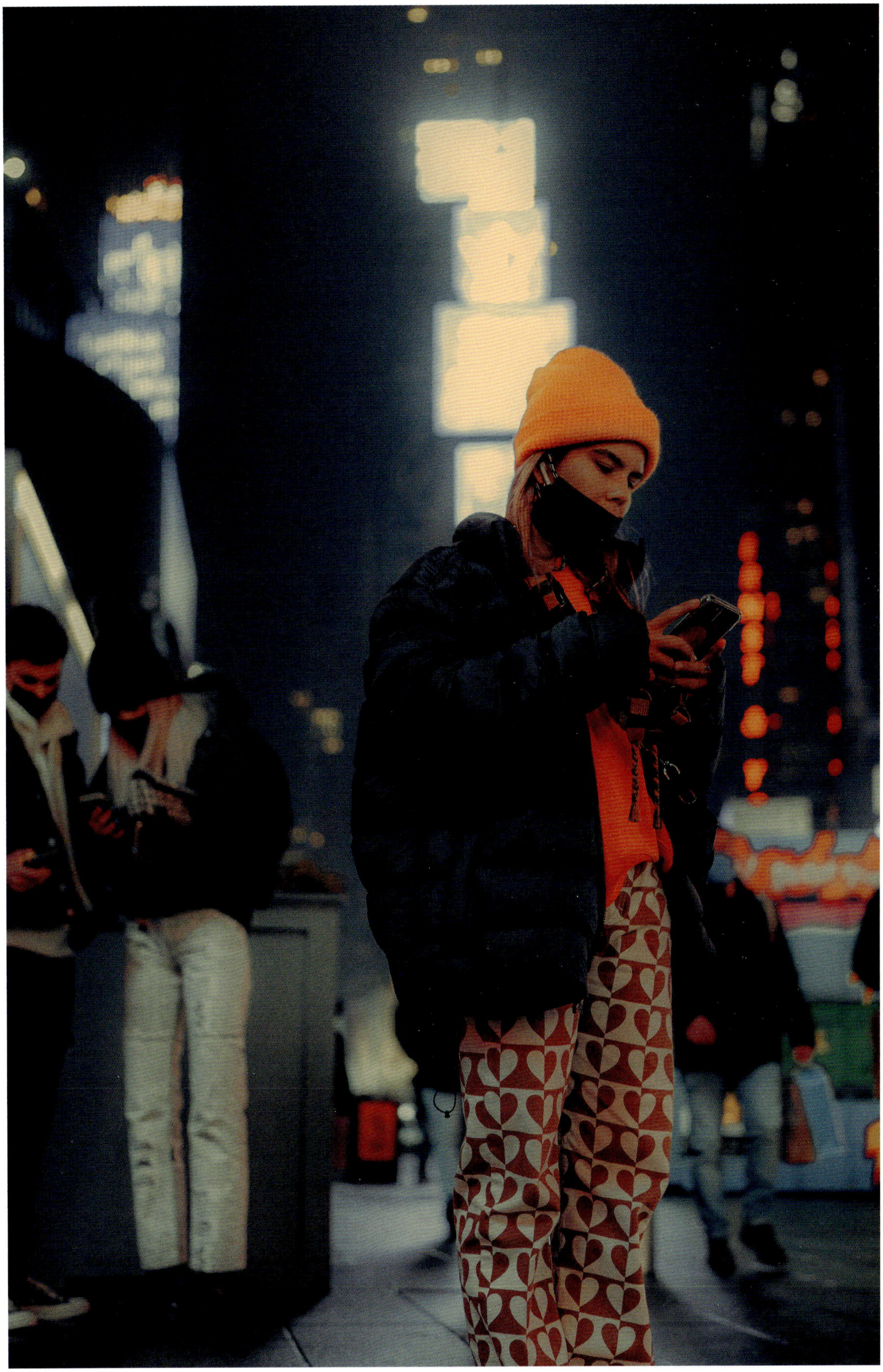

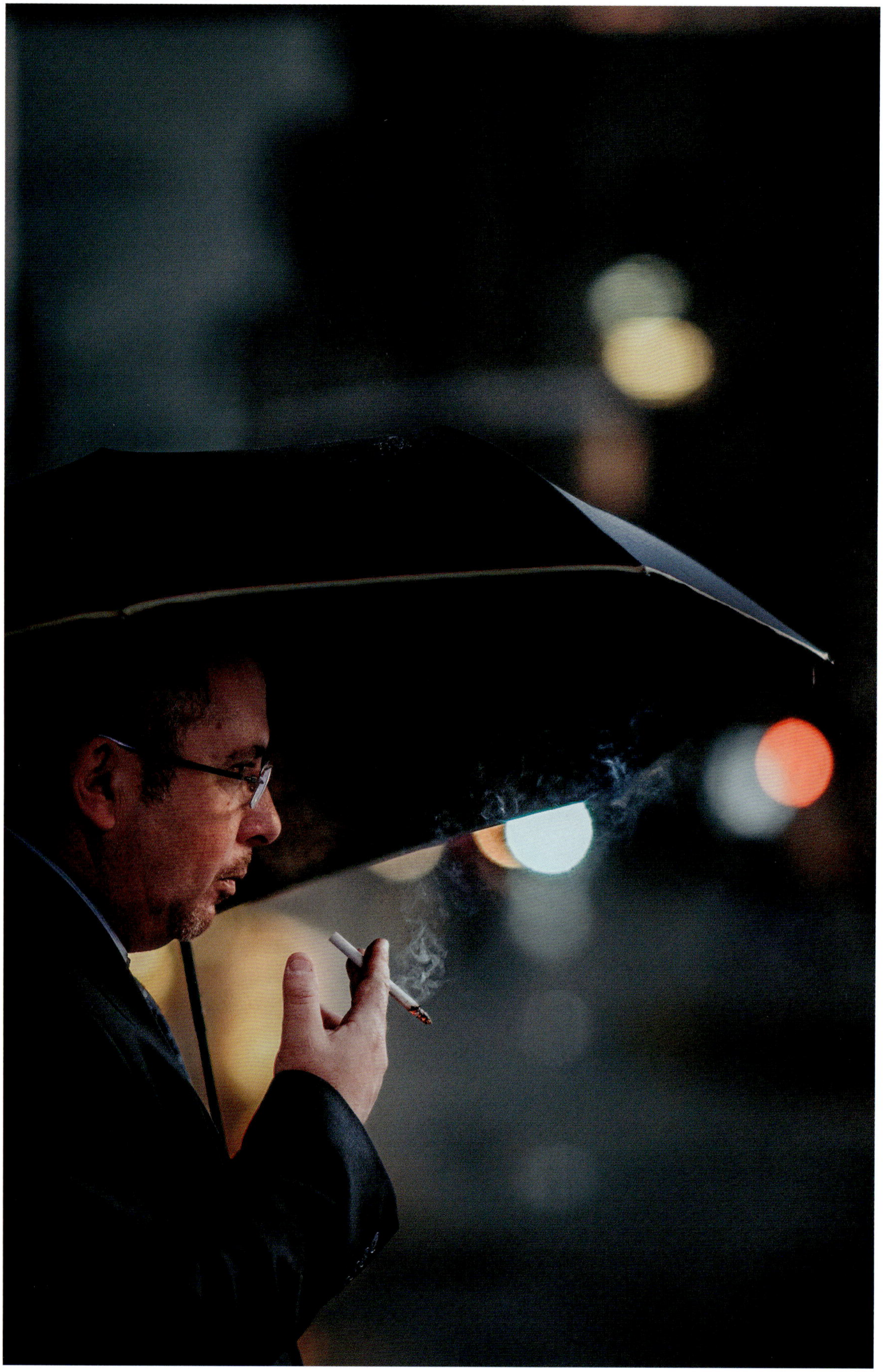

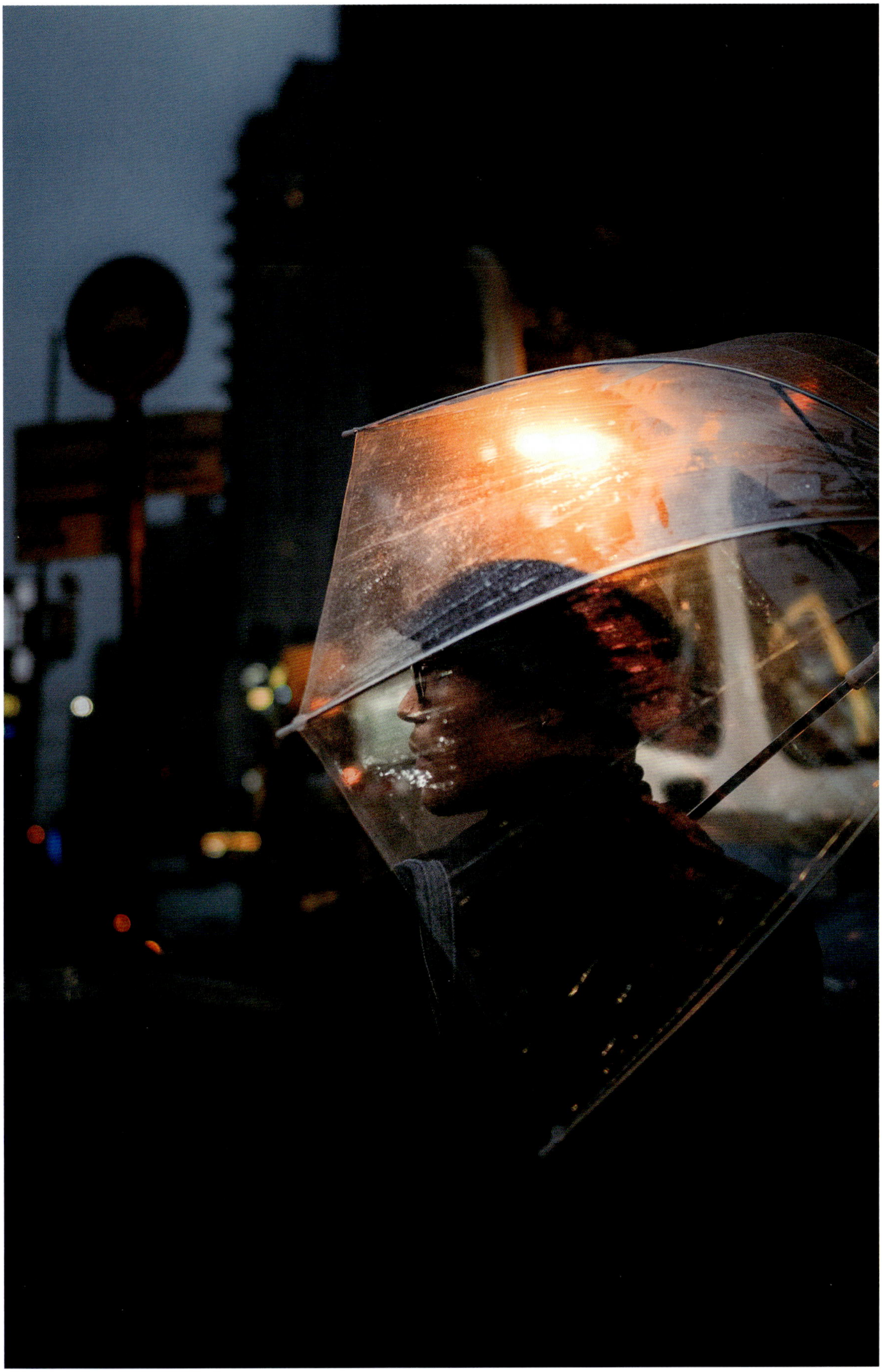

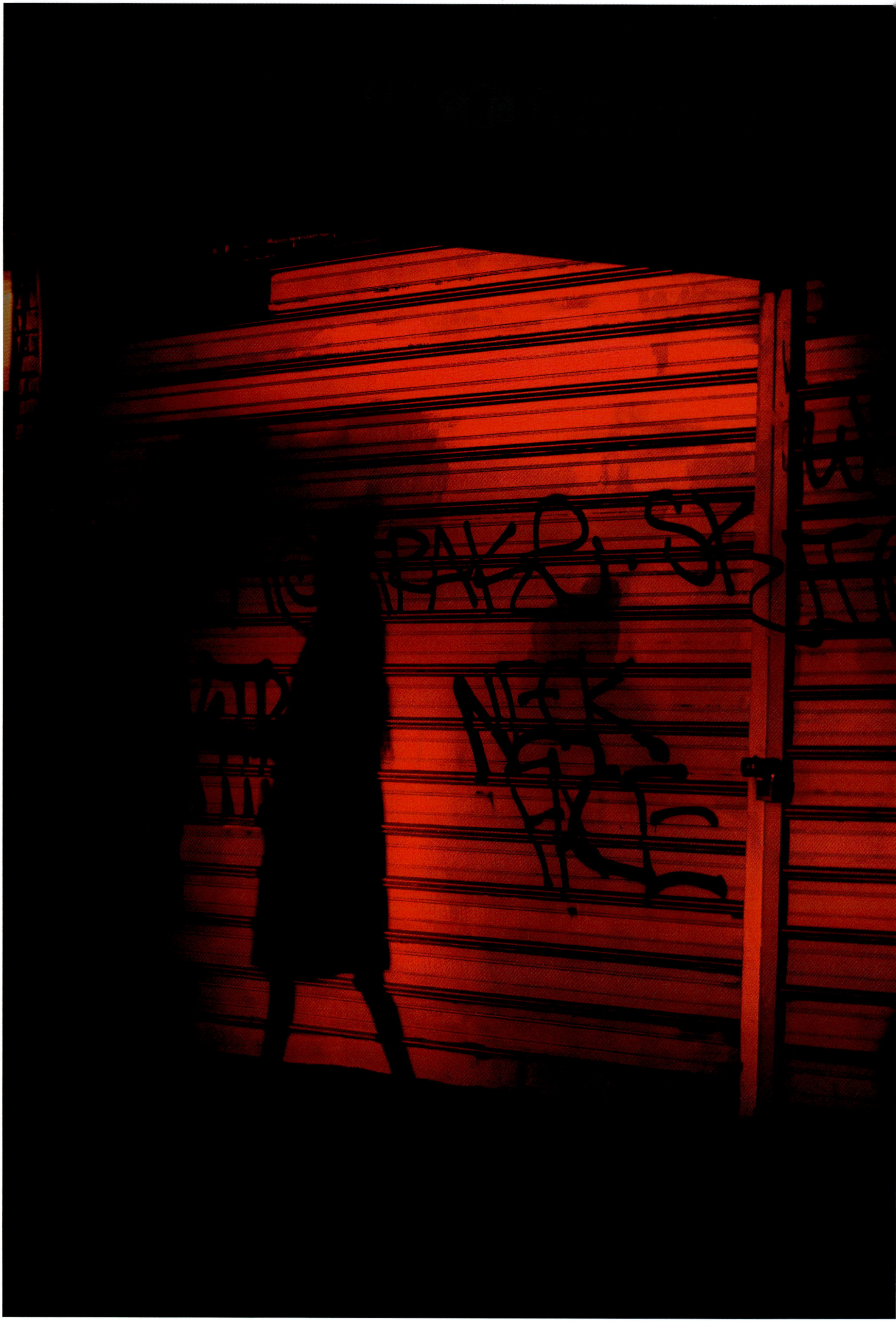

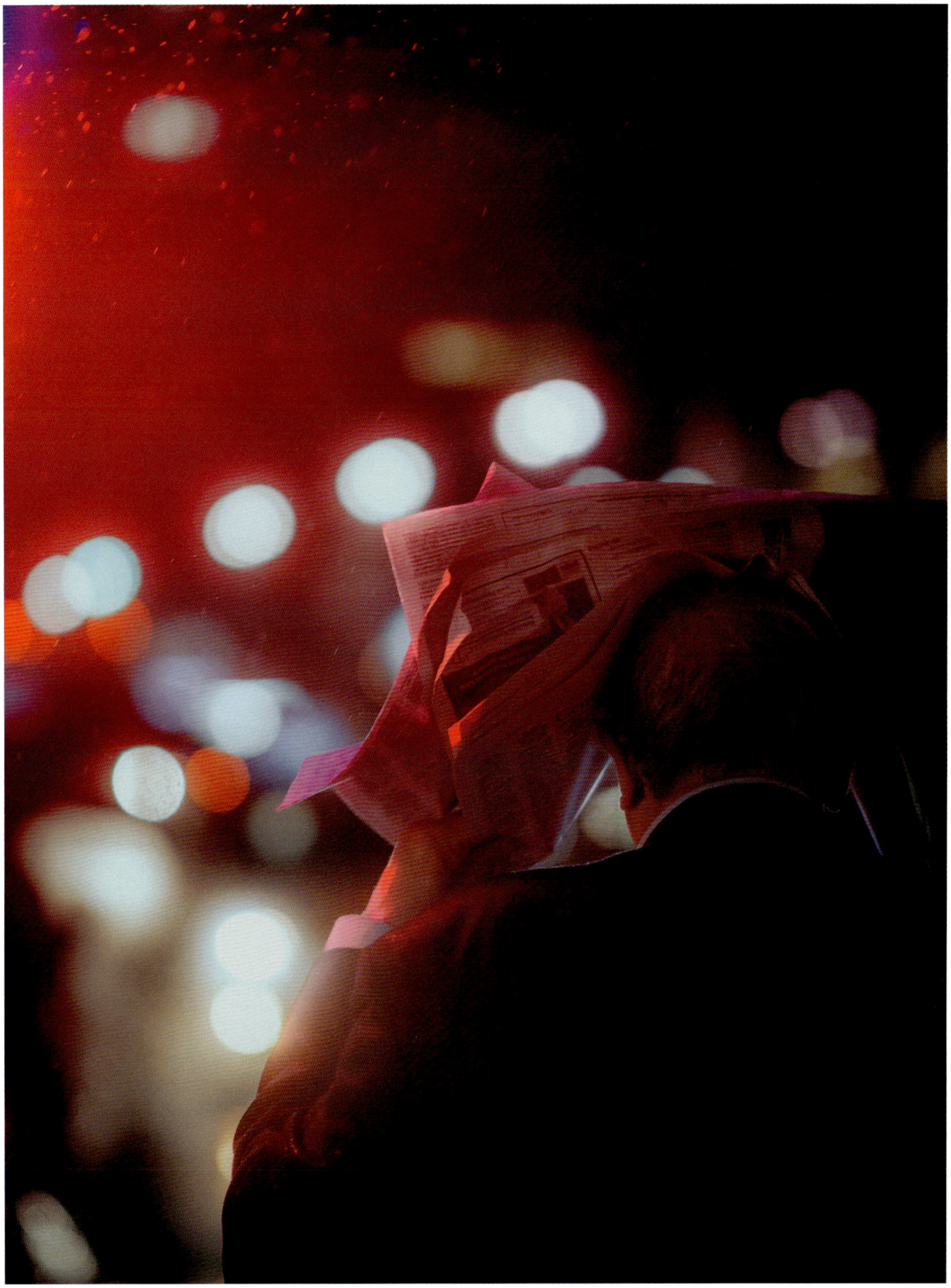

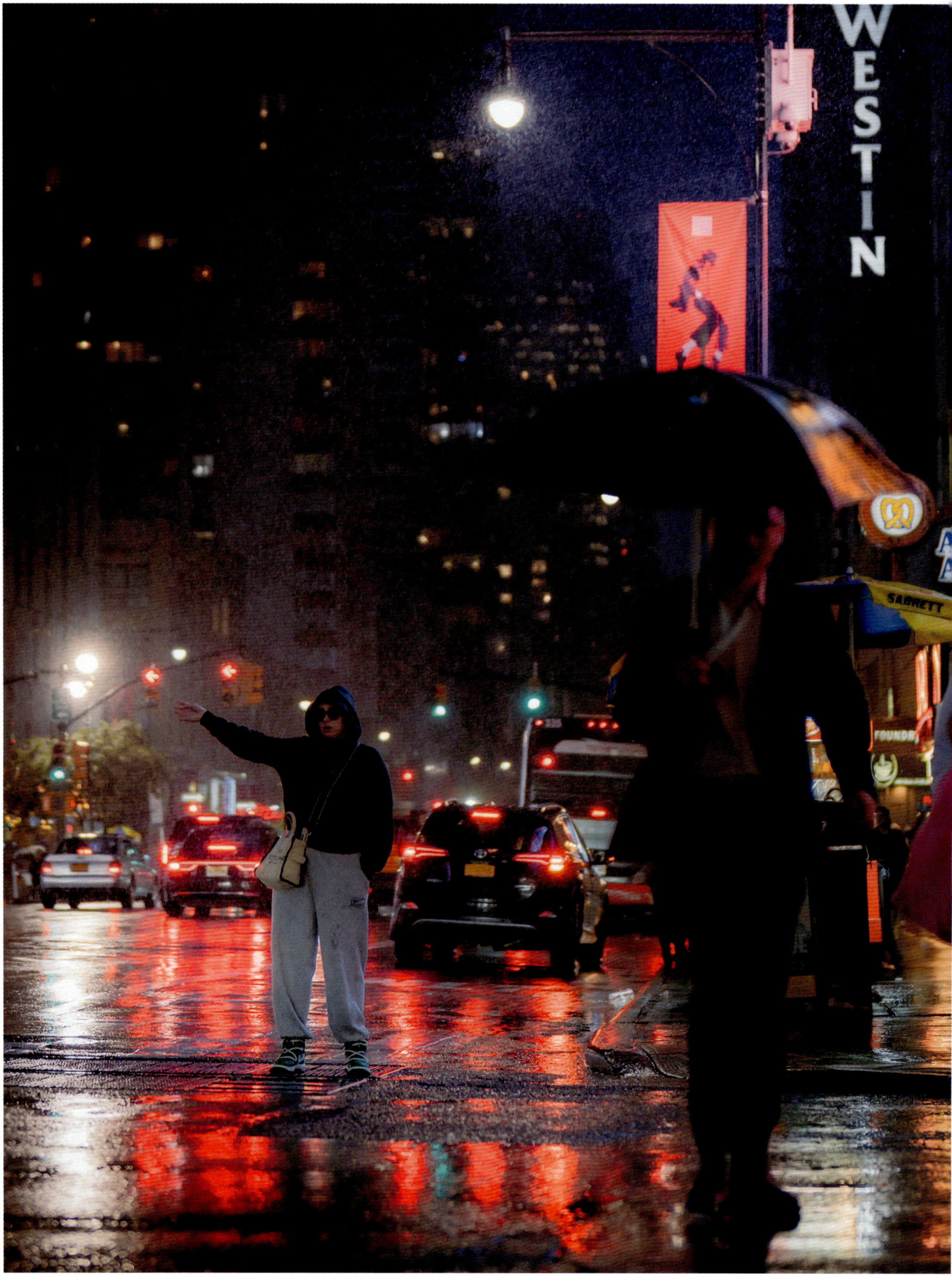
WESTIN
SABRETT

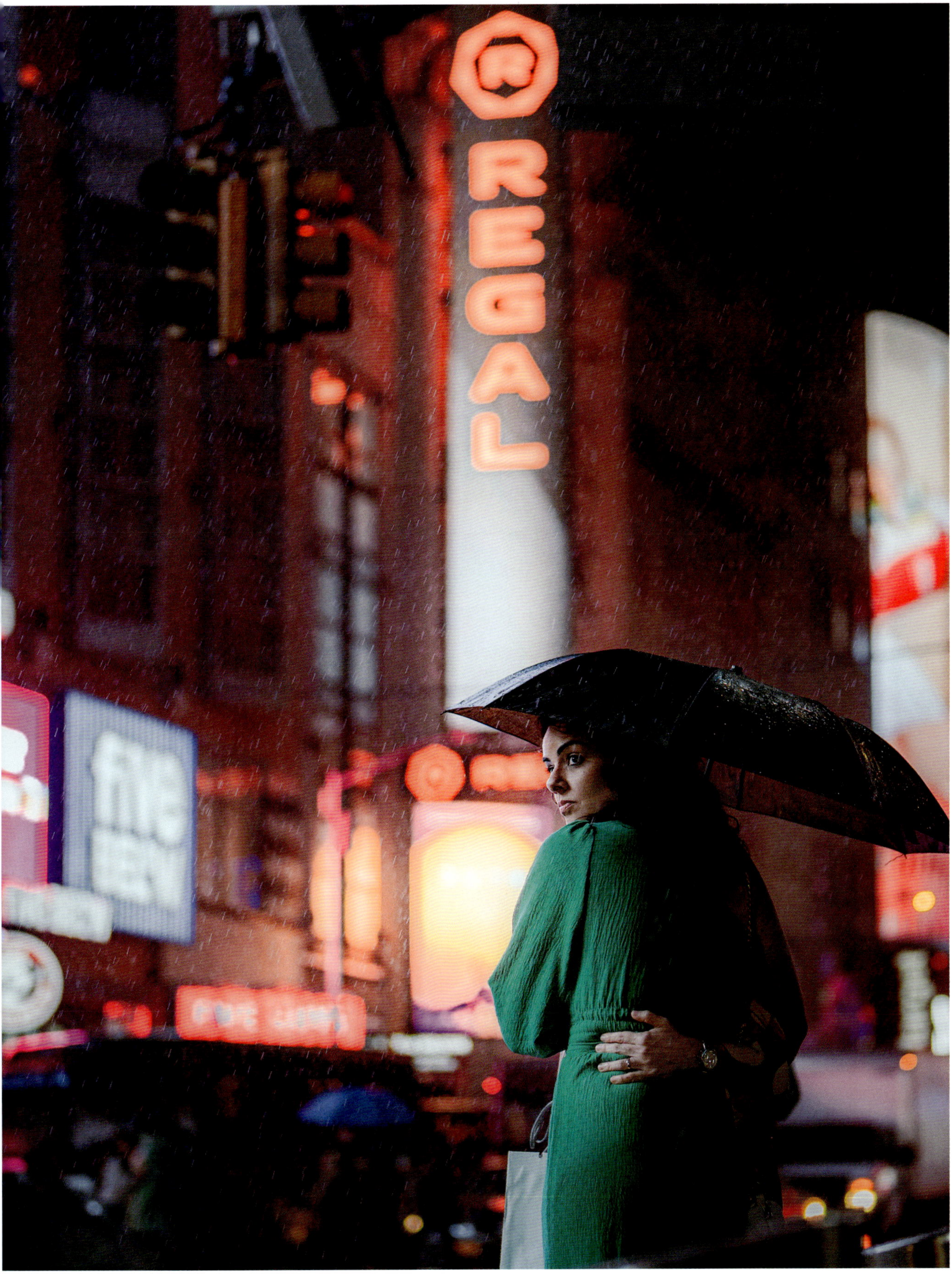
REGAL

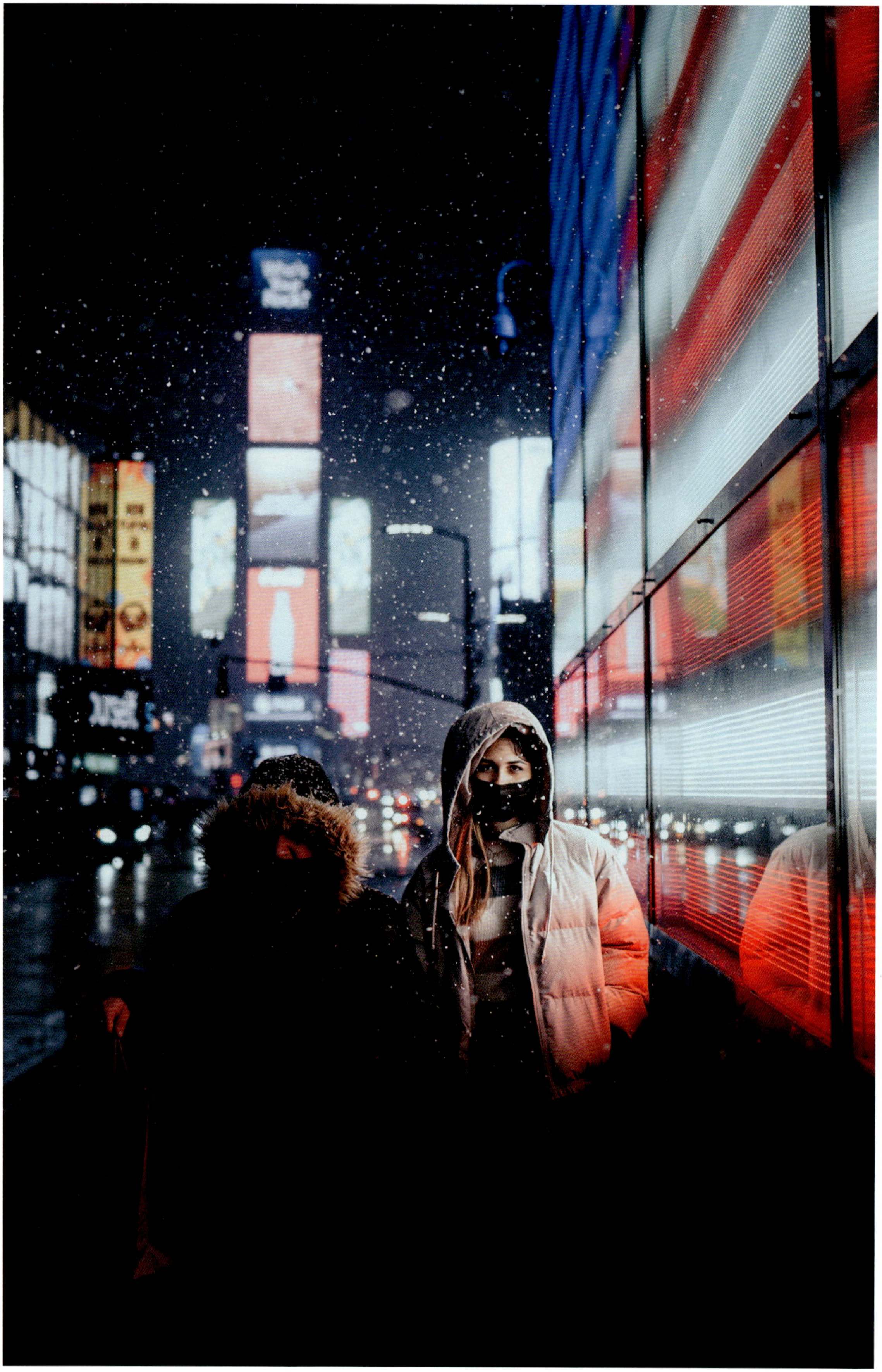

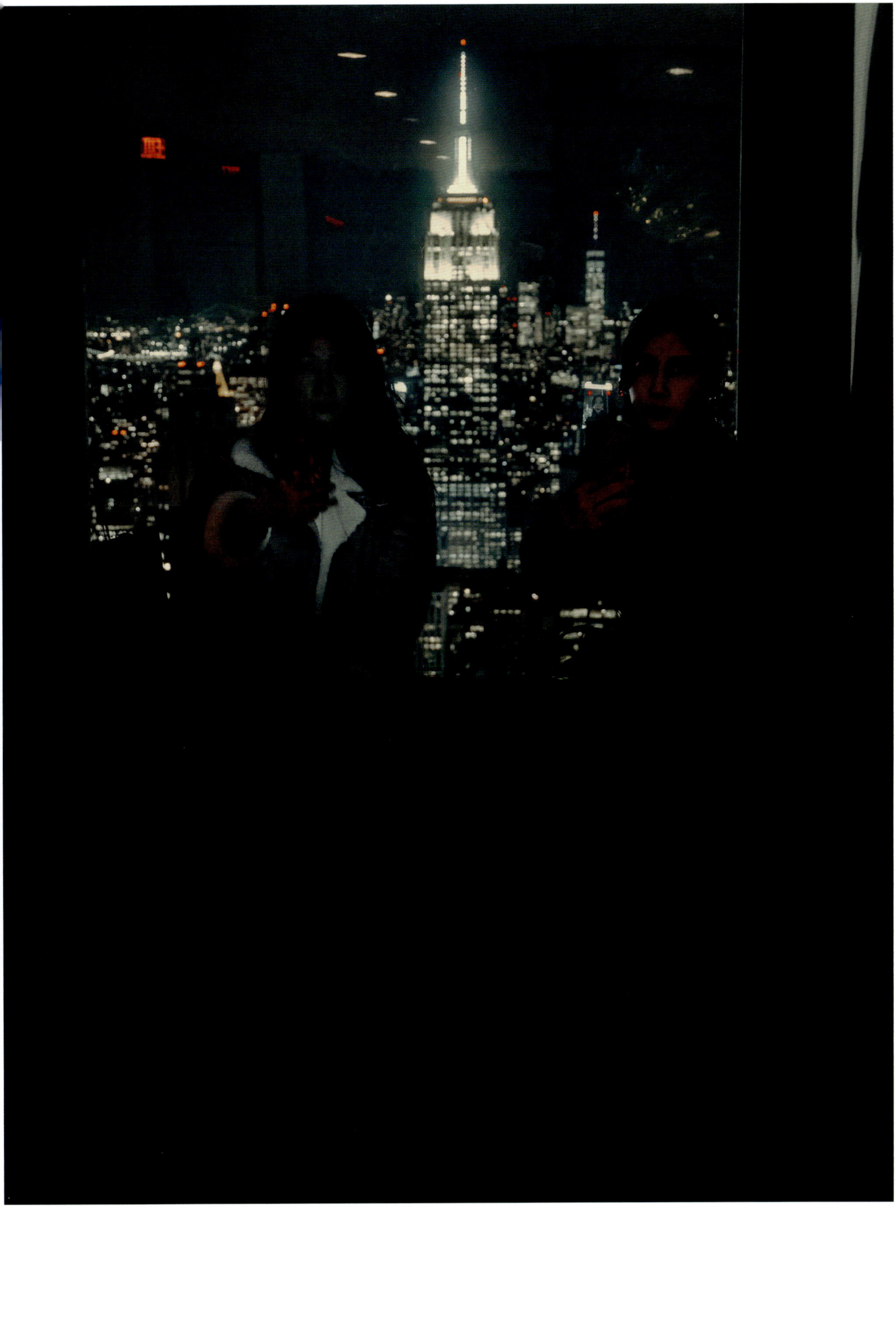

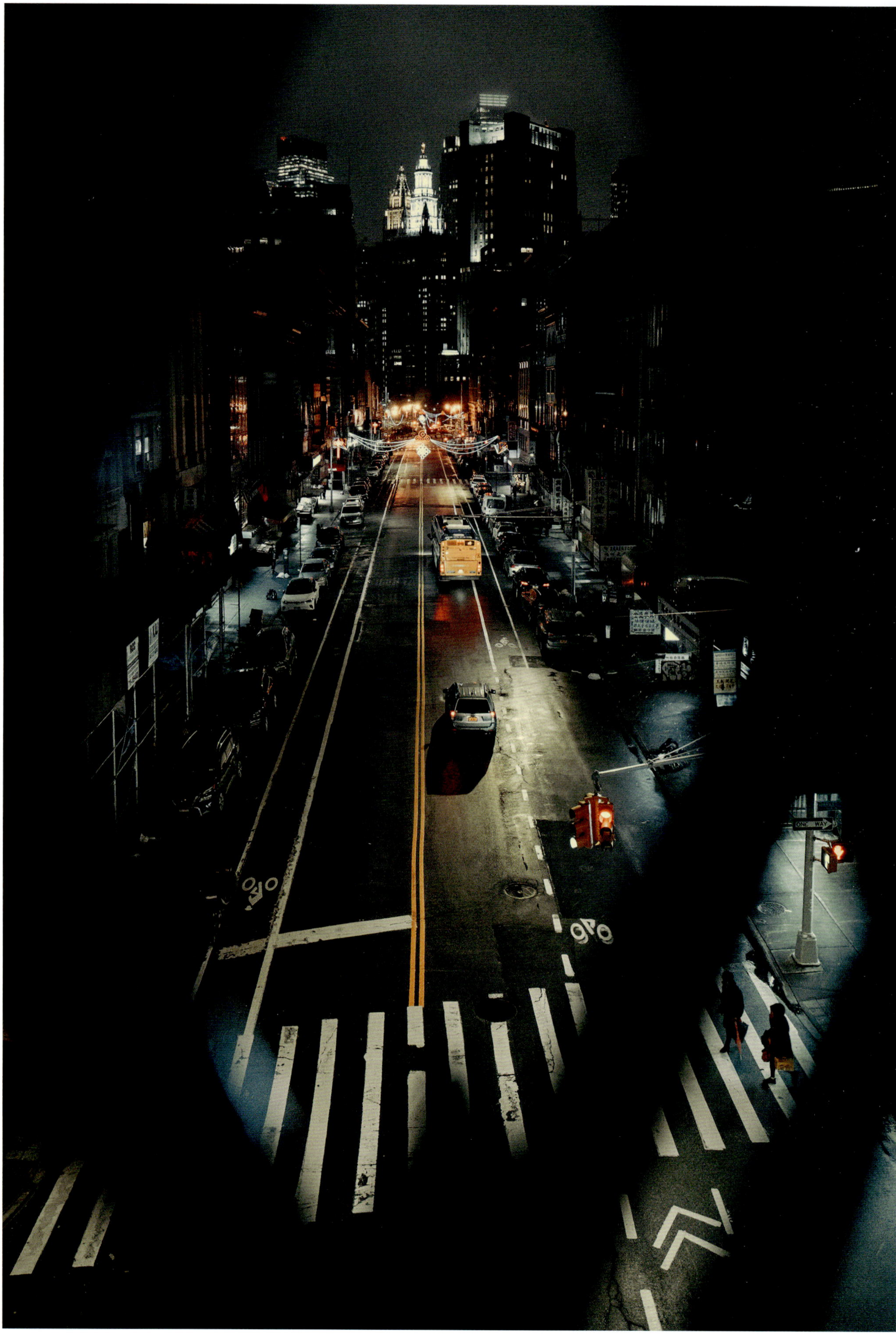

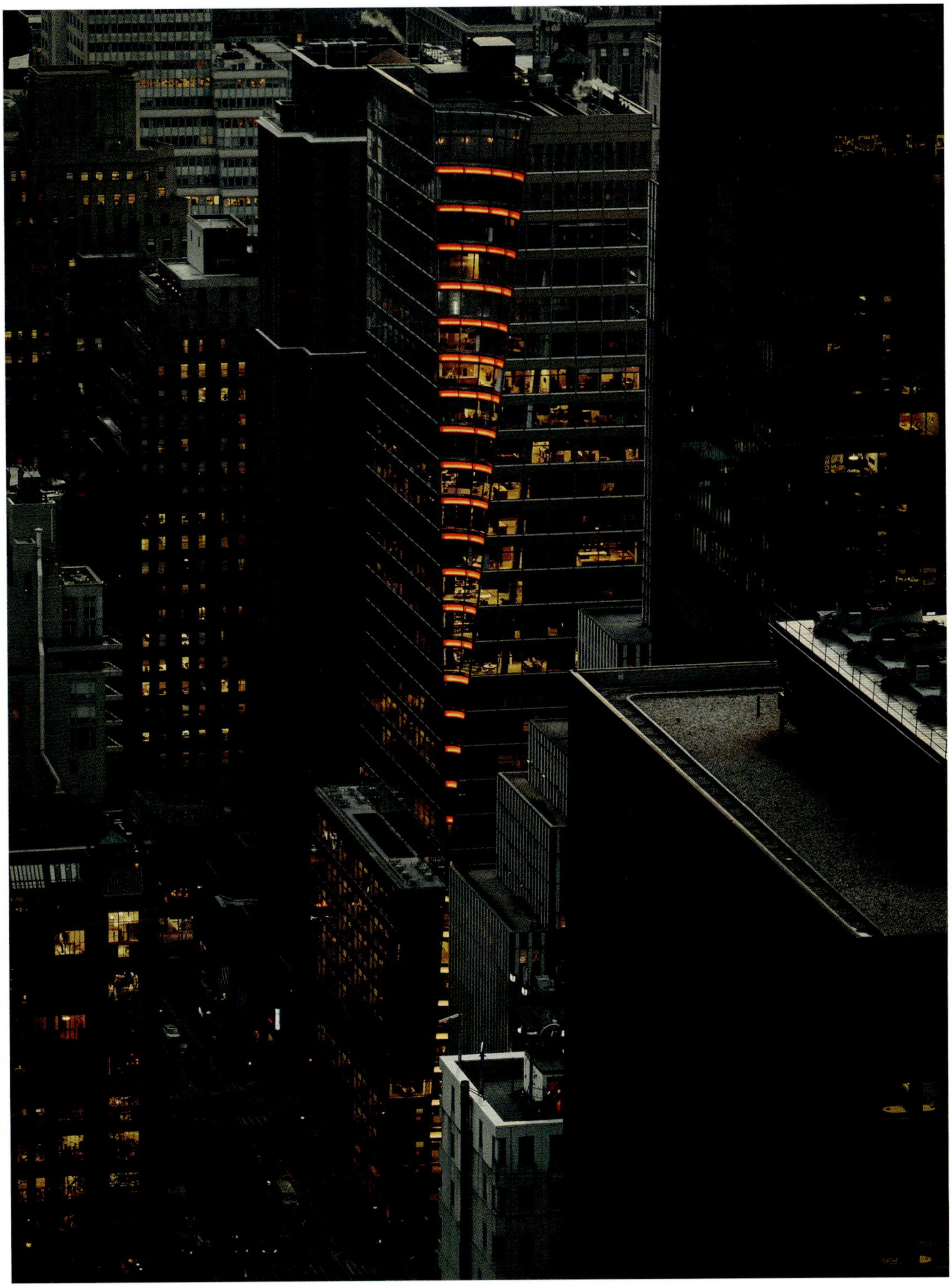

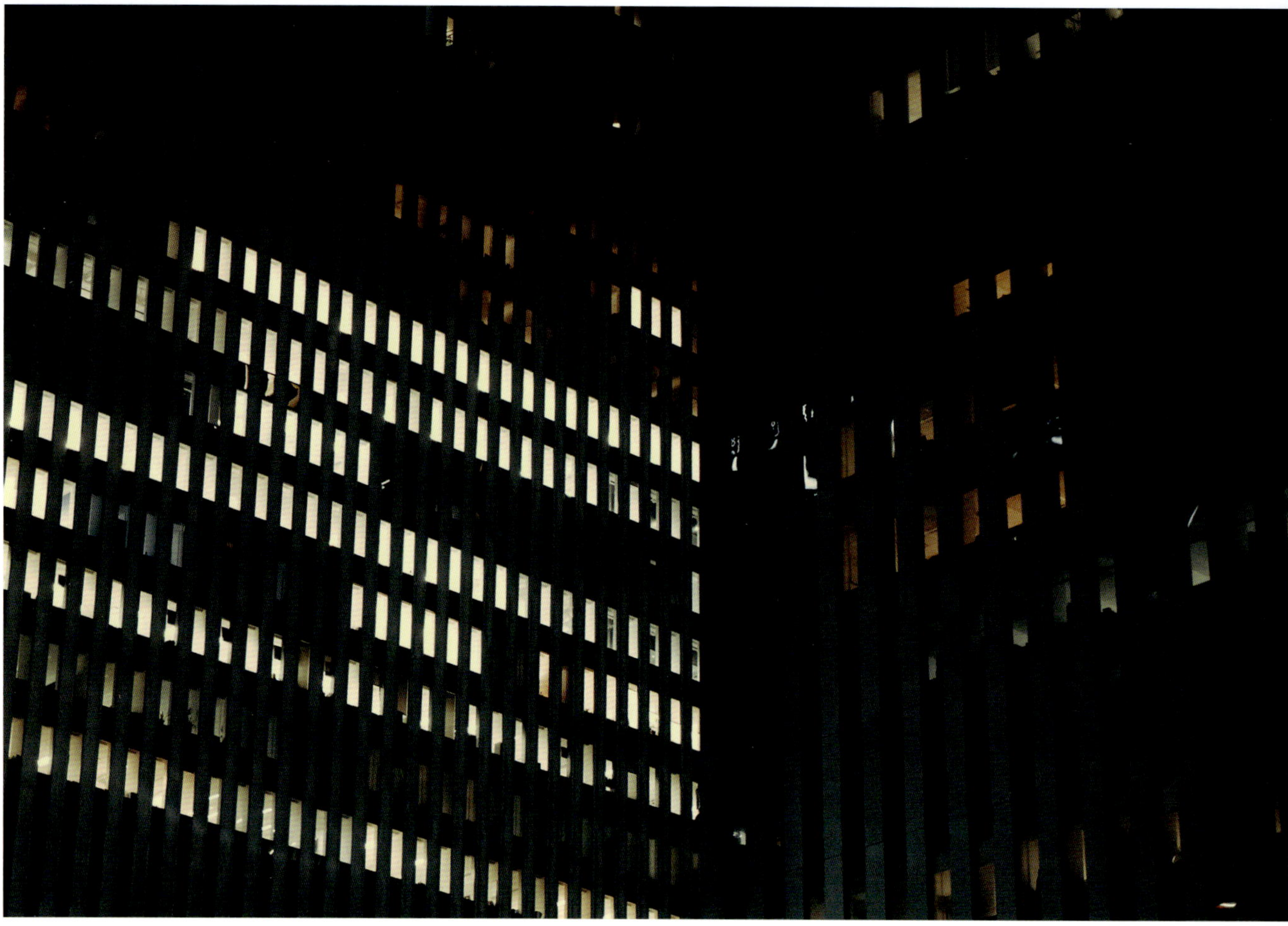

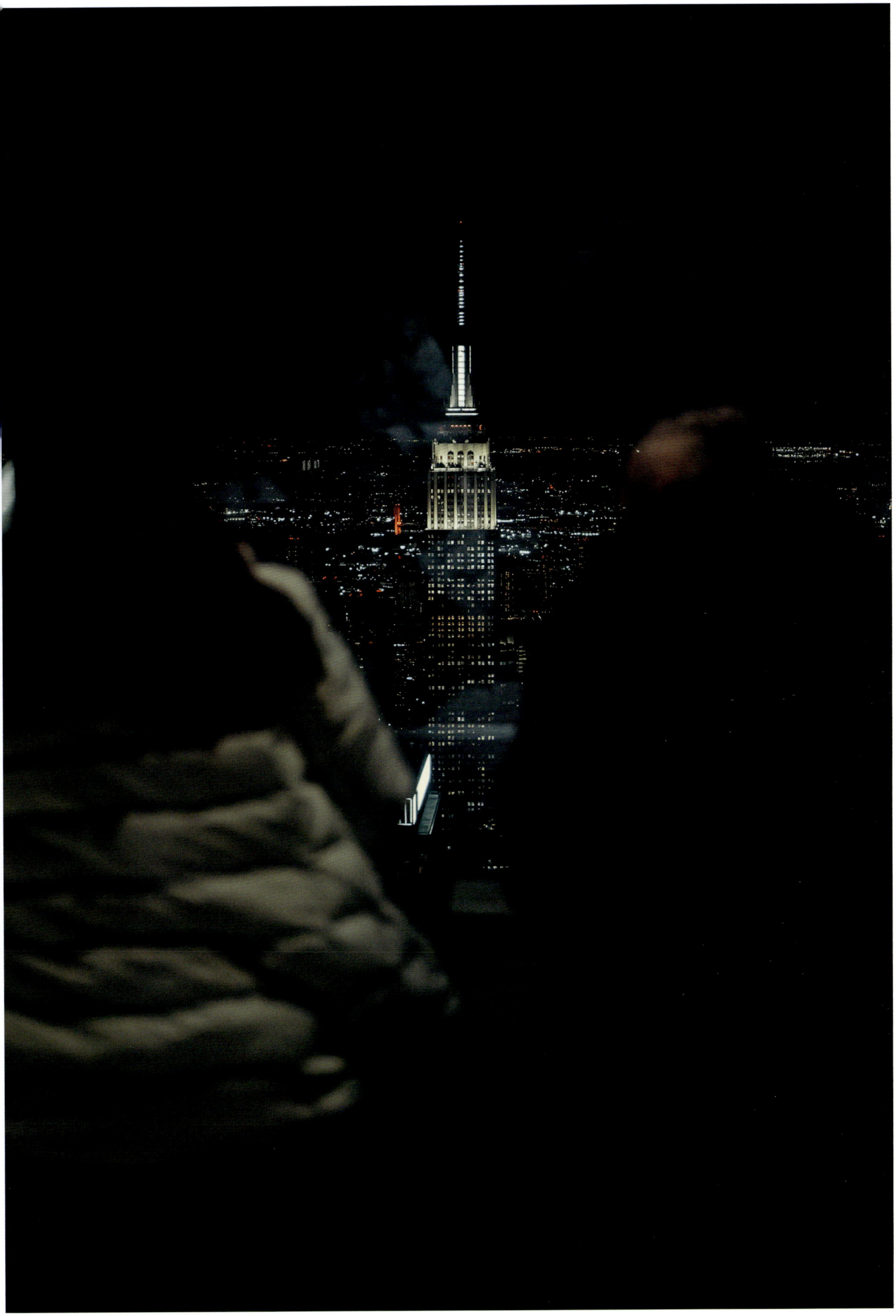

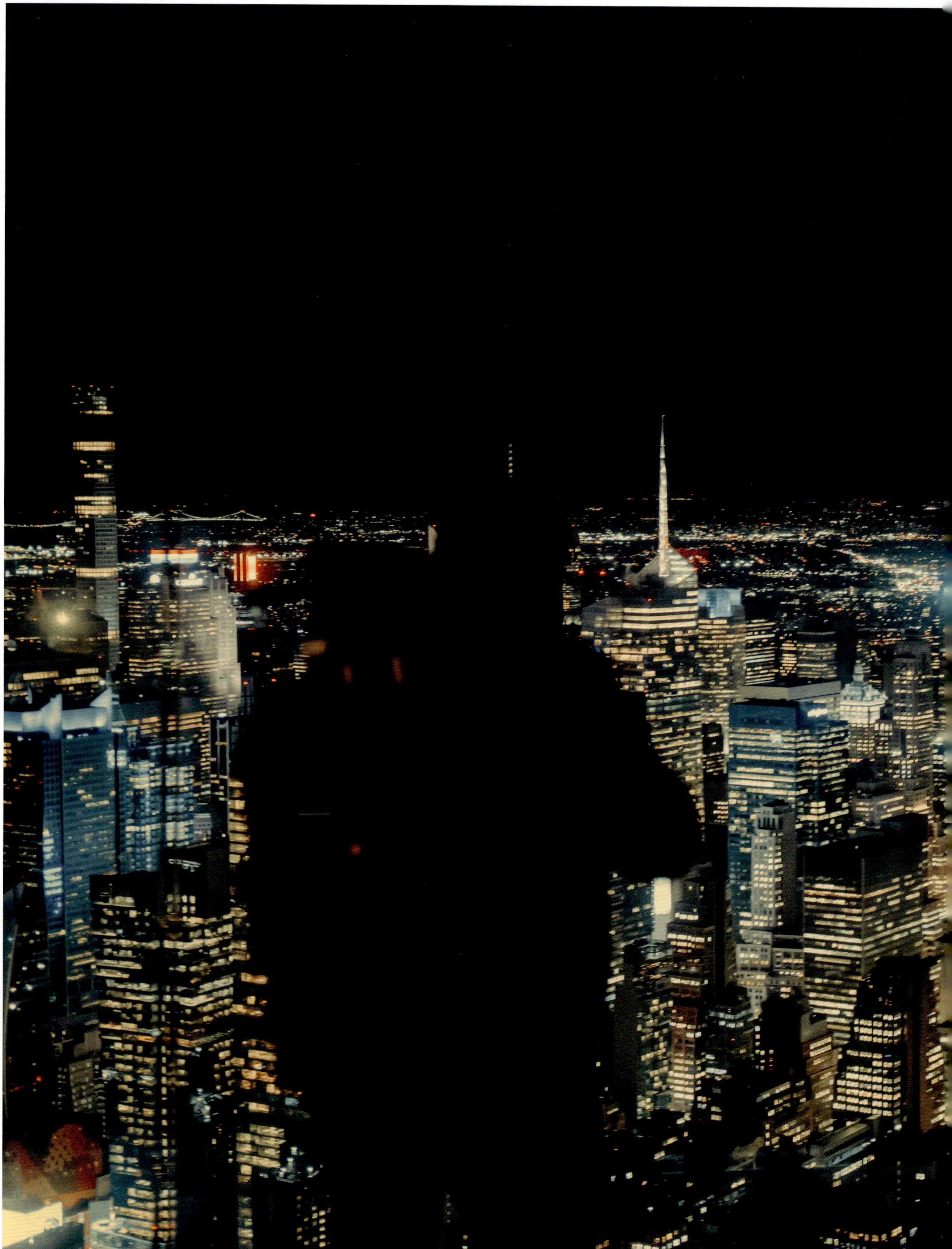

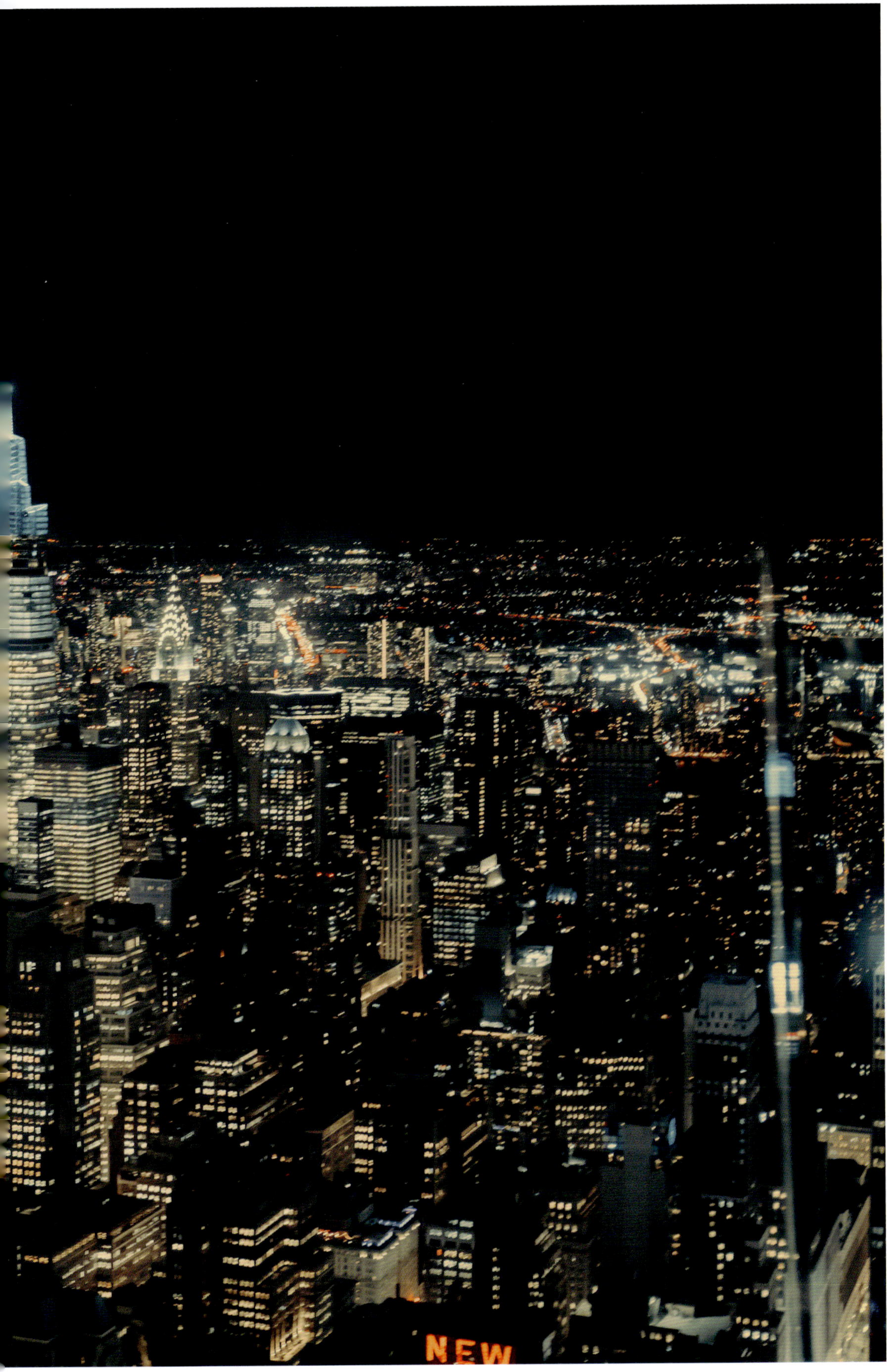
NEW

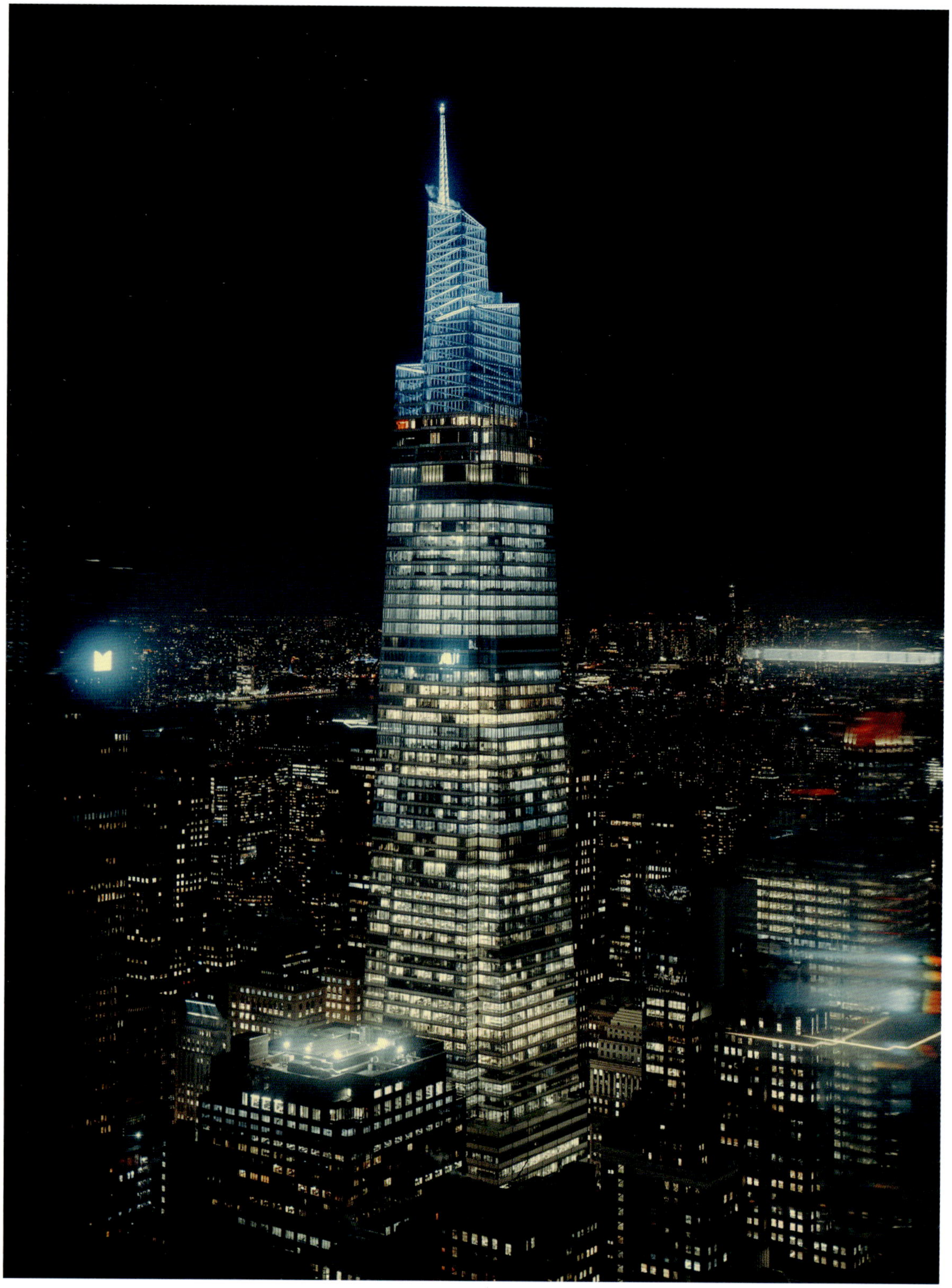

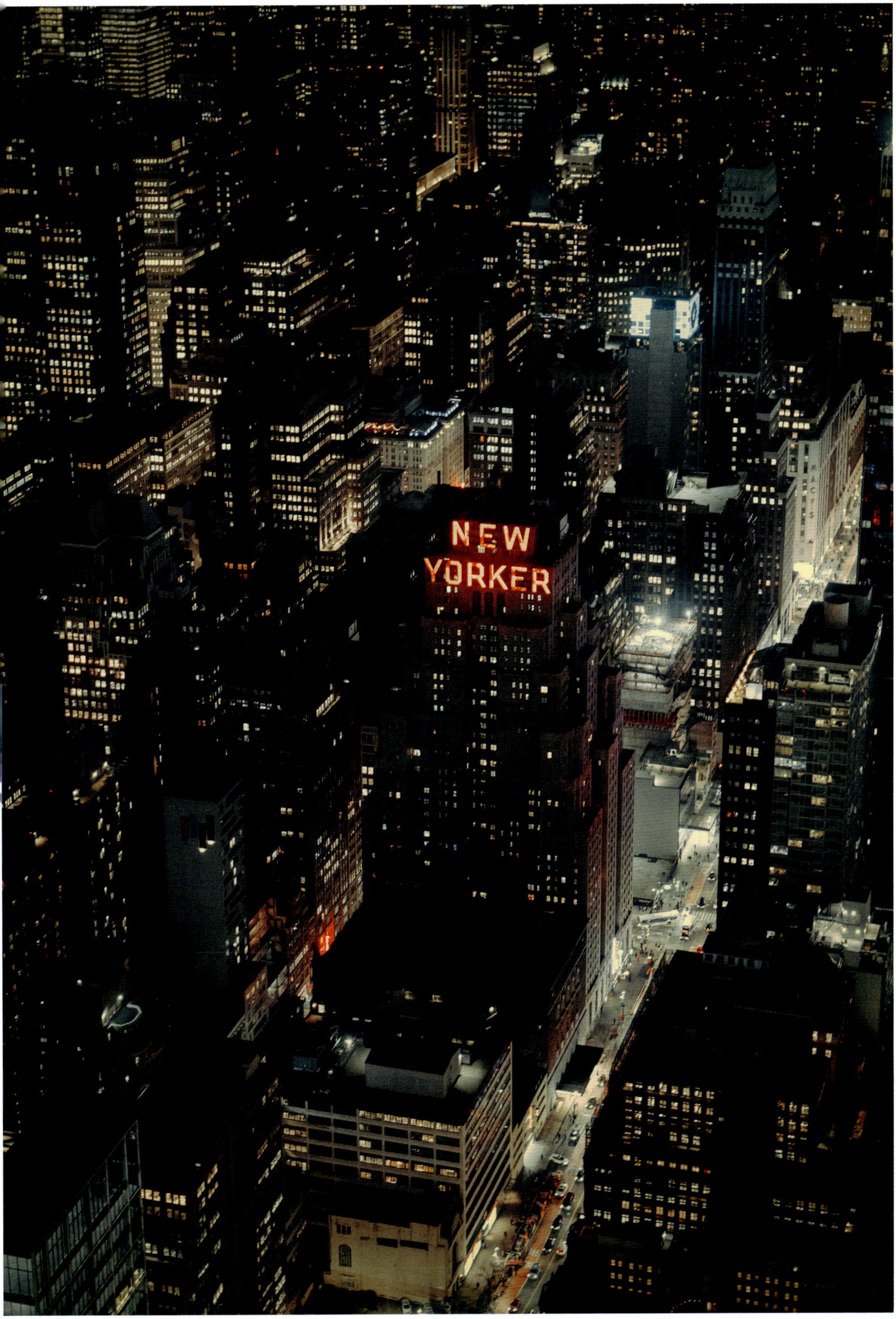
NEW
YORKER

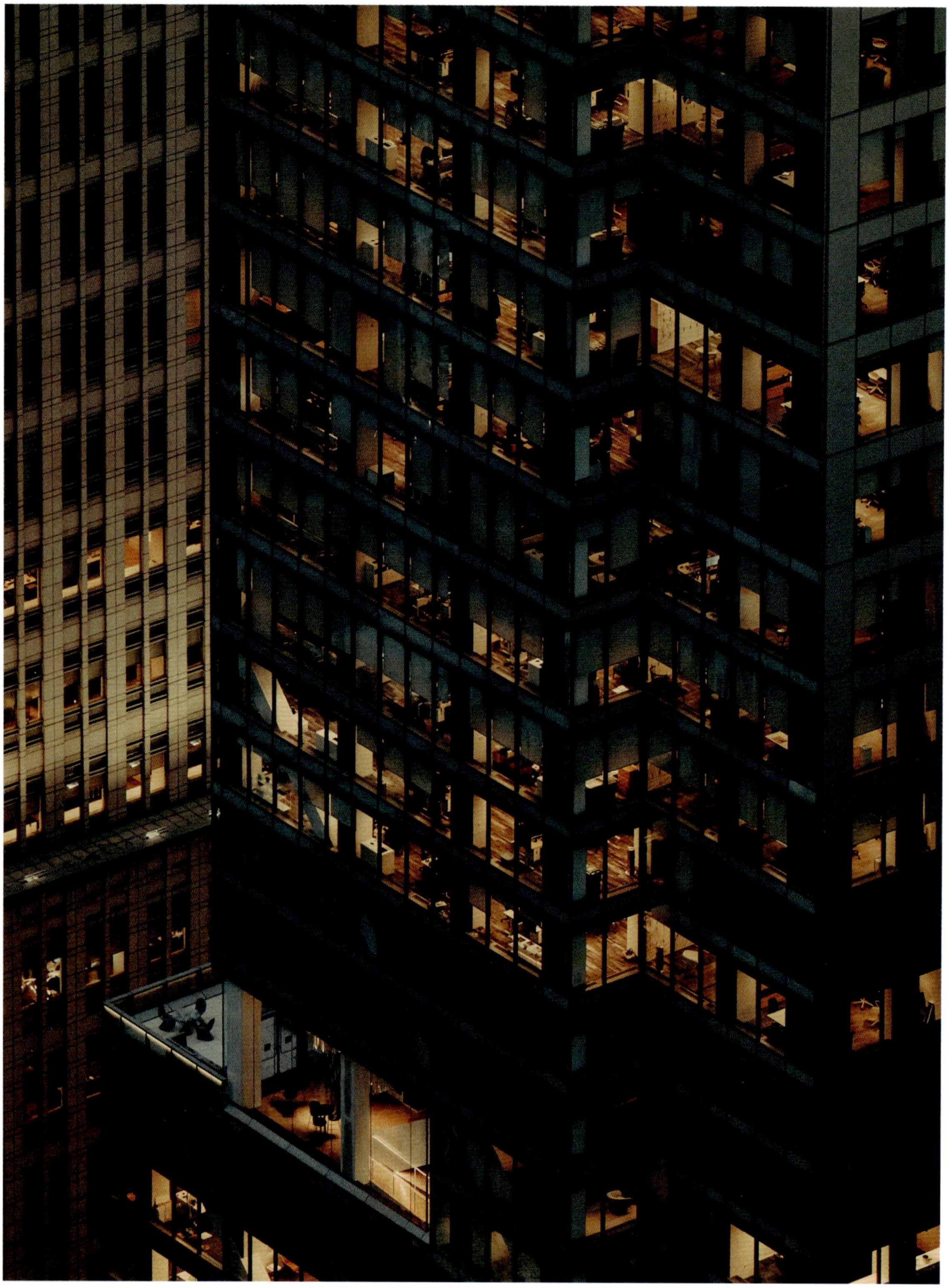

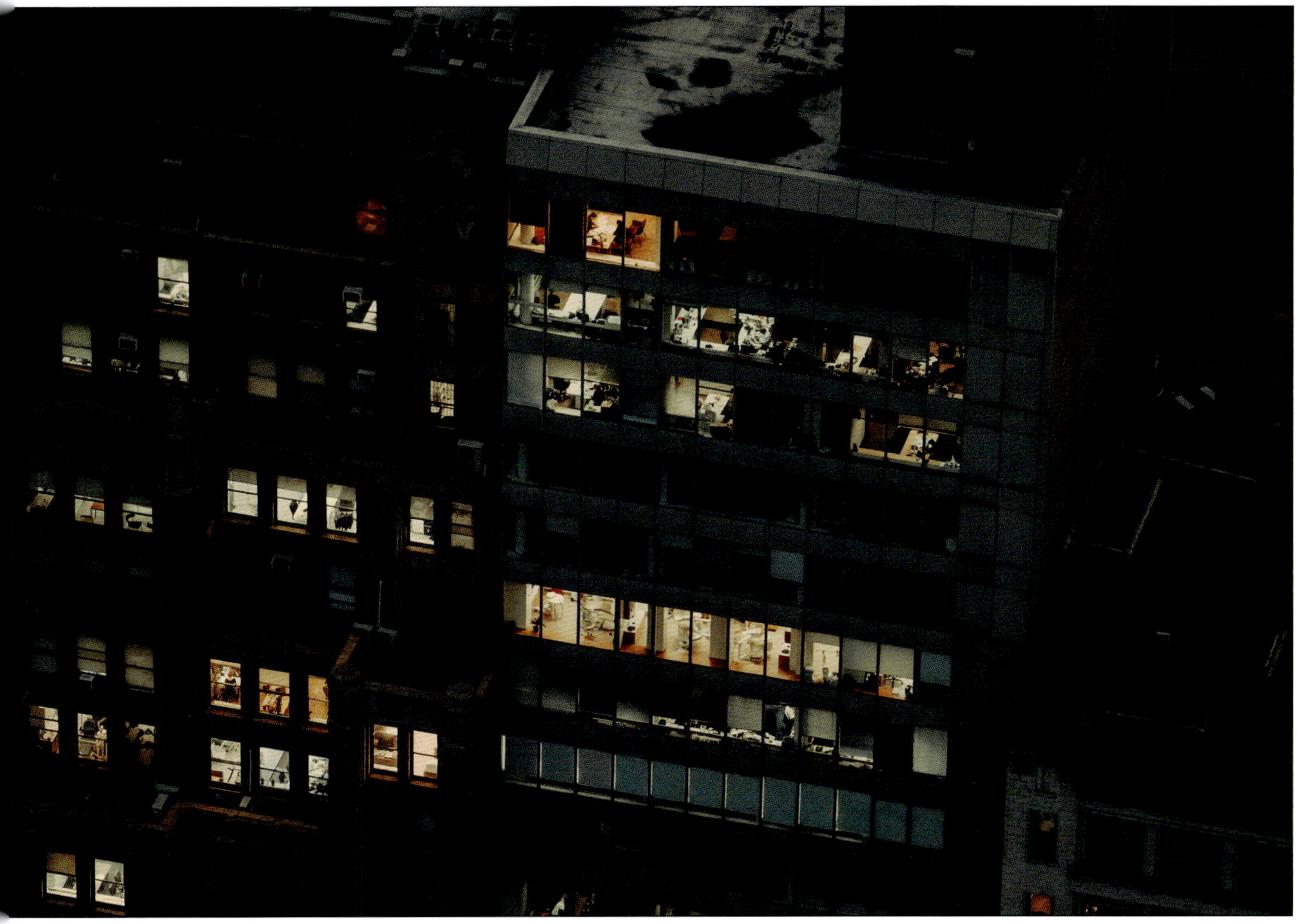

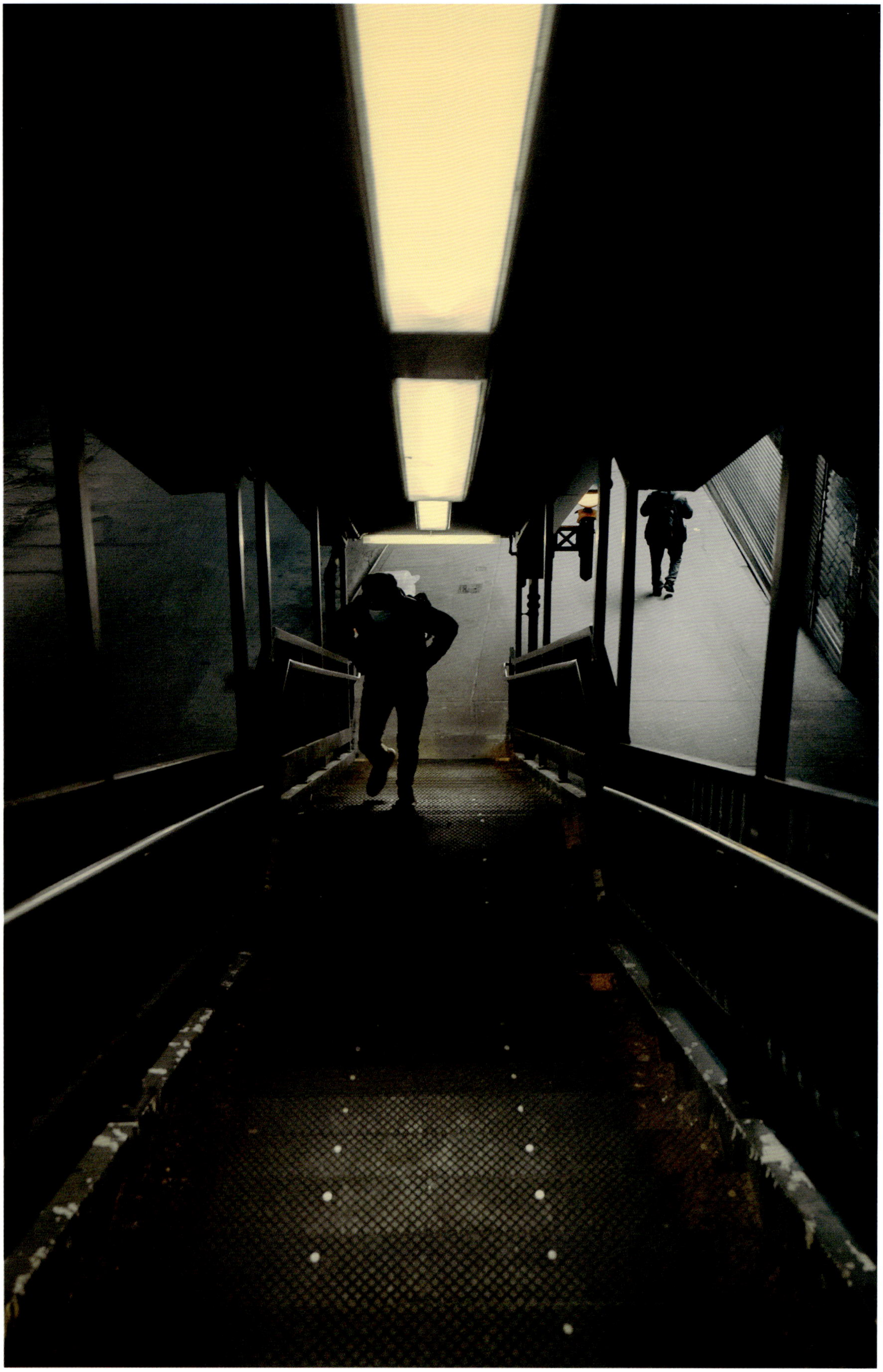

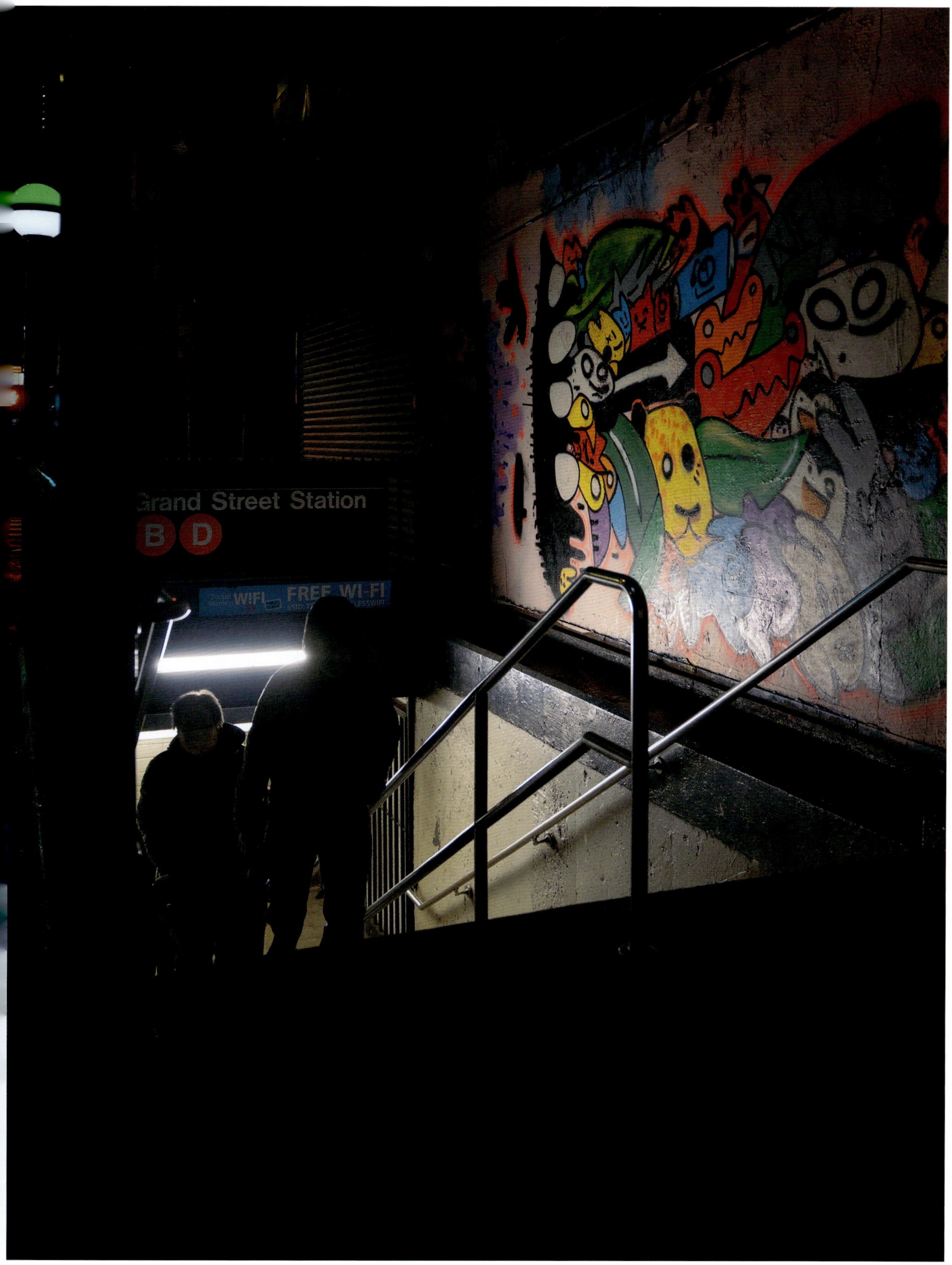
Grand Street Station
B
D
FREE WI-FI

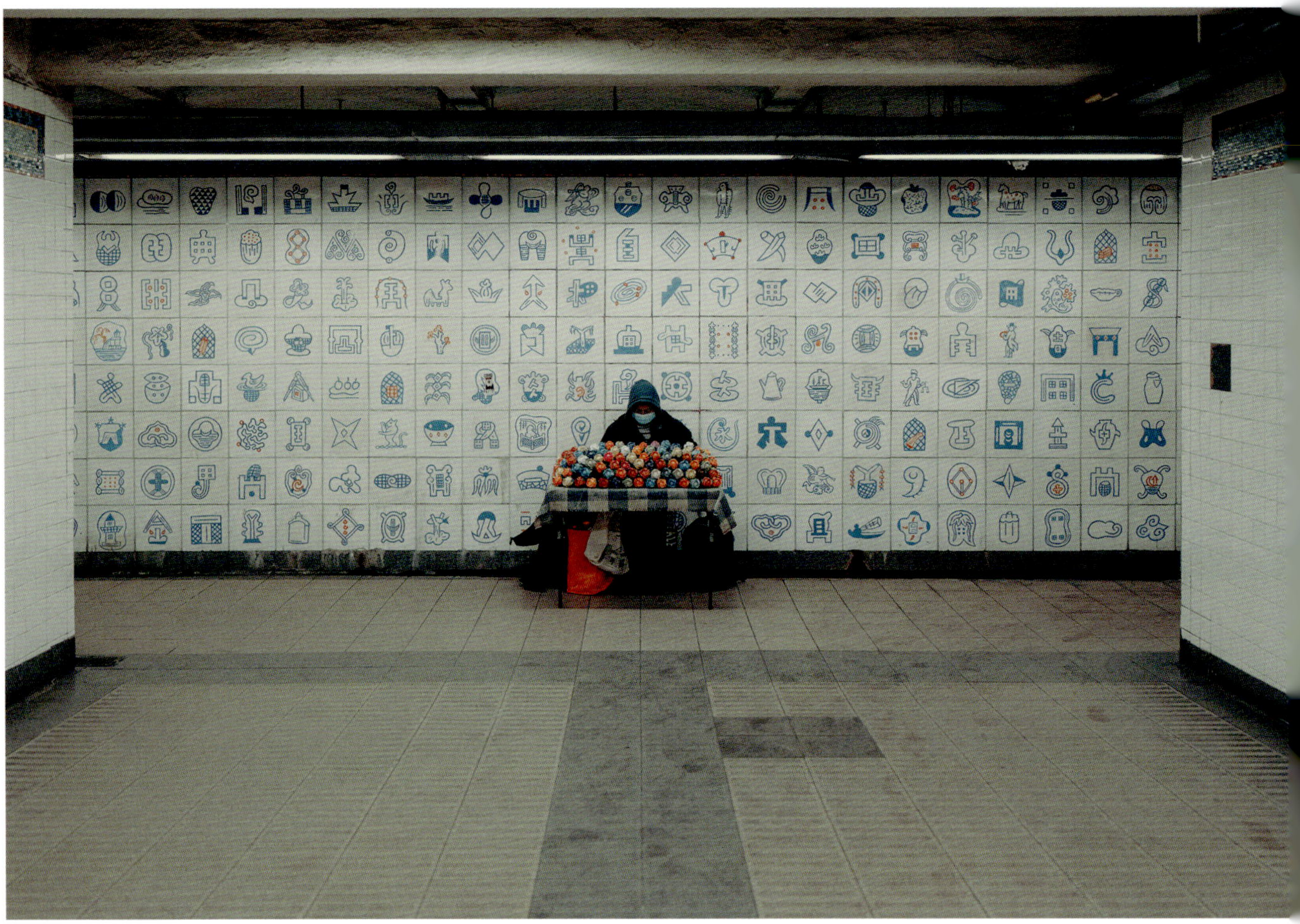

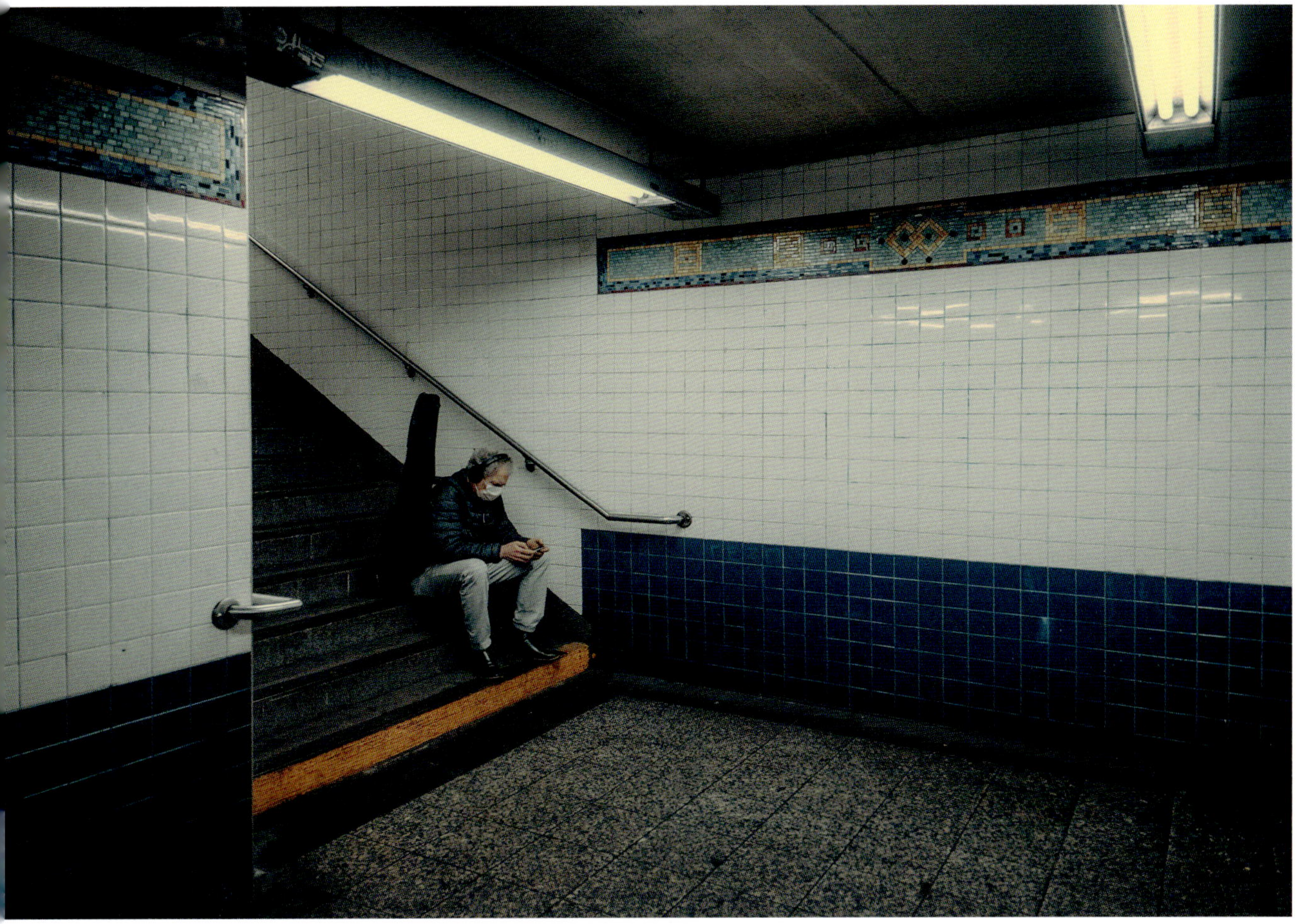

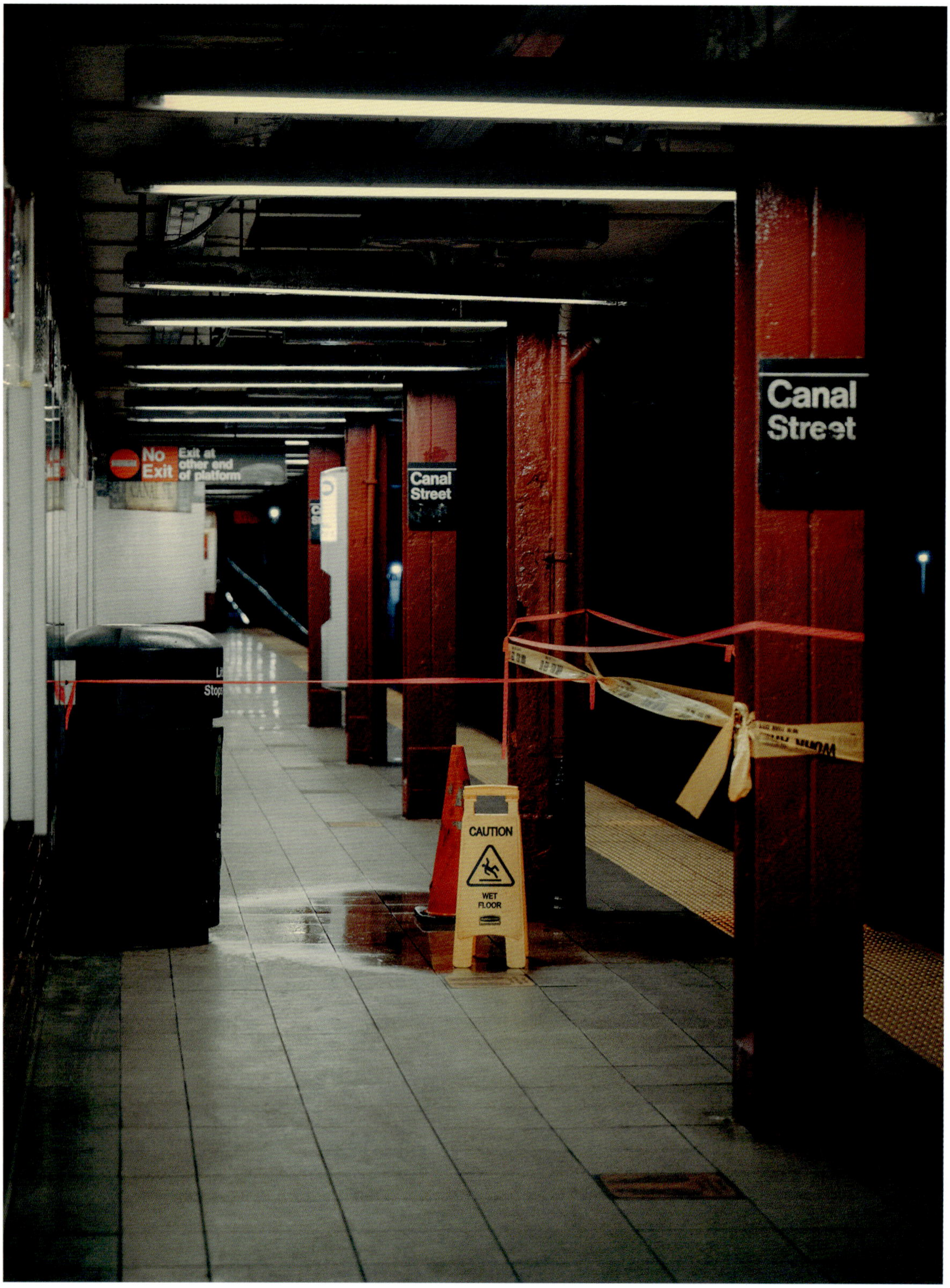

CANAL STREET STATION

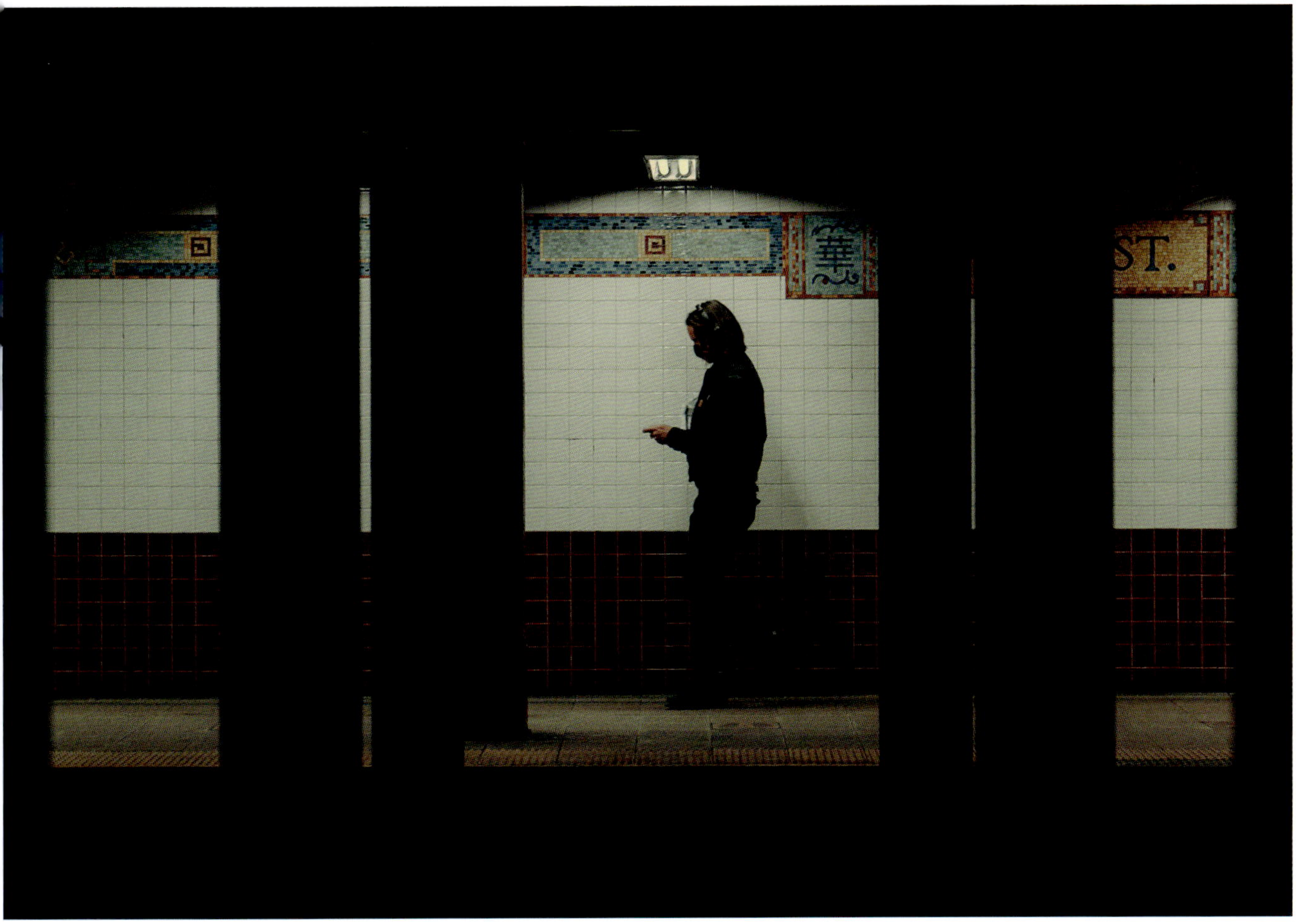
華
ST.

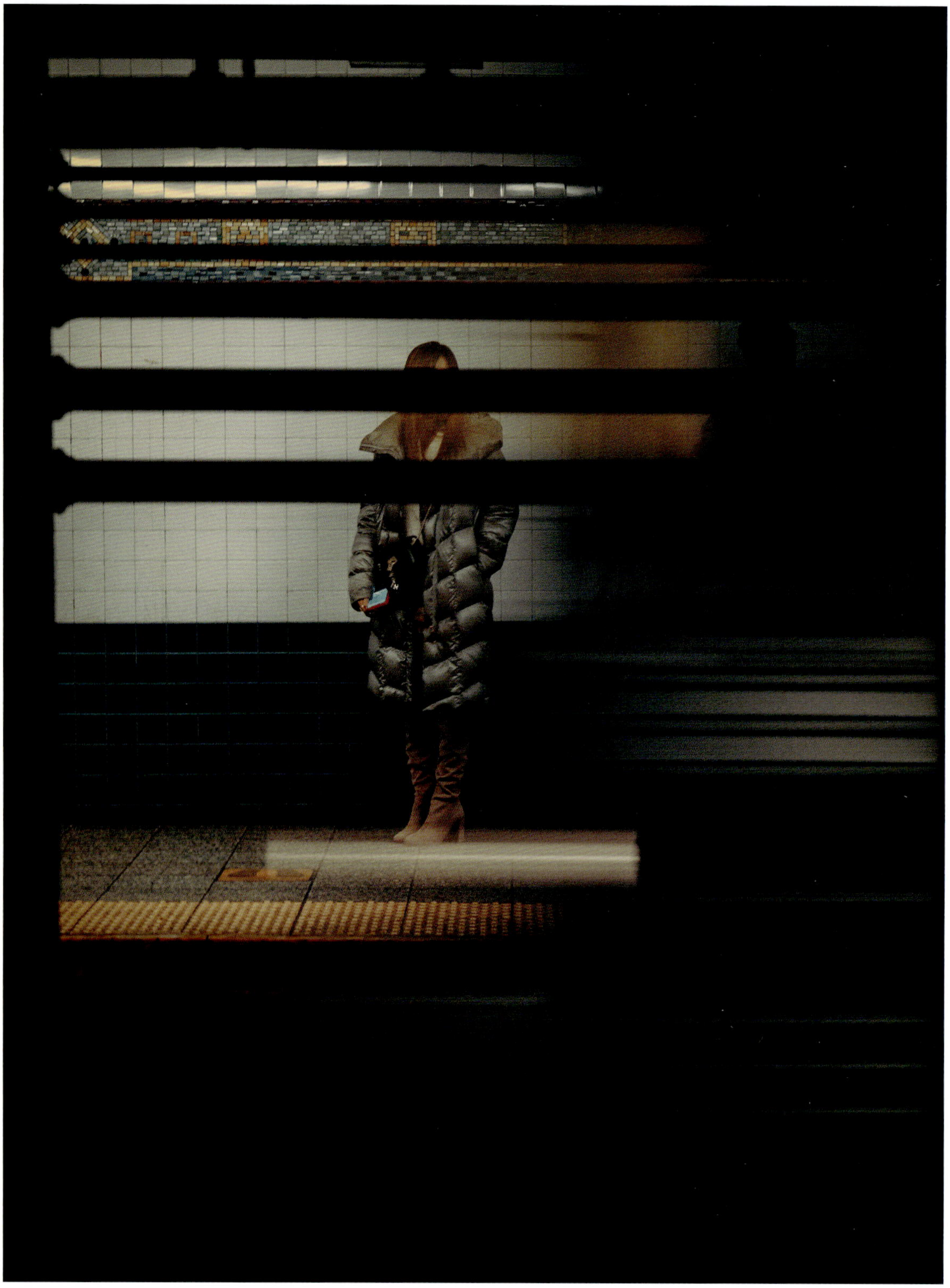

CANAL STREET STATION

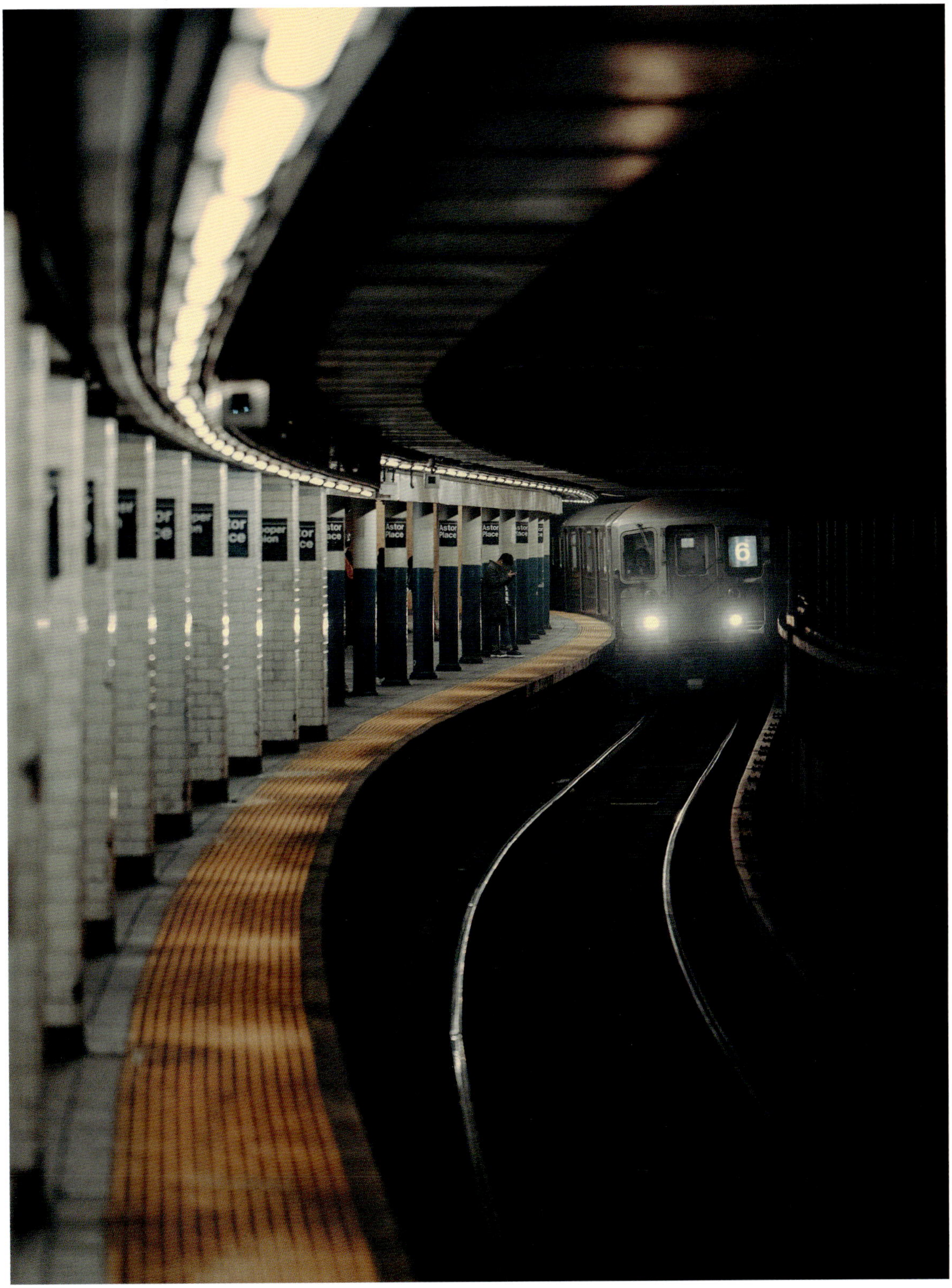

ASTOR PLACE STATION

Even at night, there's always a way to get where you're going in New York. The trains keep moving, the buses keep rolling, and the city's vast transit network continues into the overnight hours.

New York's subway system is famously open 24/7—something few global cities can claim. Between midnight and 5am, trains run less frequently and many lines switch to local stops, but crucially, the system never fully closes. Whether you're heading home from a show, clocking in for an overnight shift, or catching an early flight, there's almost always a train to get you there.

Late-night riding has its own atmosphere. Stations are quieter, platforms stretch out emptier, and the rumble of an approaching train echoes longer in tiled corridors. You'll notice more orange-vested crews, too. Overnight hours are prime time for track work, signal upgrades and station repairs, which means service changes are common. If a line is suspended for maintenance, buses step in. Some operate as overnight versions of major routes—often marked with an "N" prefix—tracing key corridors across Manhattan, Brooklyn, Queens, and the Bronx.

Regional trains slow down but also never stop running. The Long Island Rail Road and Metro-North Railroad run late-evening departures and early-morning arrivals into hubs like Penn Station and Grand Central, feeding not only the city's nightlife but also the early morning workforce. The Staten Island Ferry continues its 24-hour schedule as well, traveling across New York Harbor with significantly lighter crowds and stunning skyline views.

And then there's everything above ground: yellow cabs cruising under streetlights, green borough taxis in Upper Manhattan and beyond, and rideshare drivers orbiting busy nightlife zones. Bike lanes stay active, too, with delivery riders and night cyclists moving steadily through avenues that feel wider after dark.

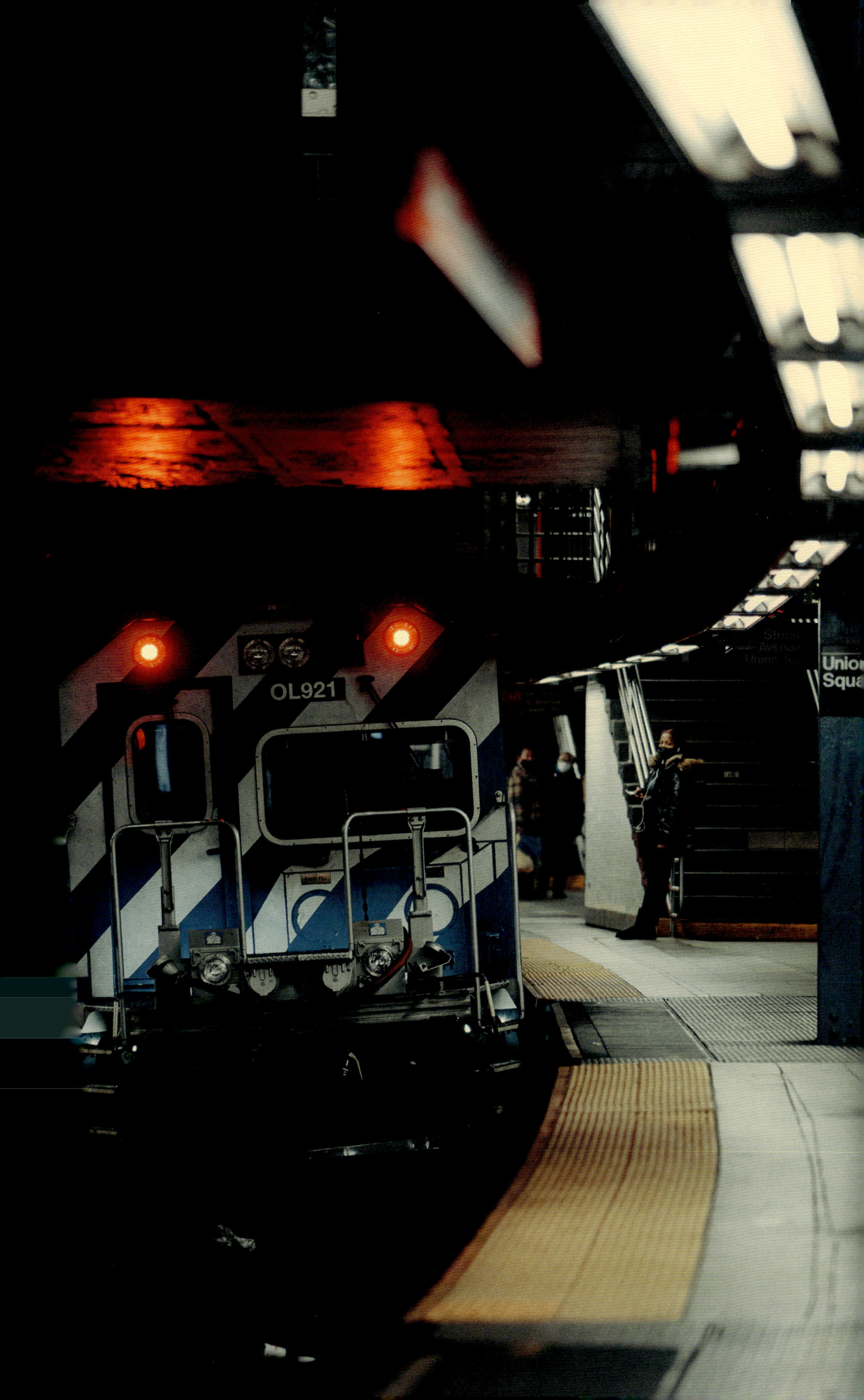
OL921

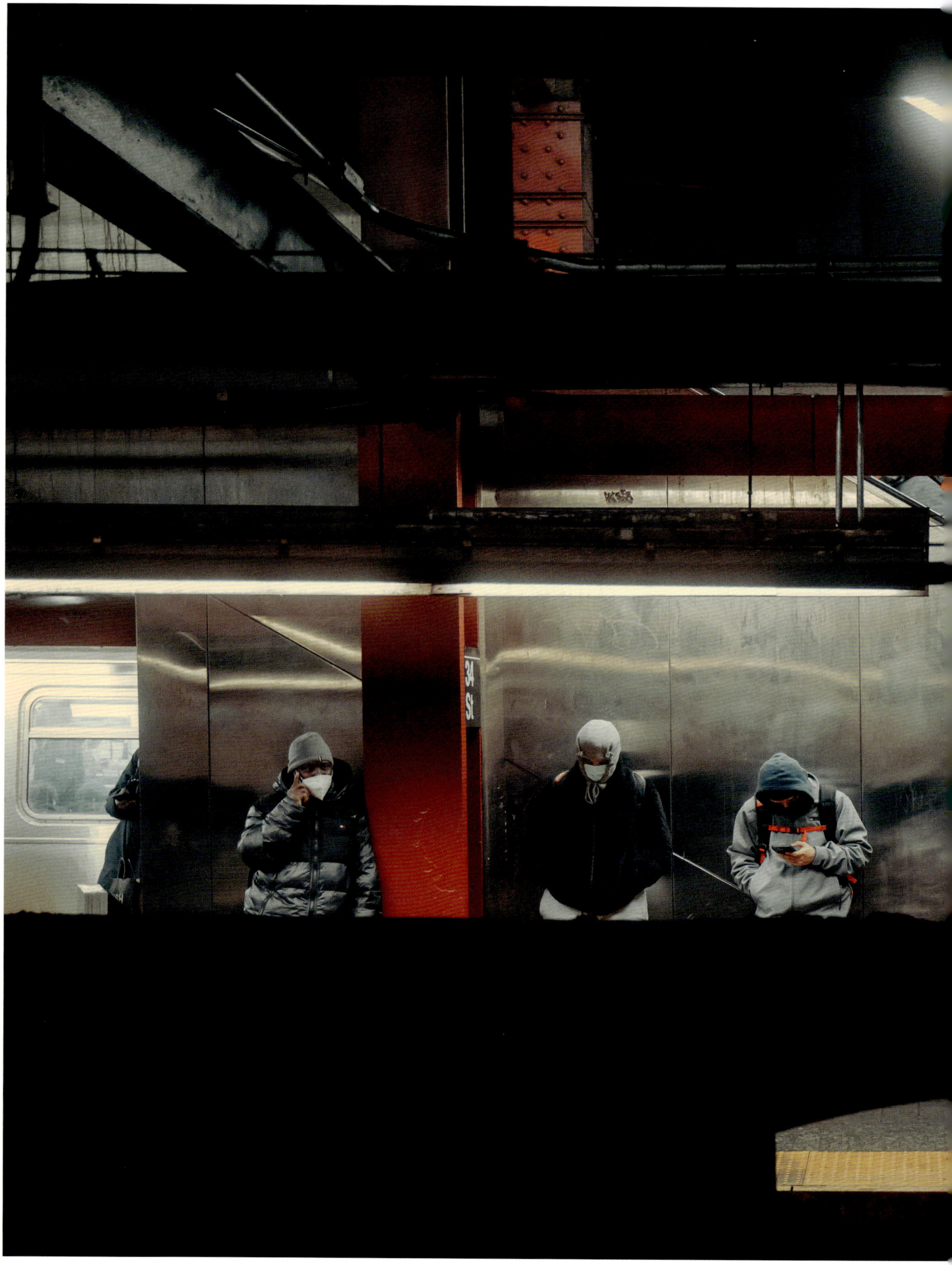

34TH STREET - HERALD SQUARE STATION

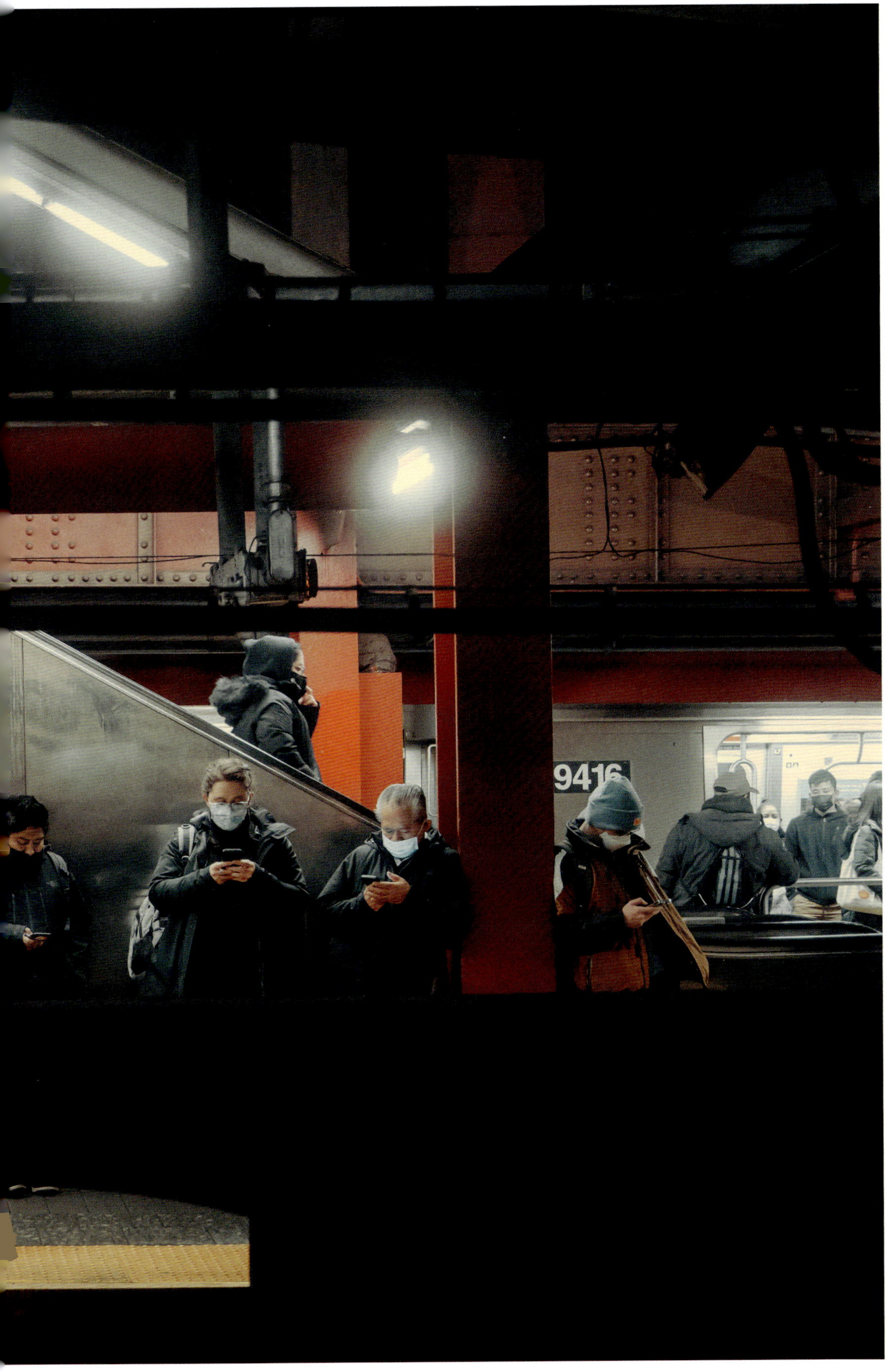
9416

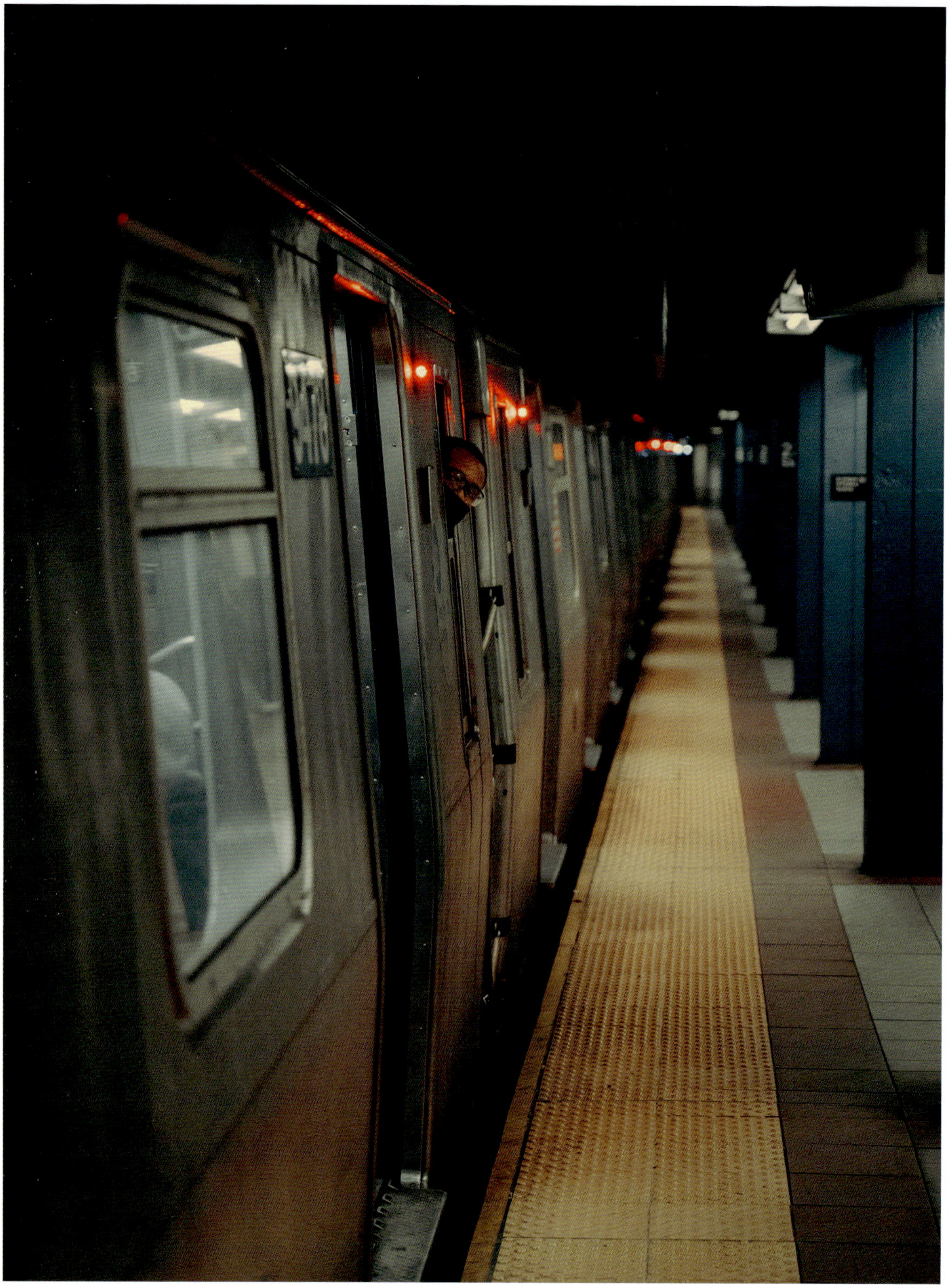

23RD STREET STATION

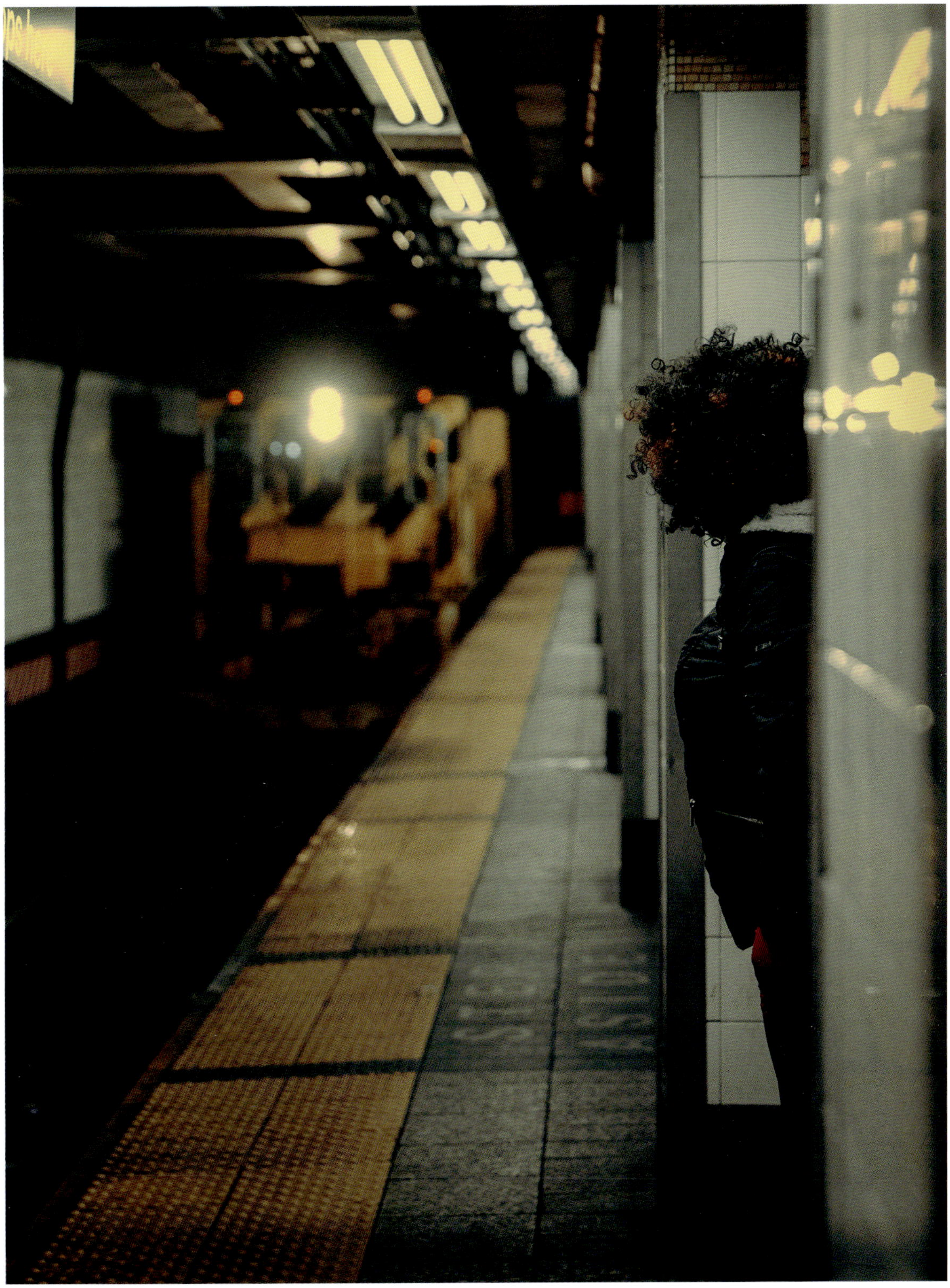

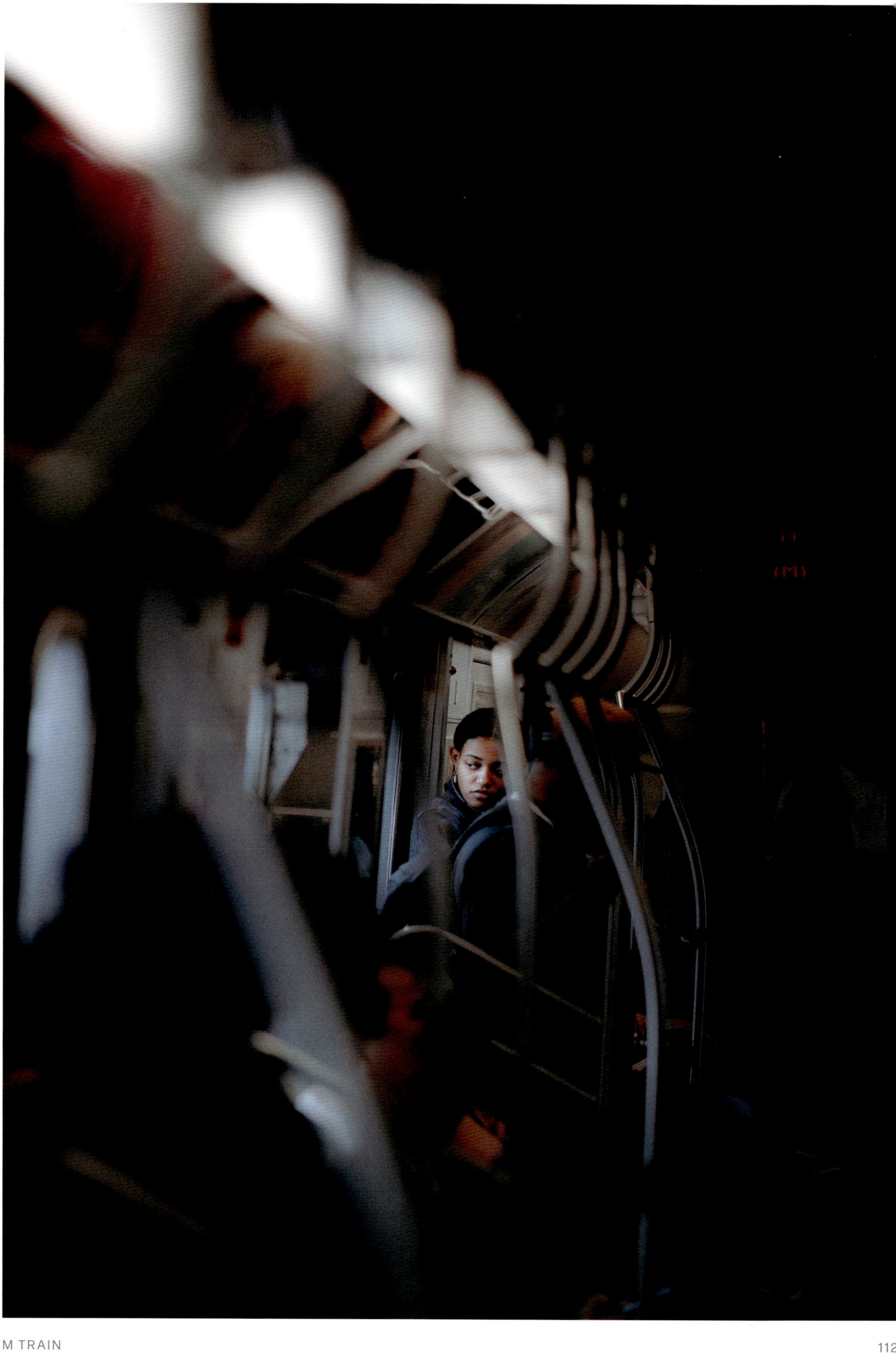

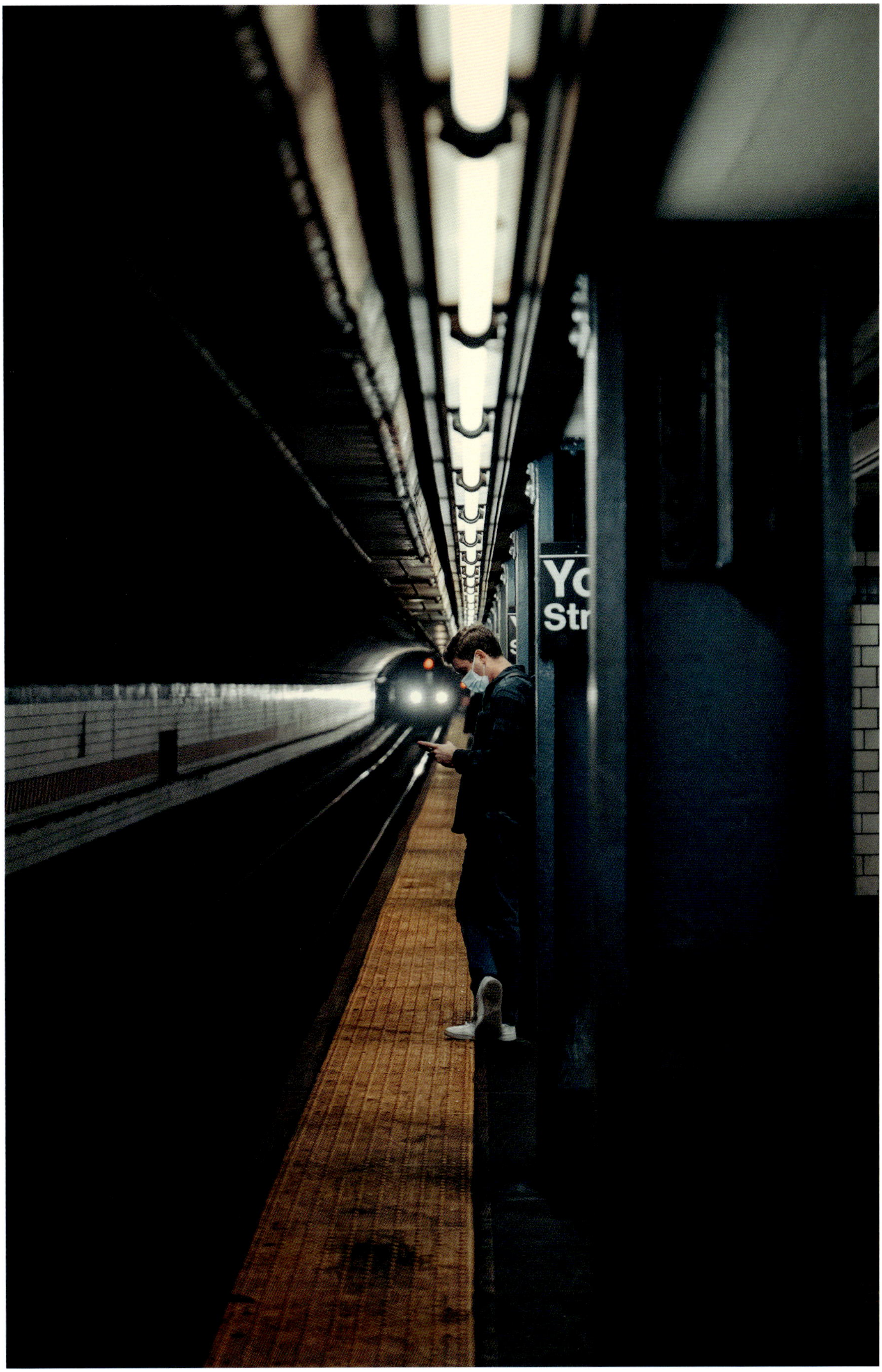
Yo
Str

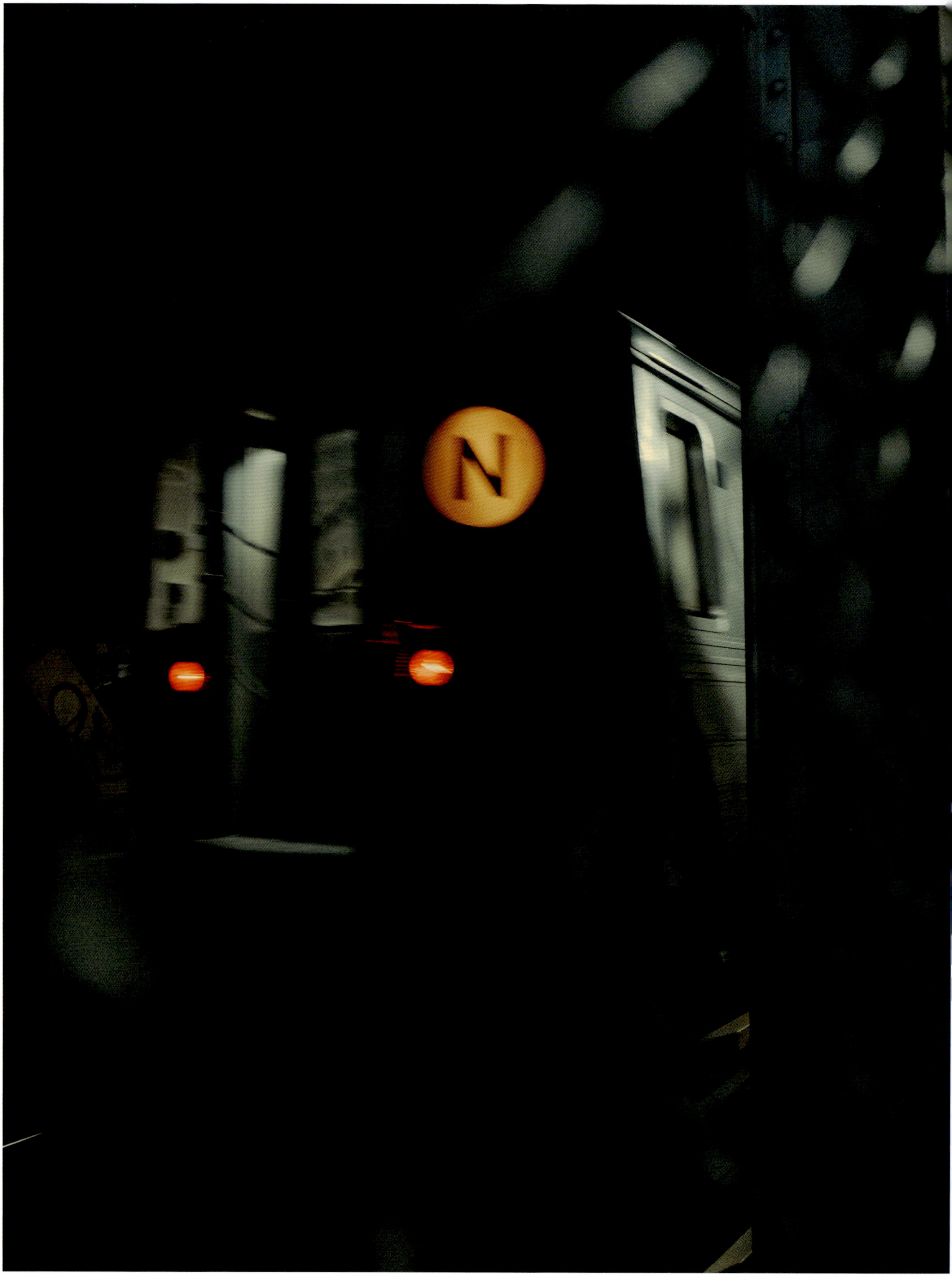
N

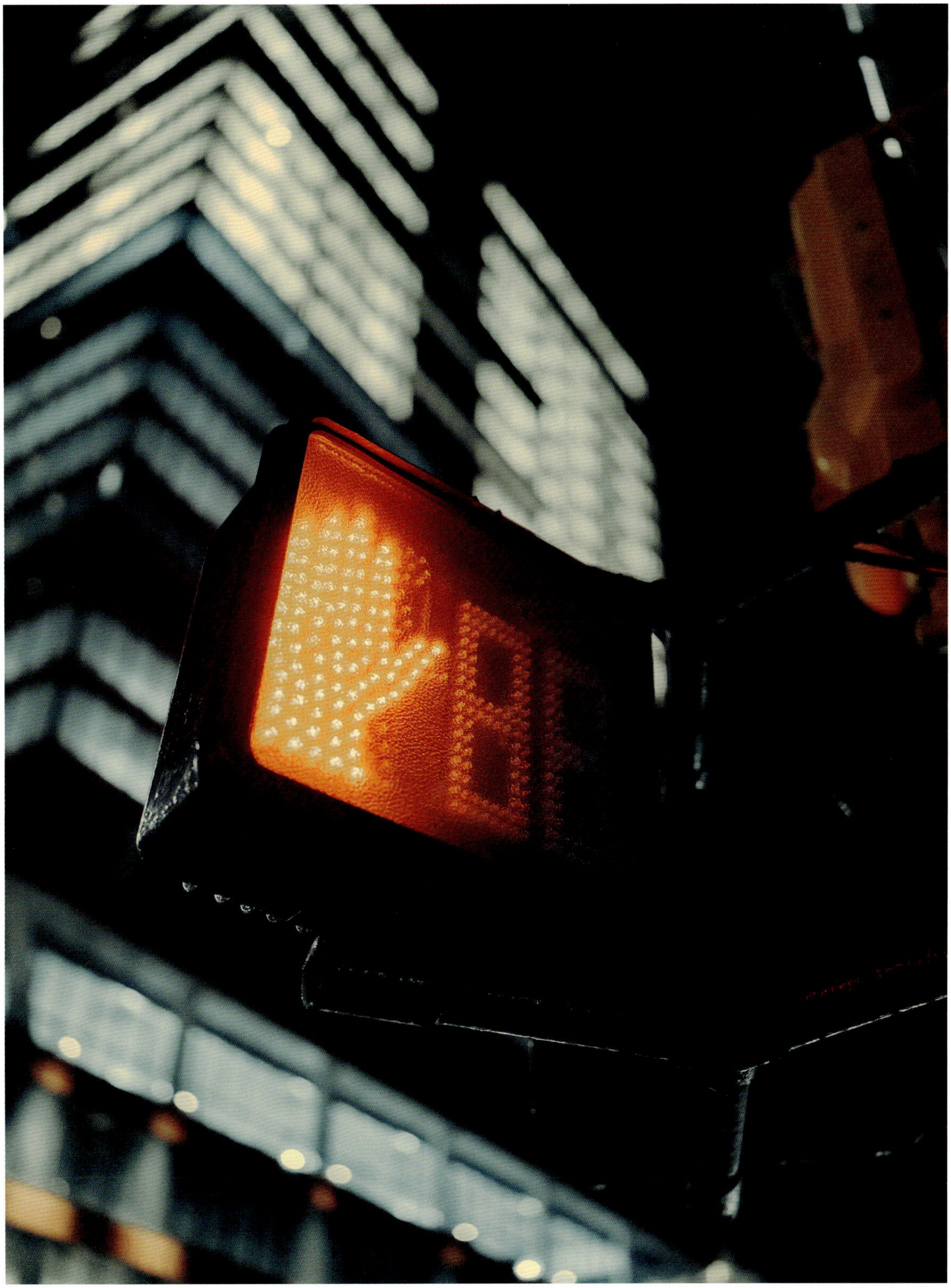

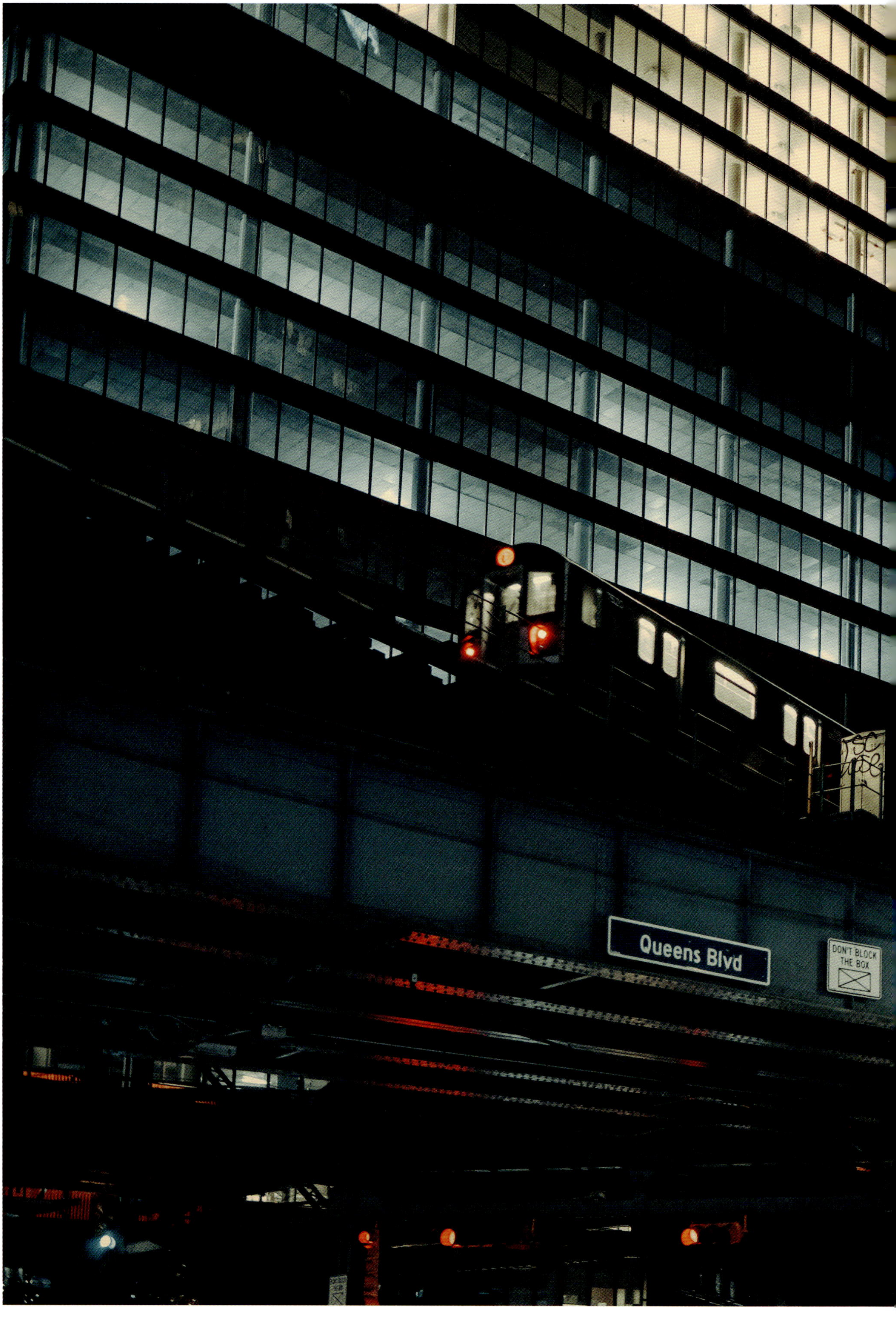

HUNTERS POINT

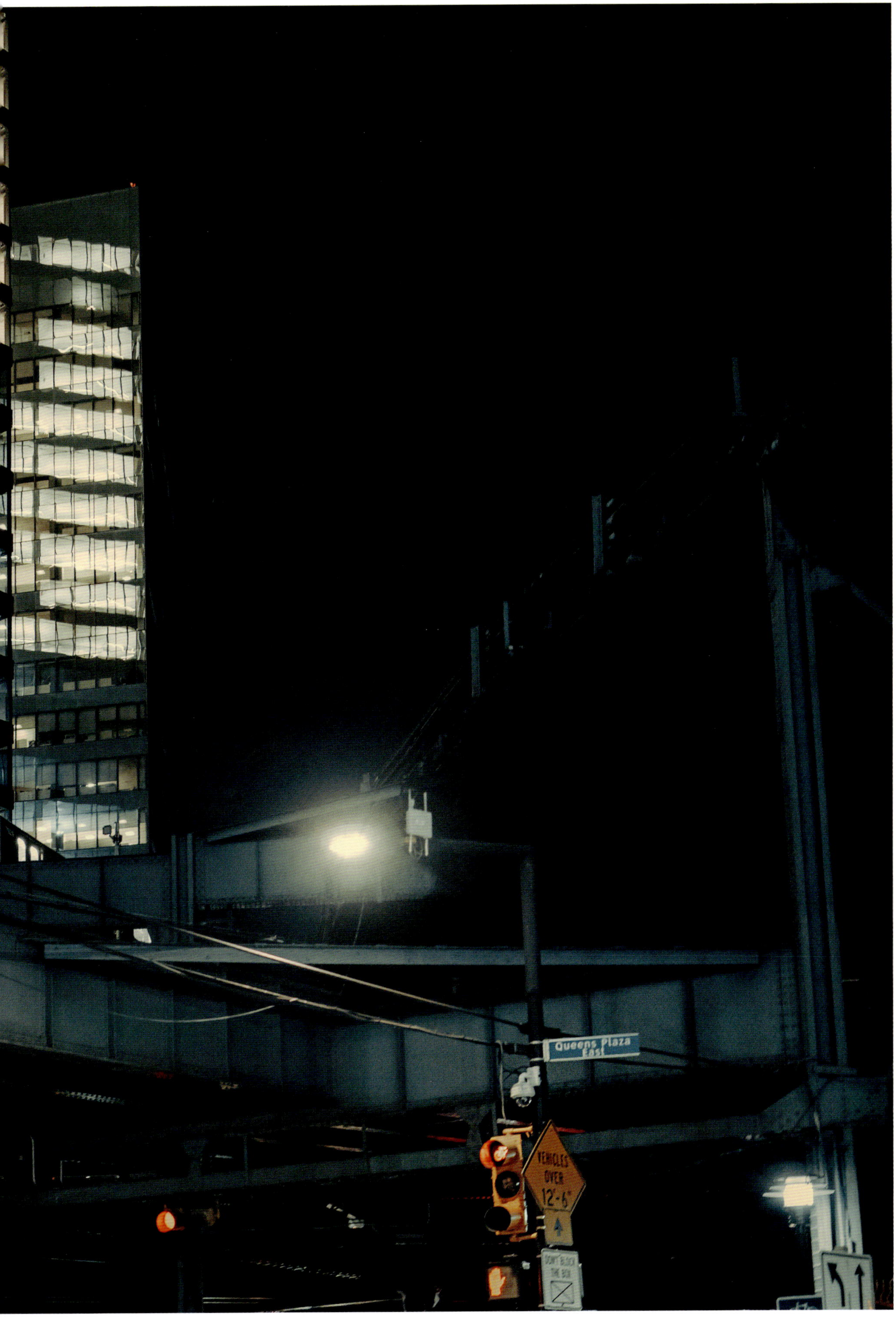
Queens Plaza
East
VEHICLES
OVER
12'-6"

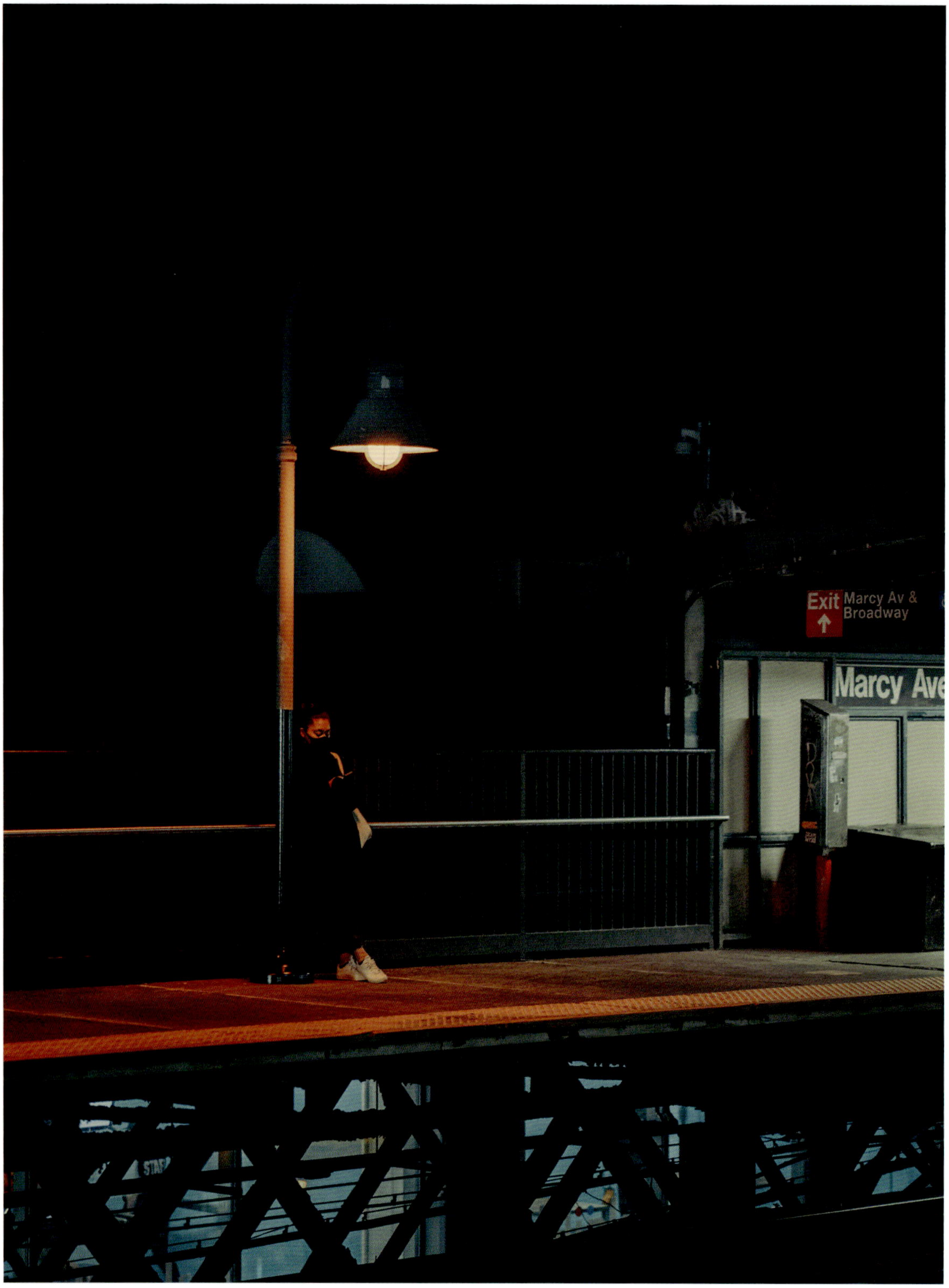
Exit
Marcy Av &
Broadway
Marcy Ave

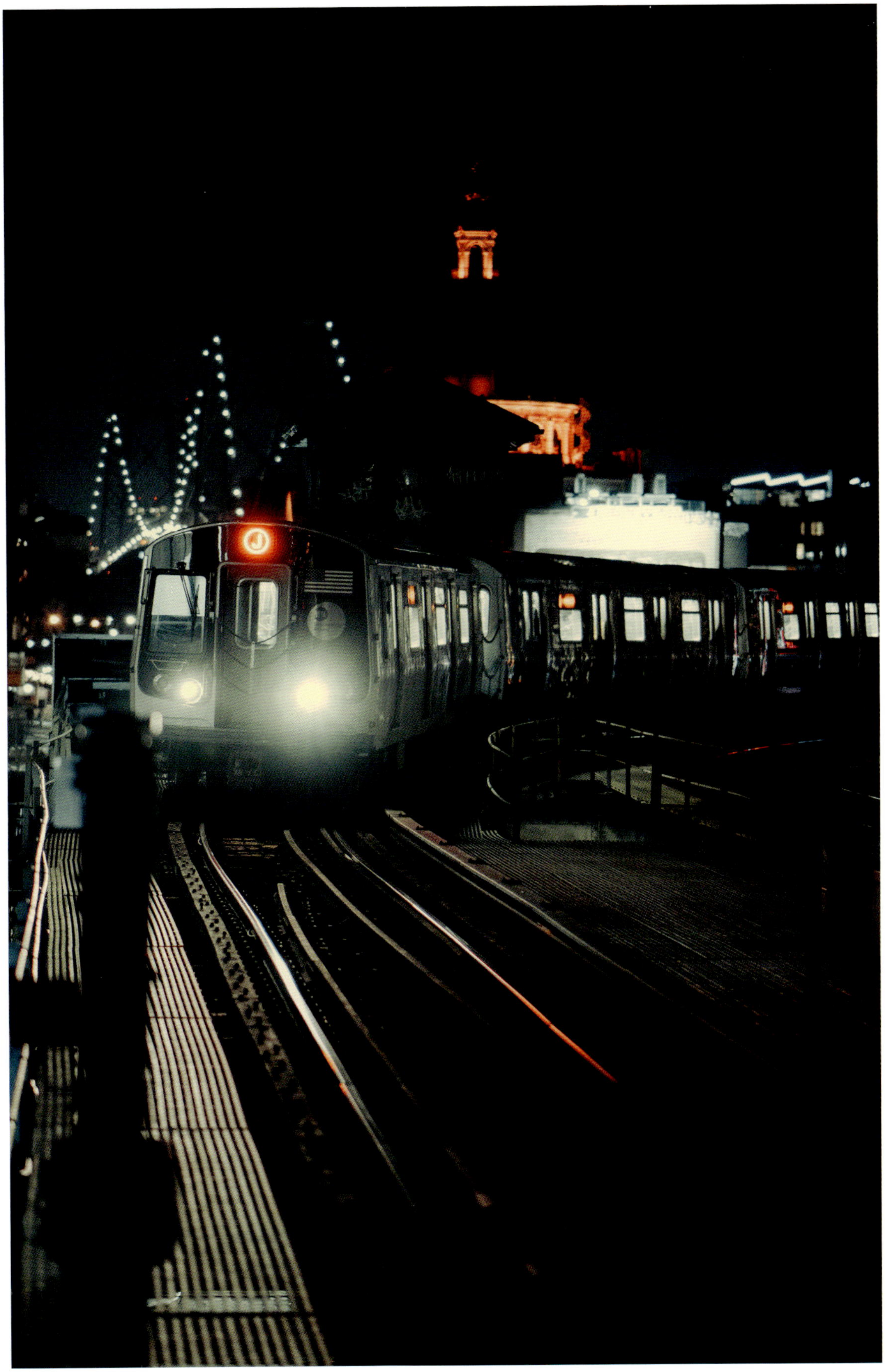

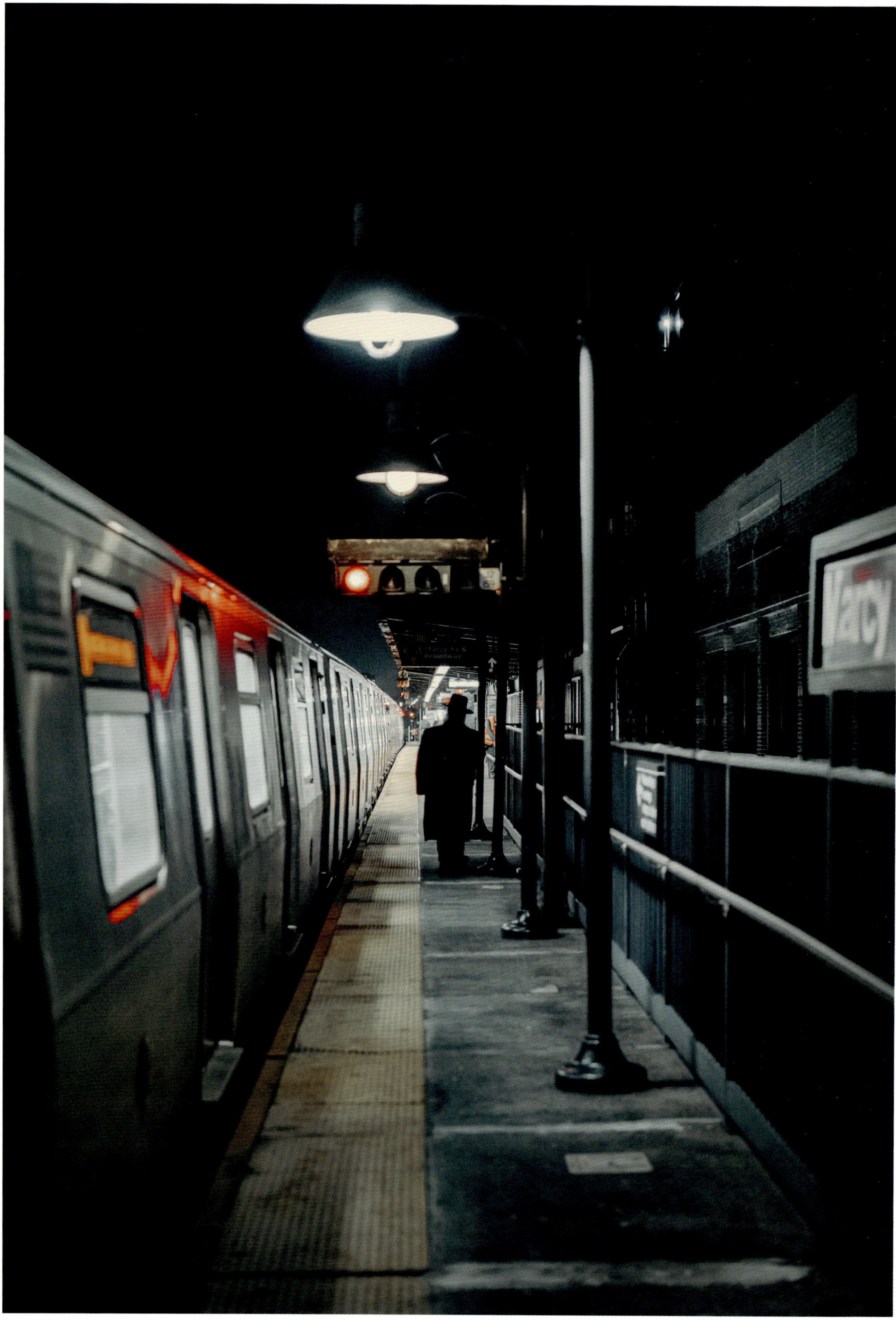
Marcy

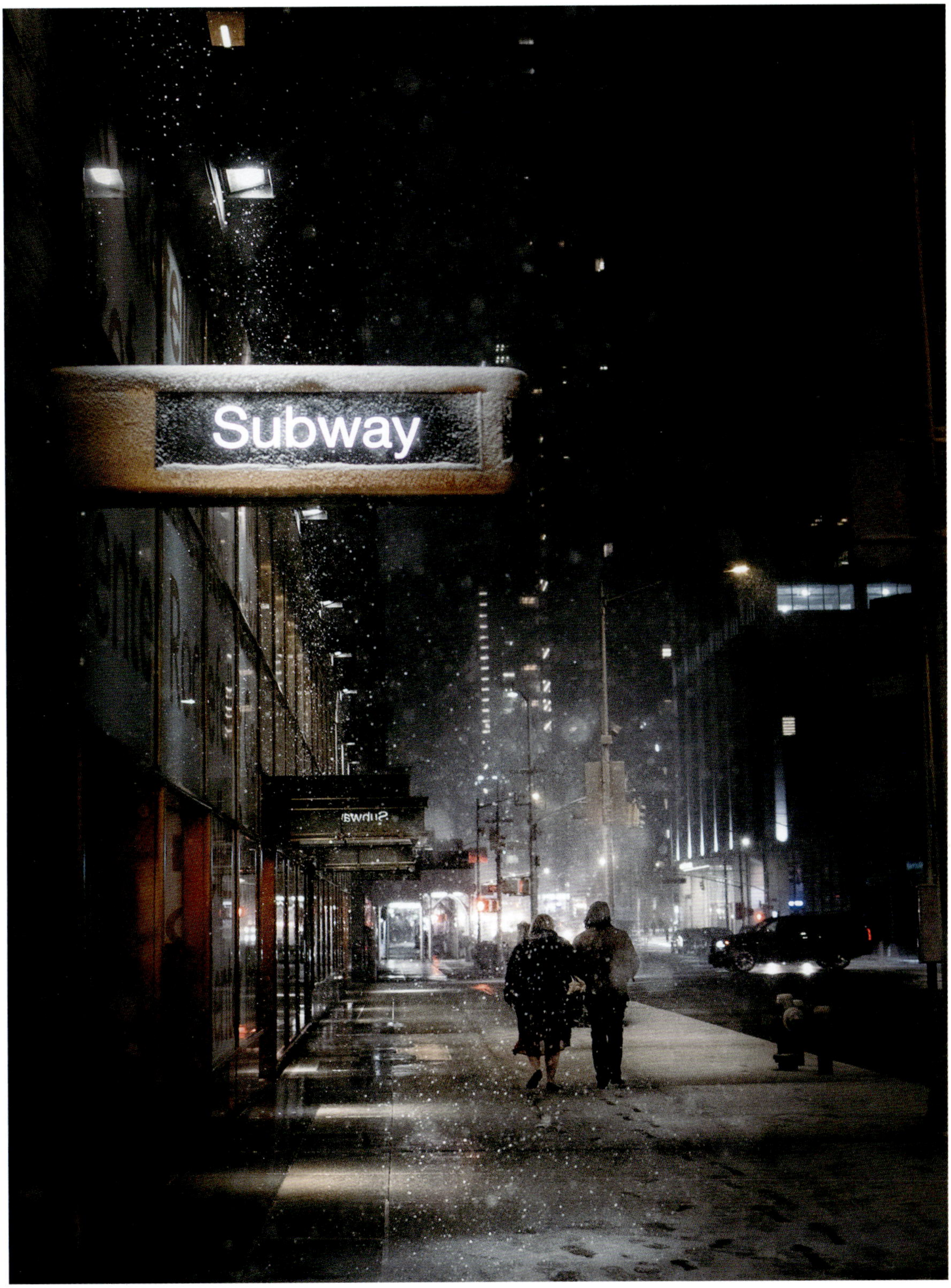
Subway

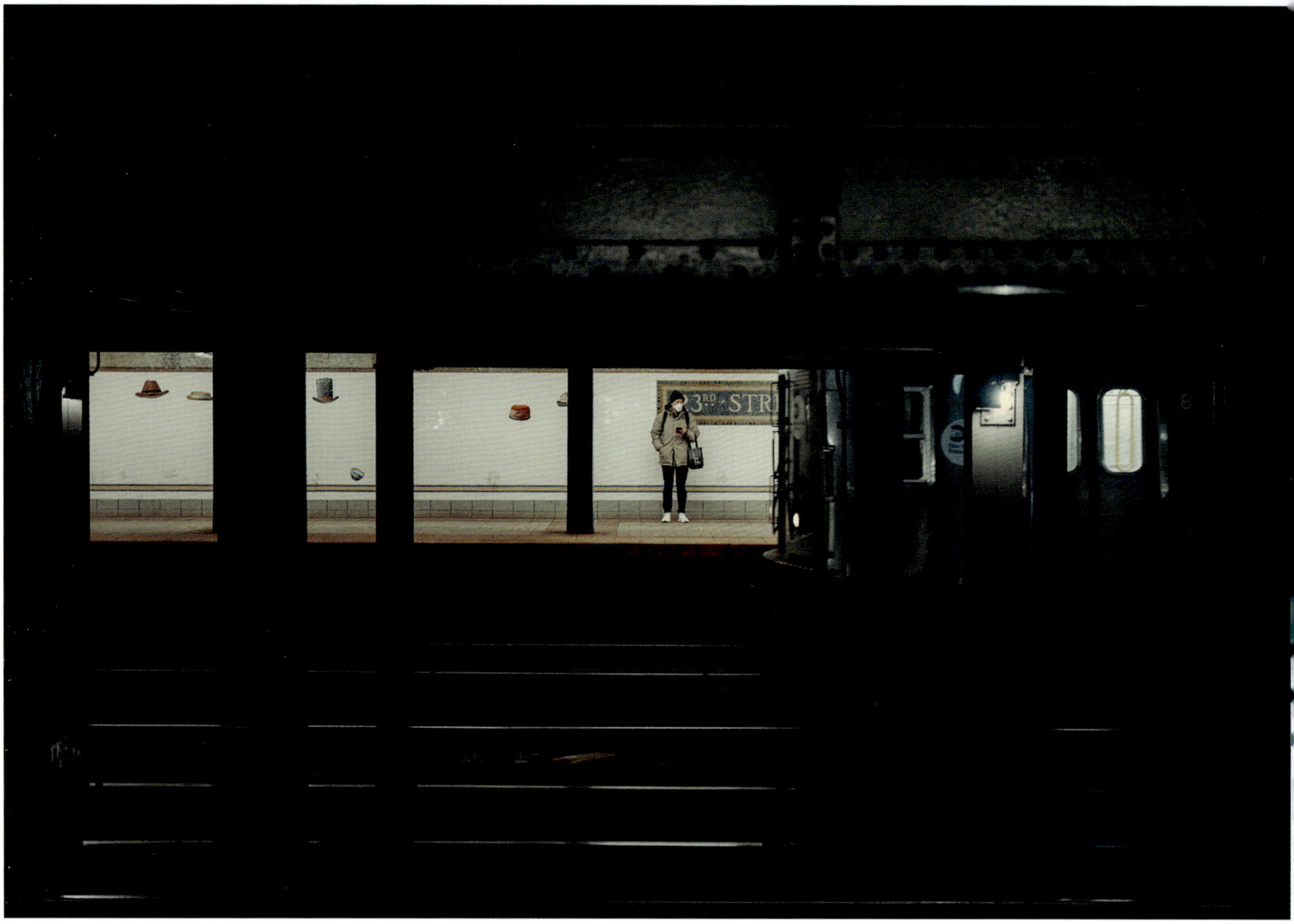

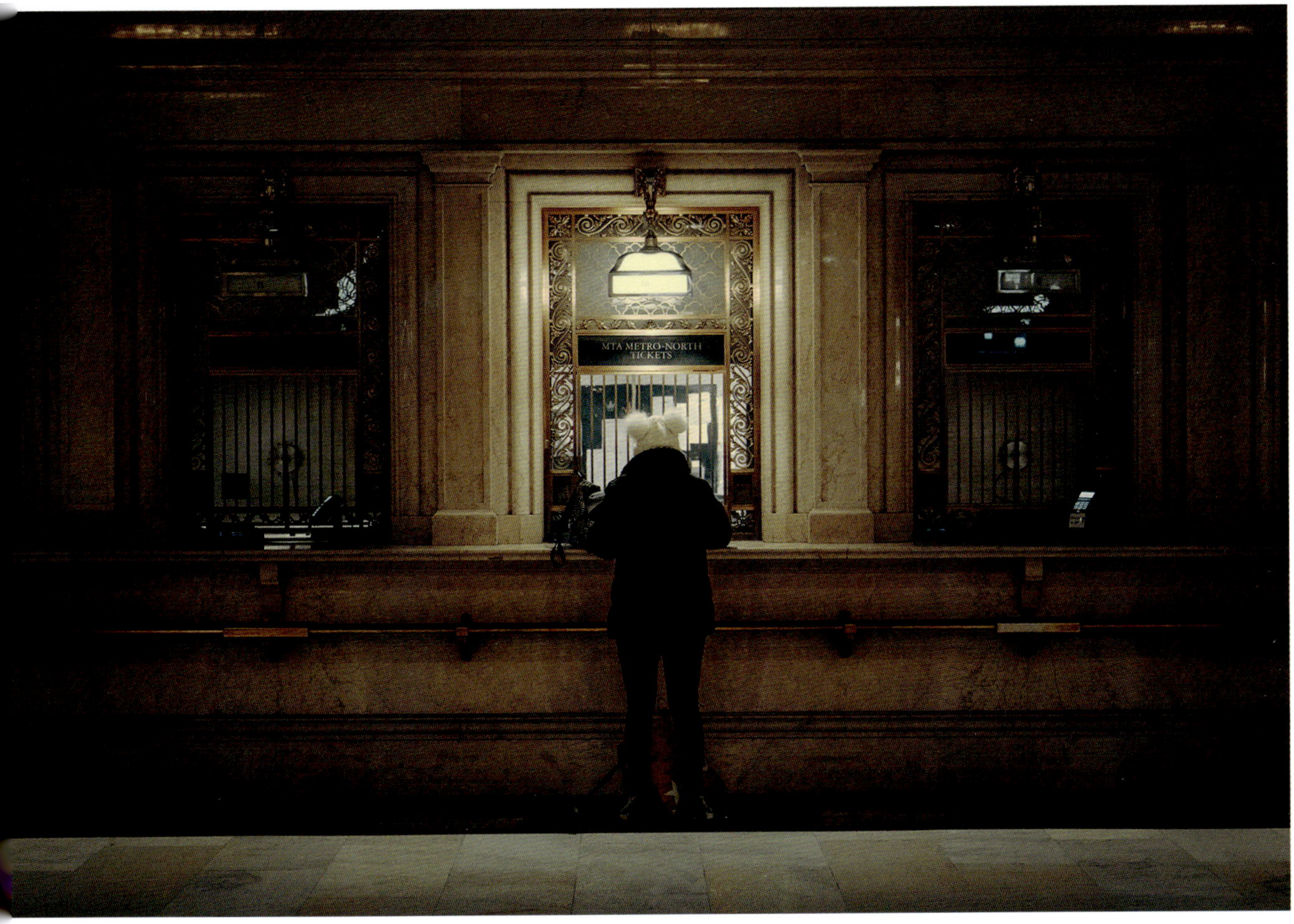
MTA METRO-NORTH
TICKETS

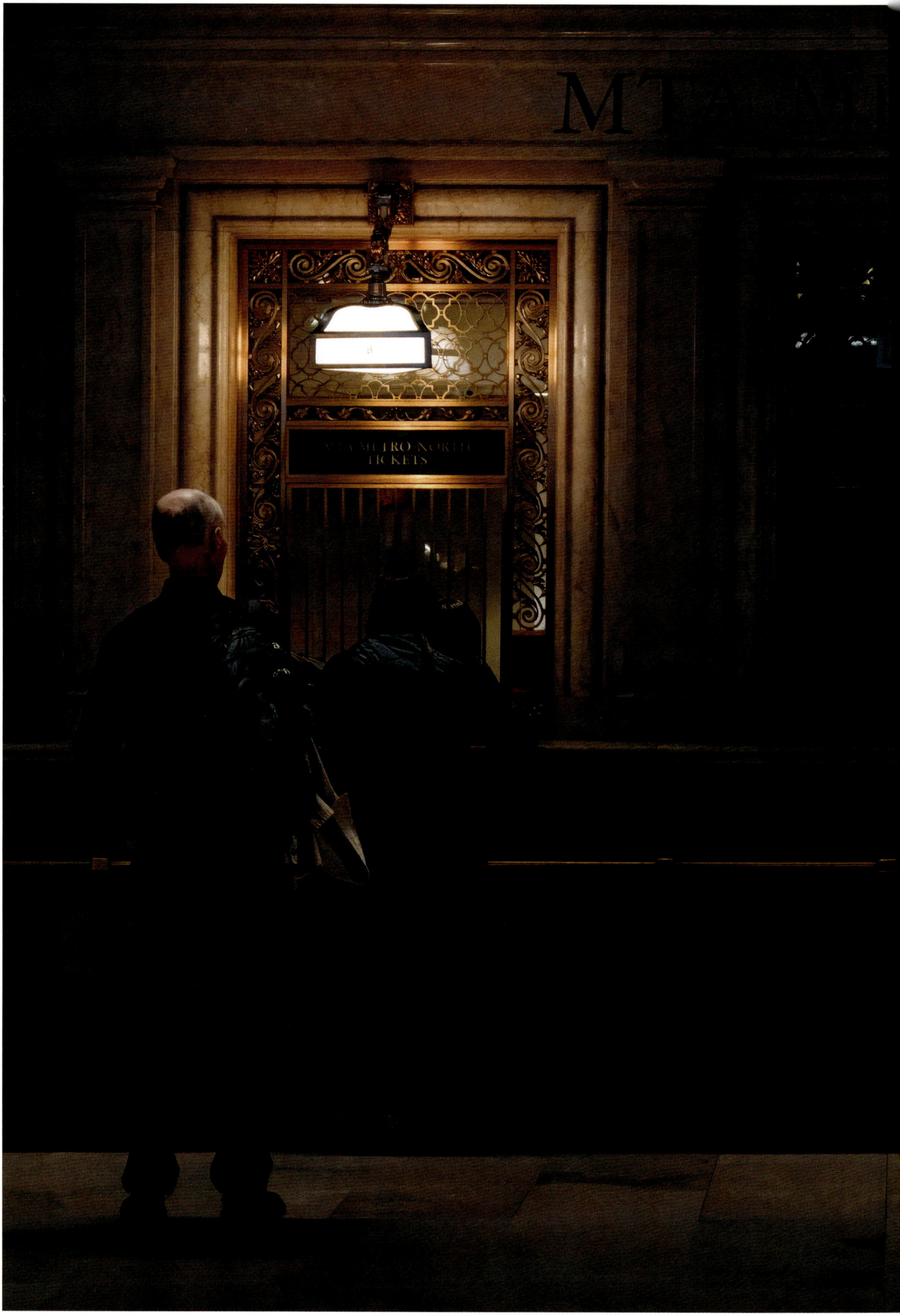

GRAND CENTRAL TERMINAL

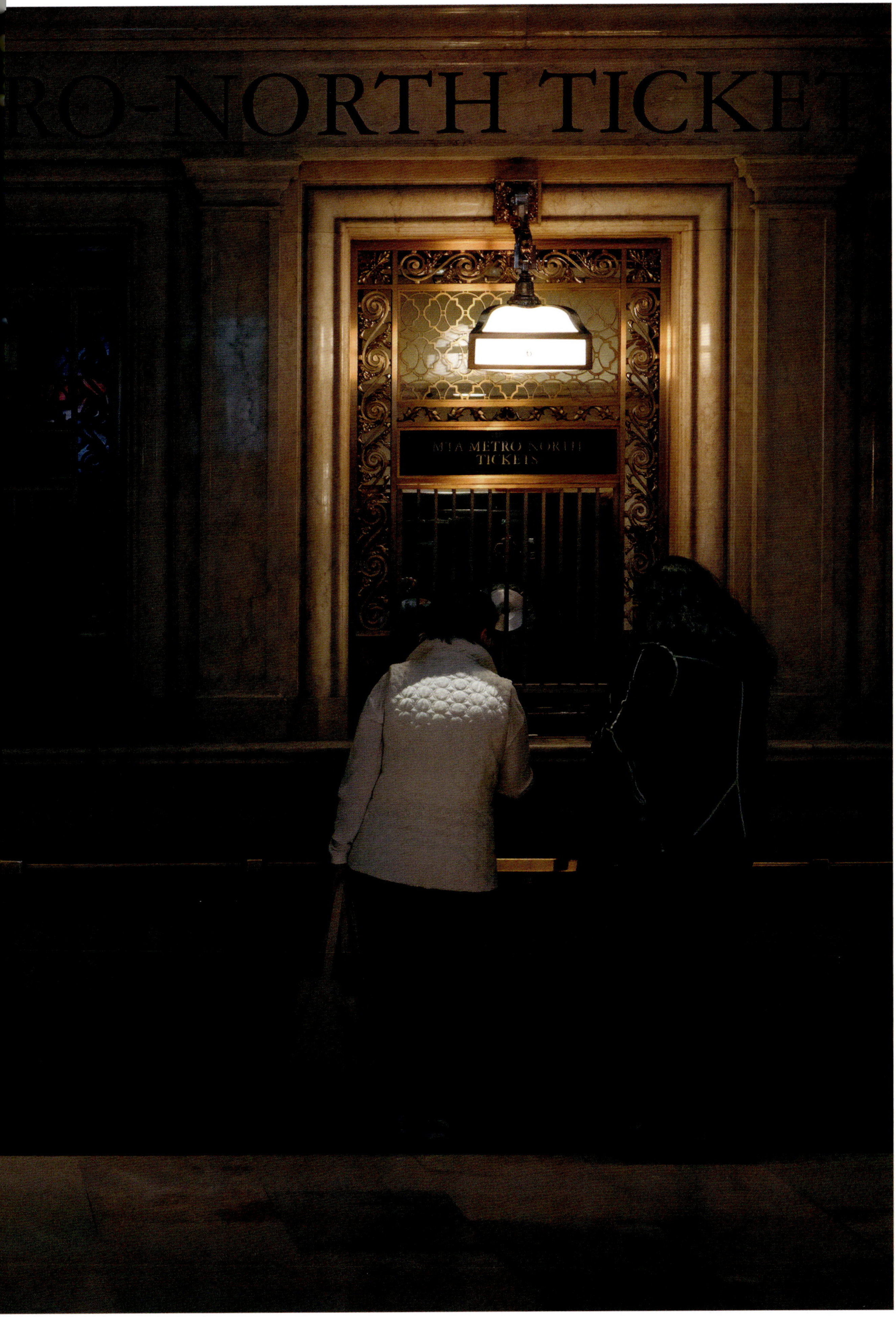
RO-NORTH TICKE
MTA METRO NORTH
TICKETS

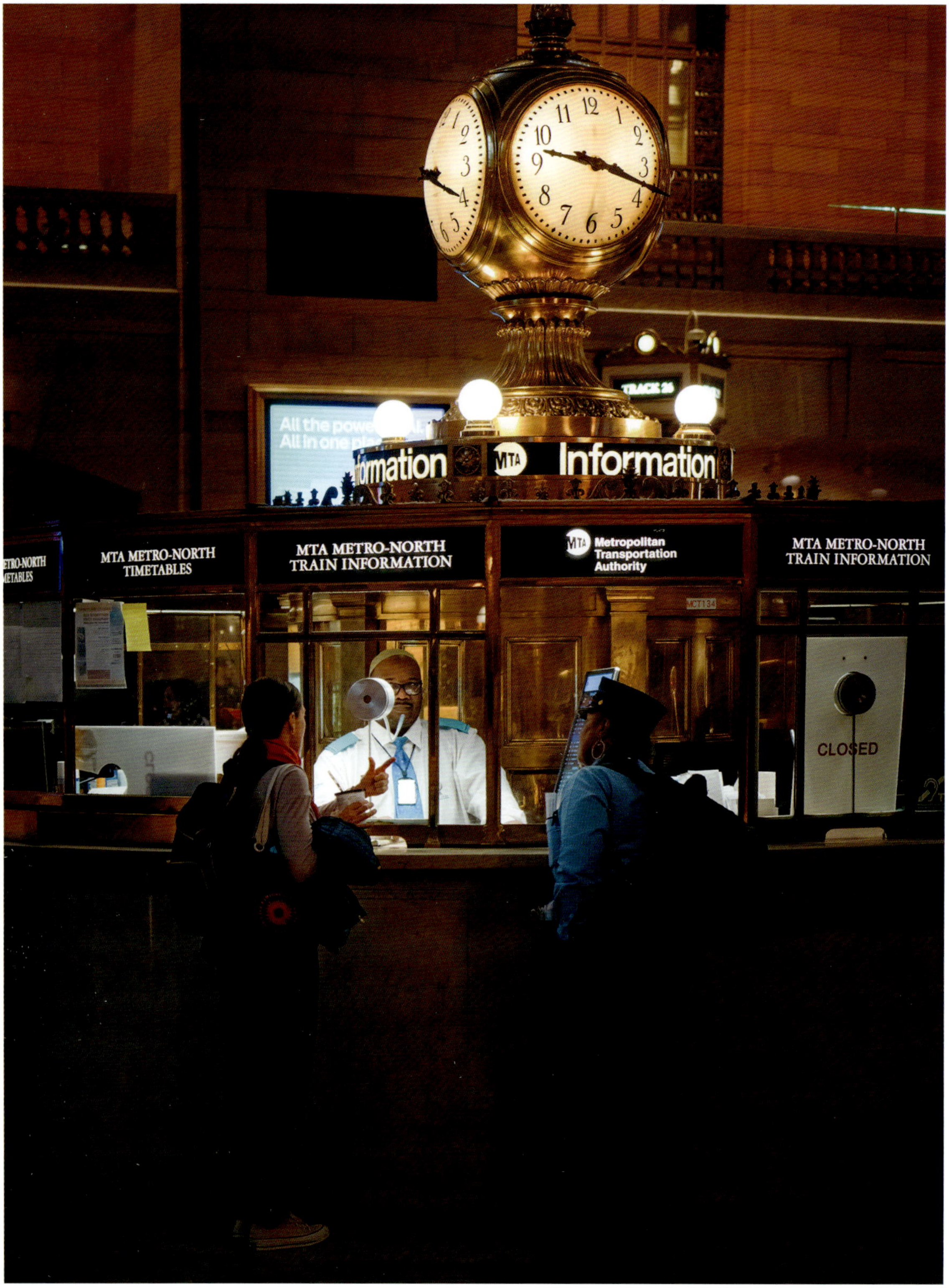
Information
MTA
Information
MTA METRO-NORTH TIMETABLES
MTA METRO-NORTH TRAIN INFORMATION
MTA Metropolitan Transportation Authority
MTA METRO-NORTH TRAIN INFORMATION
CLOSED

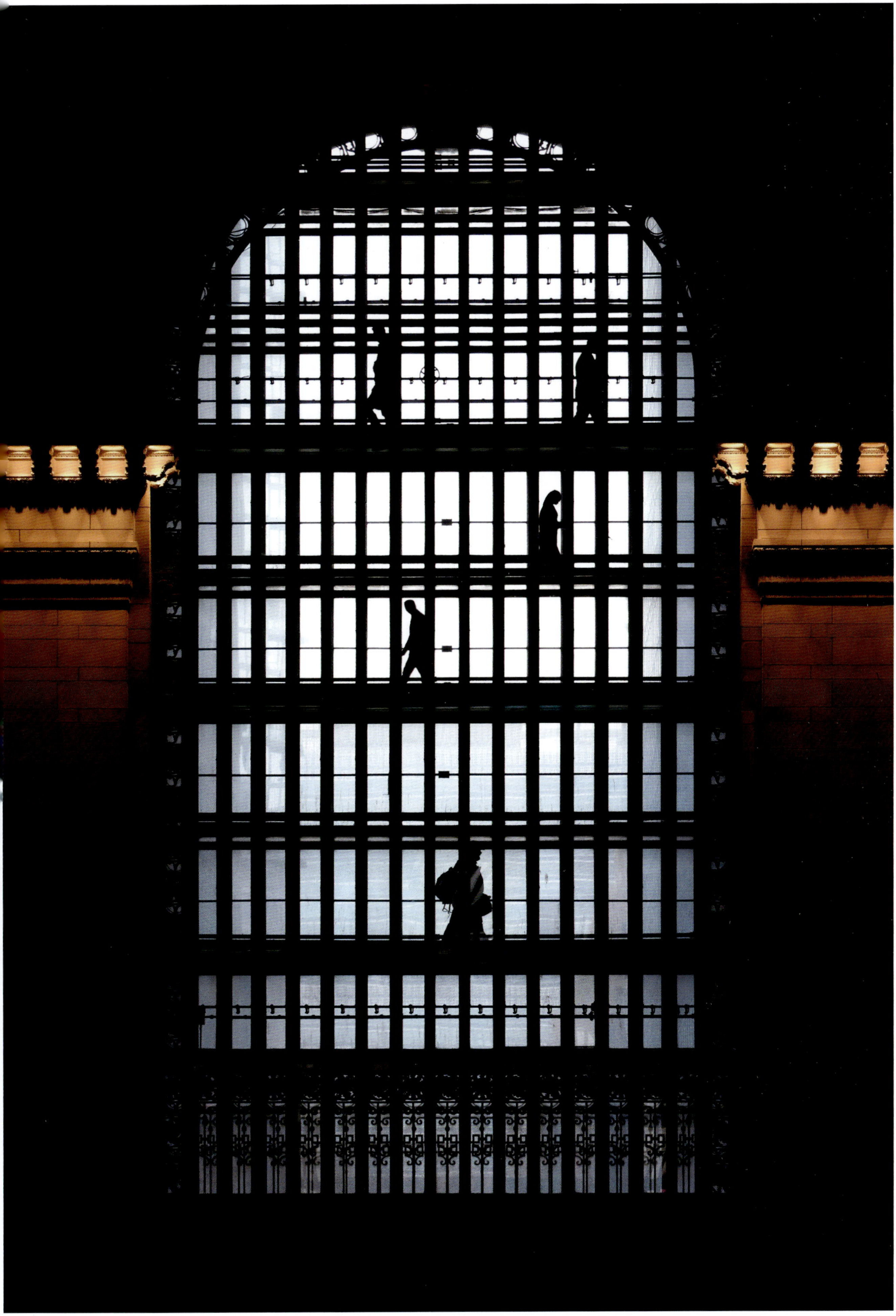

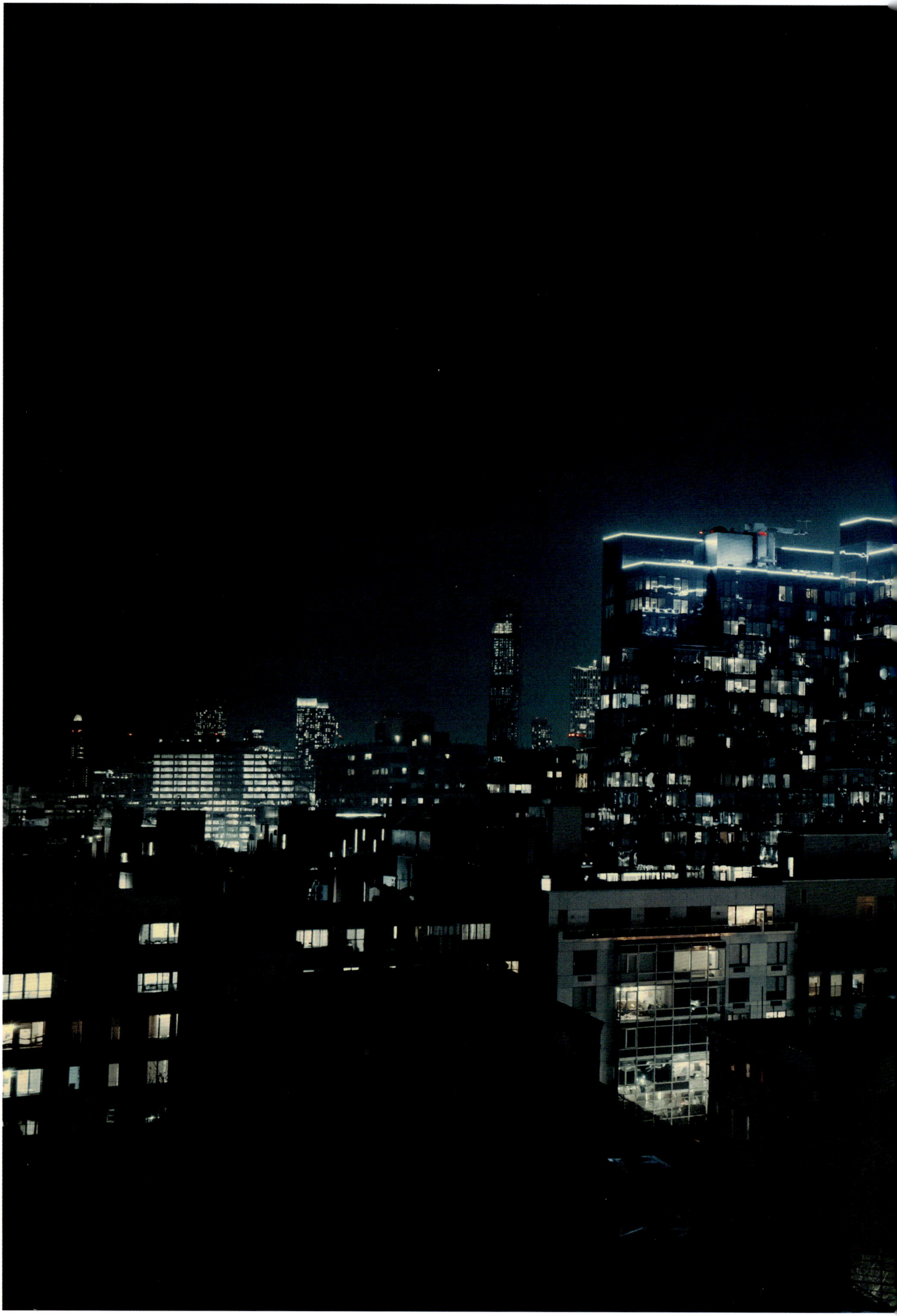

WILLIAMSBURG

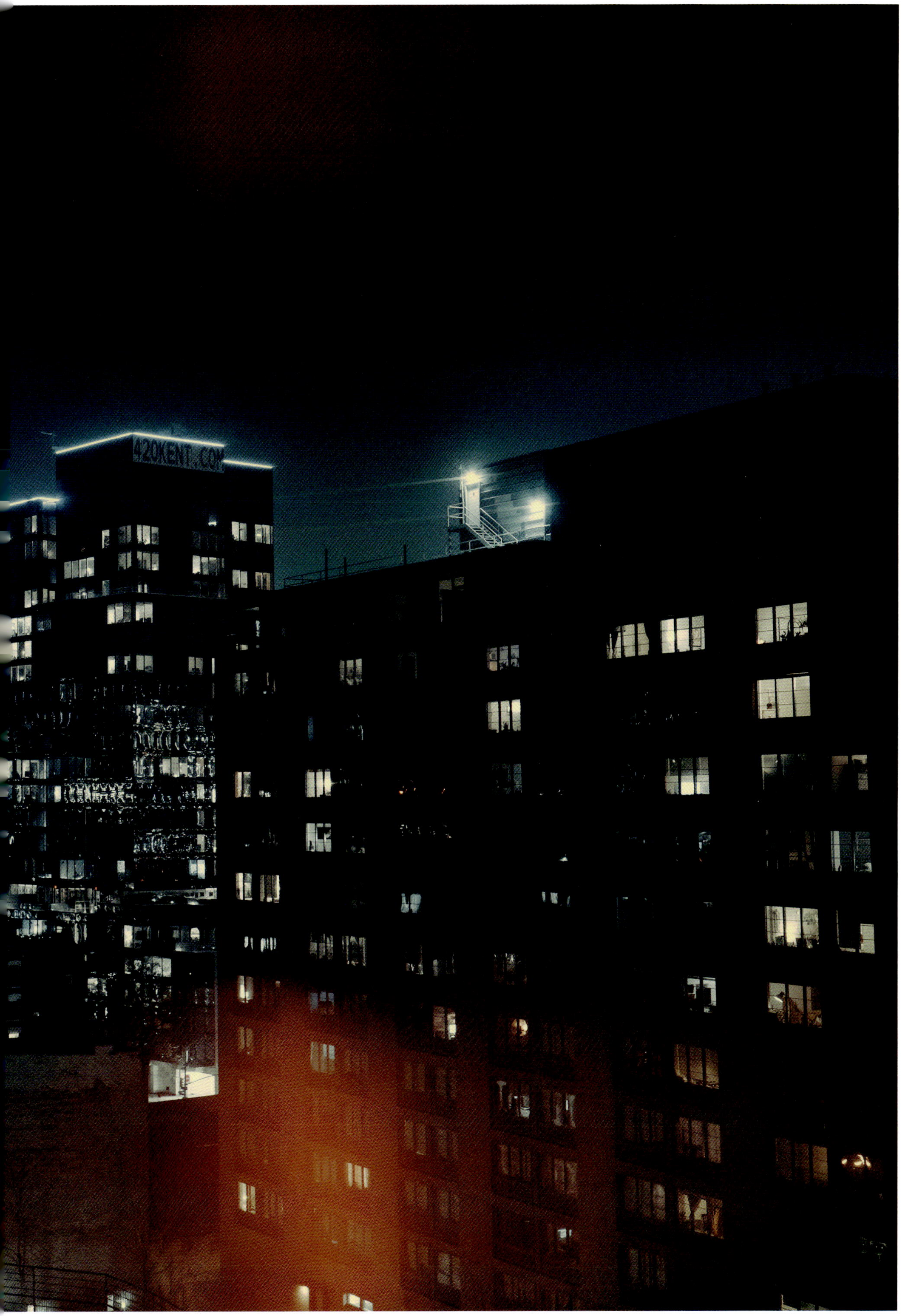
420KENT.COM

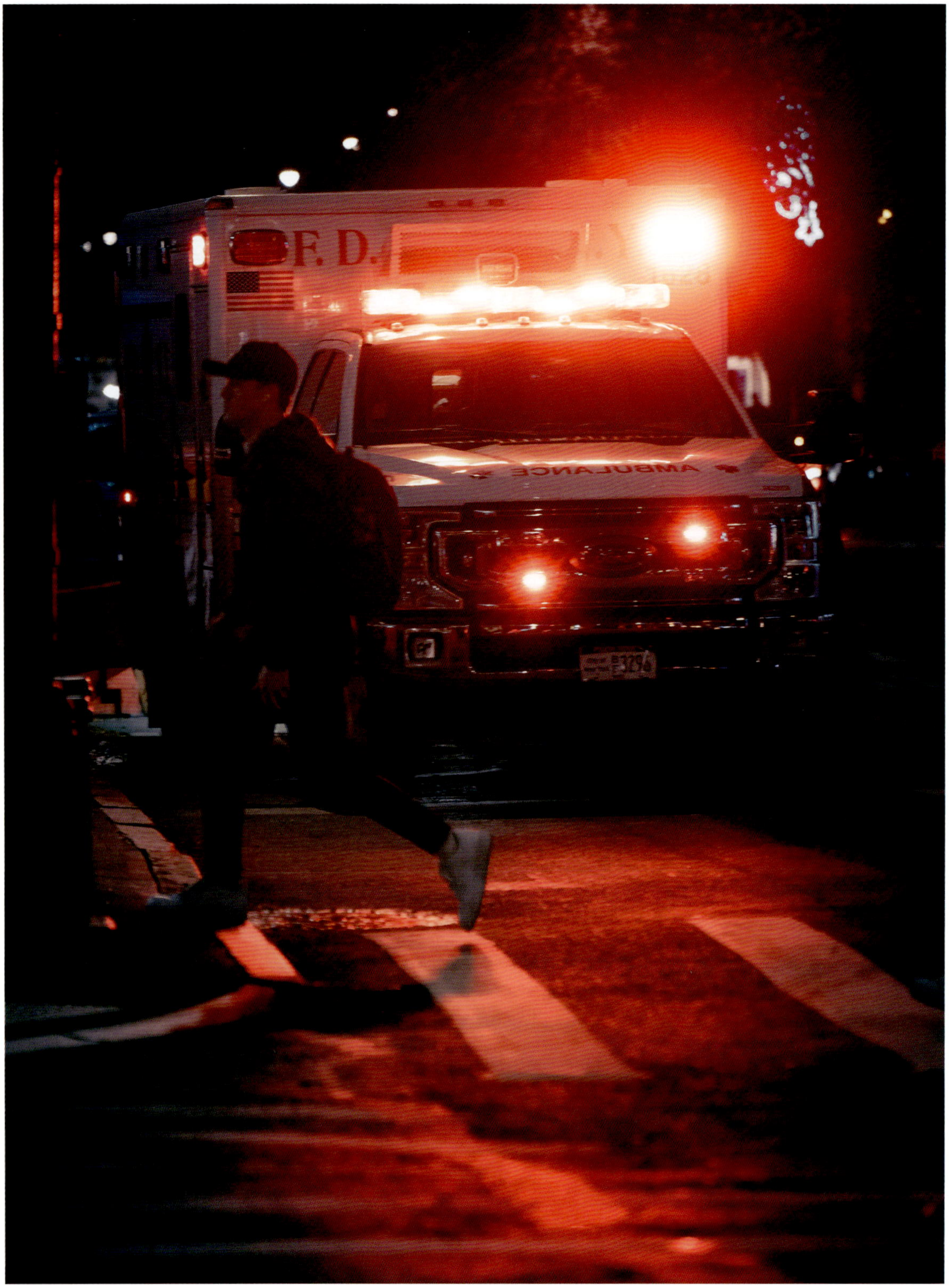
F. D.

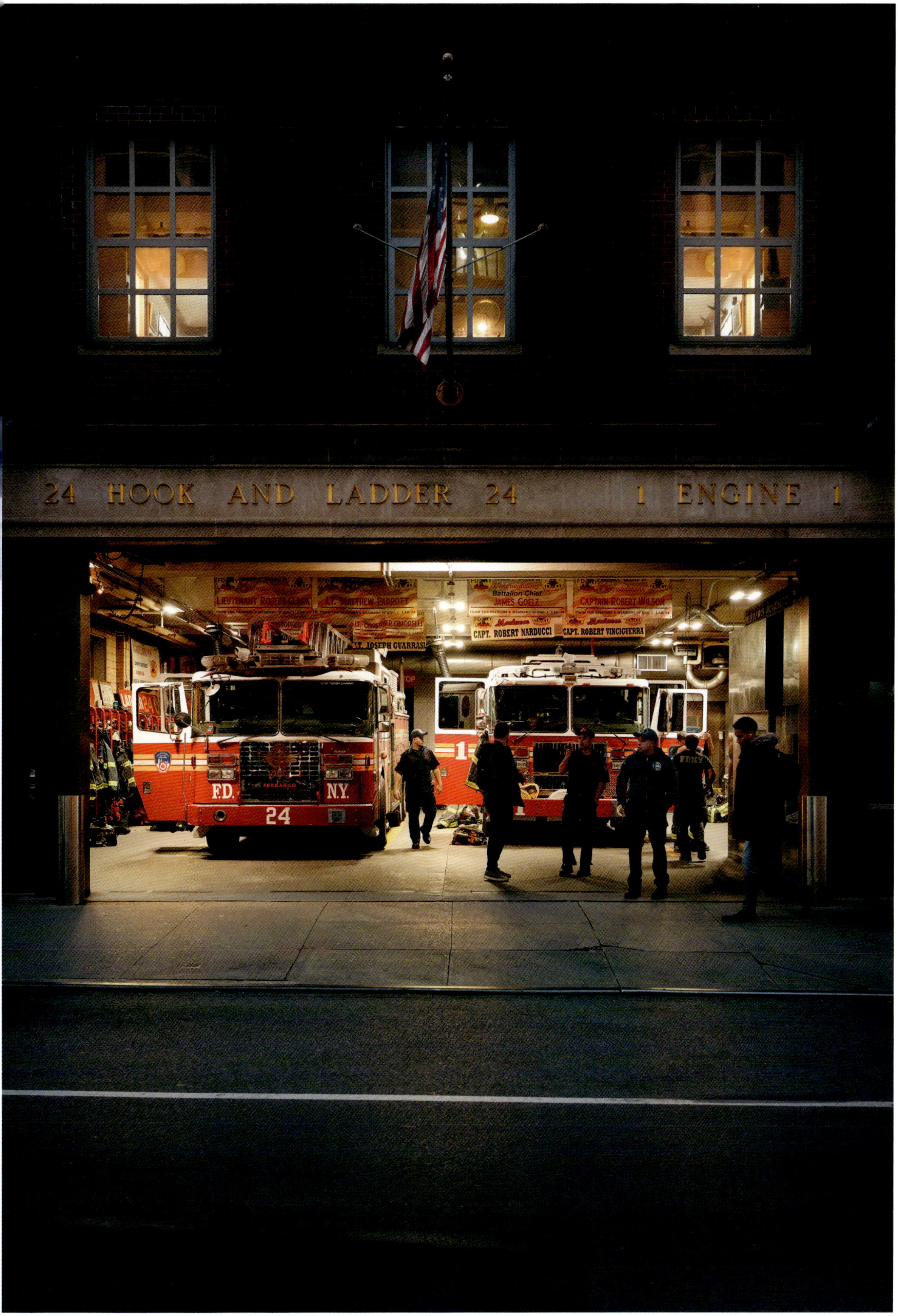
24 HOOK AND LADDER 24 1 ENGINE 1
LIEUTENANT ROBERT CLARK
LT. MATTHEW PARROTT
Battalion Chief
JAMES GOELZ
CAPTAIN ROBERT WILSON
CAPT. ROBERT NARDUCCI
CAPT. ROBERT VINCIGUERRA
LT. JOSEPH GUARRASI
F.D. N.Y.
24
FDNY

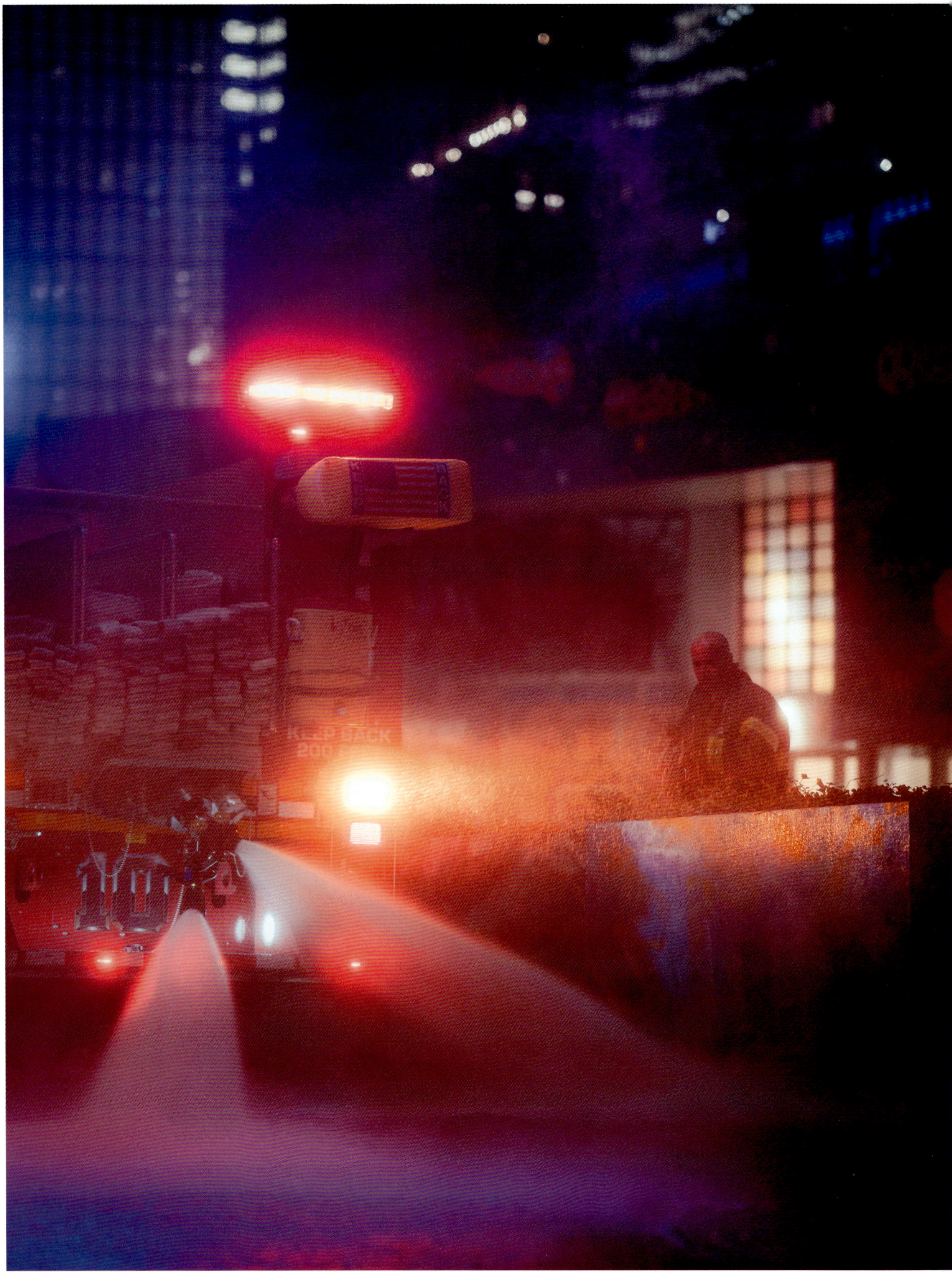
KEEP BACK
200

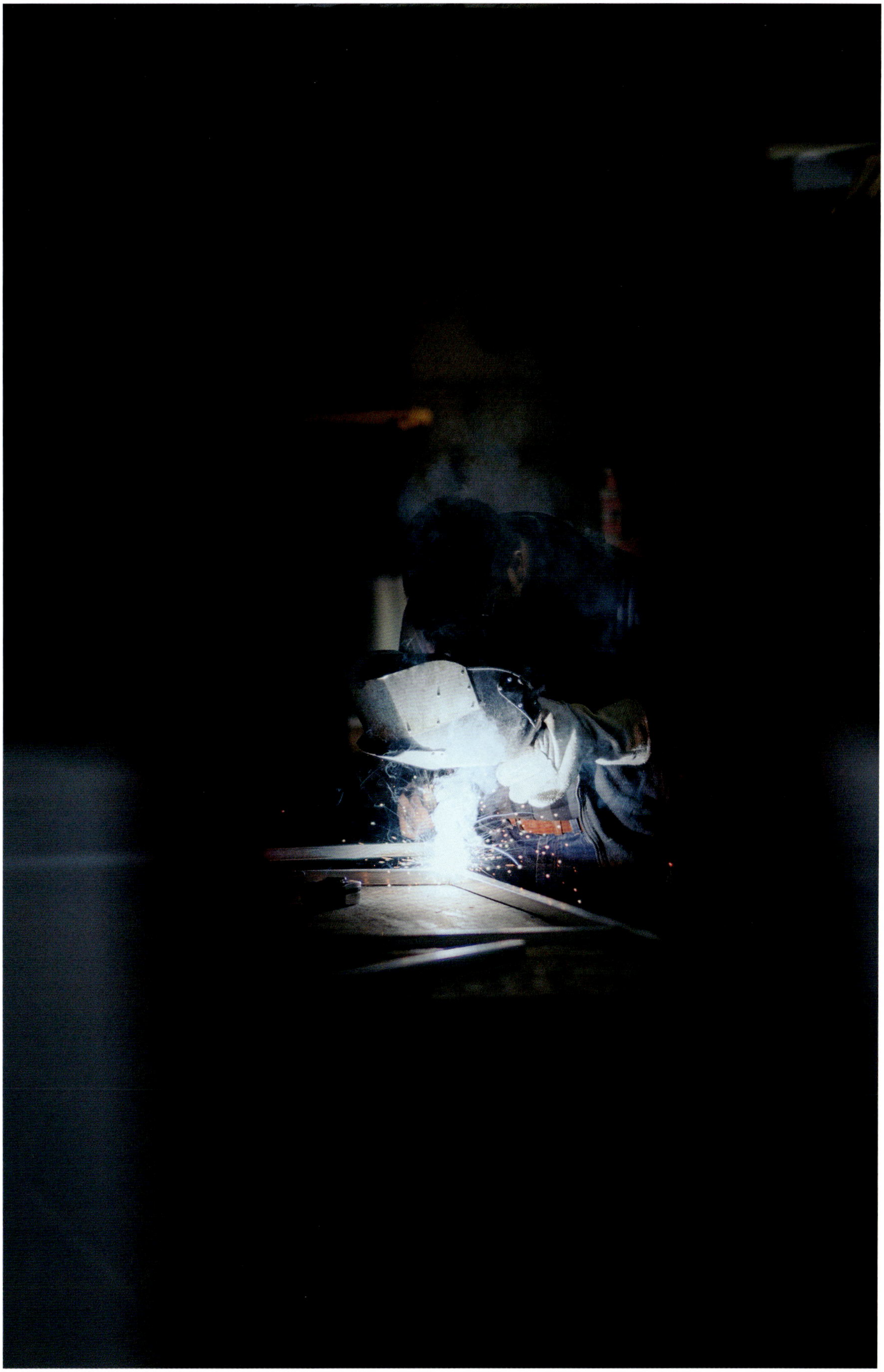

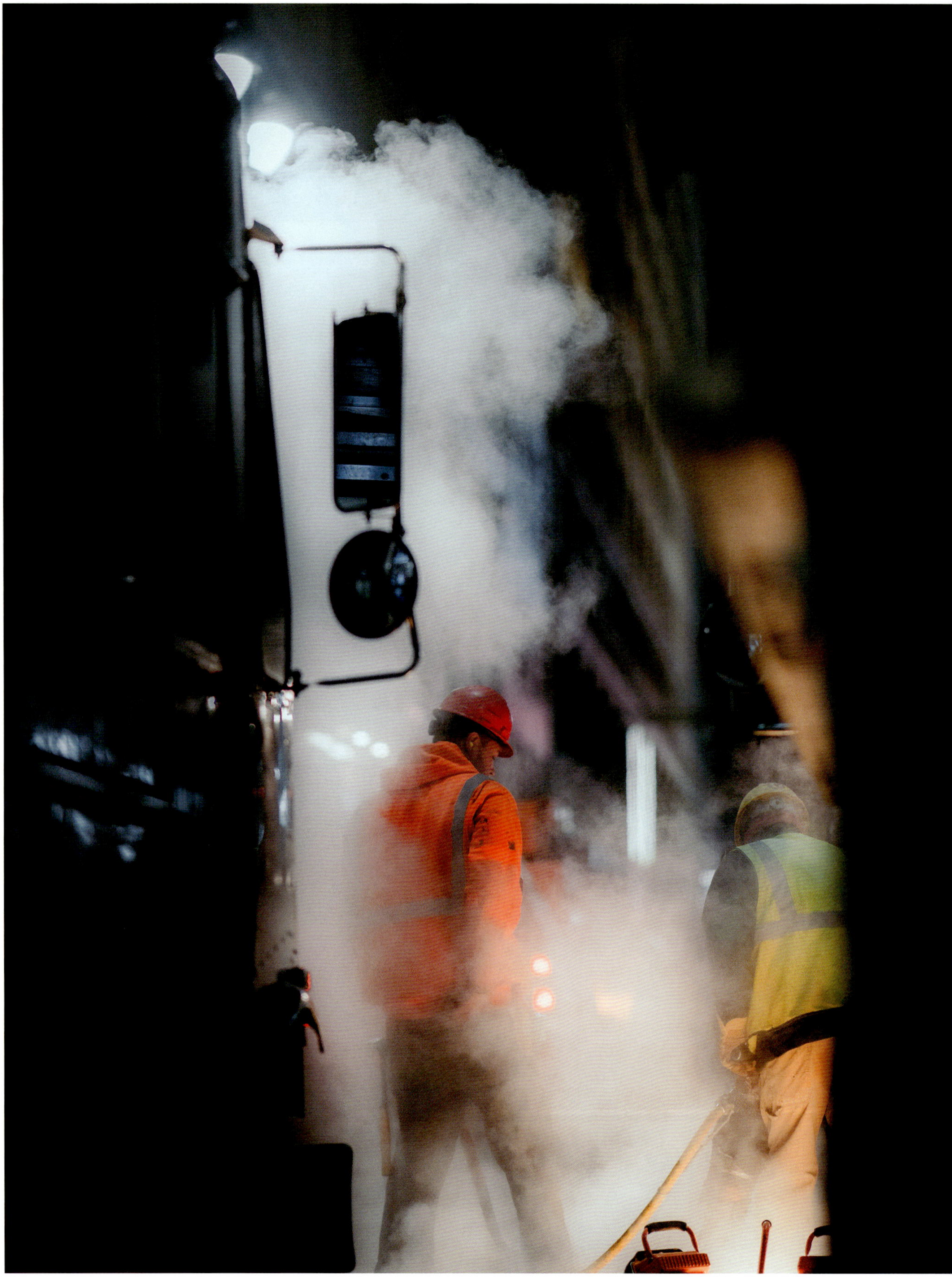

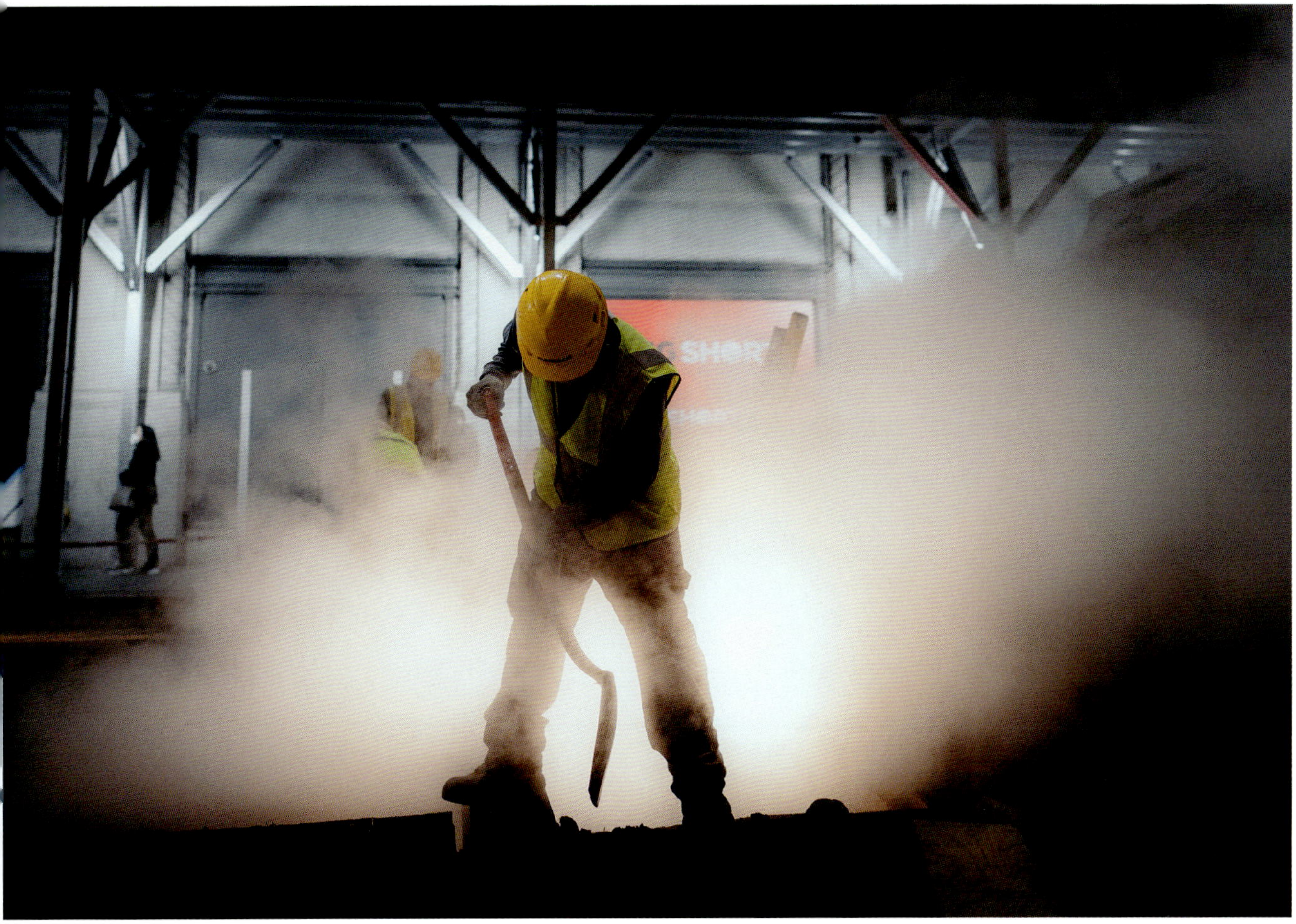

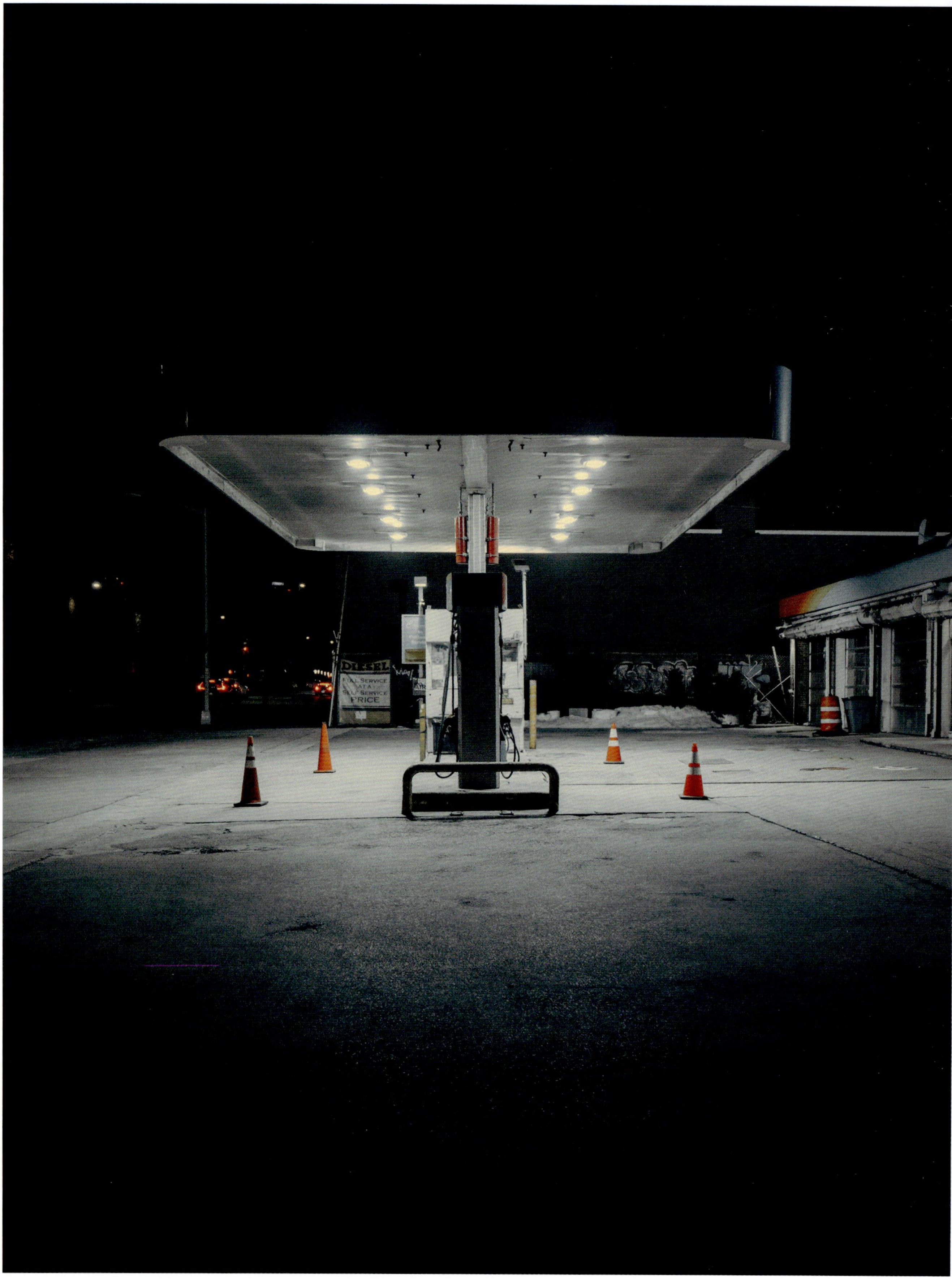
PRICE

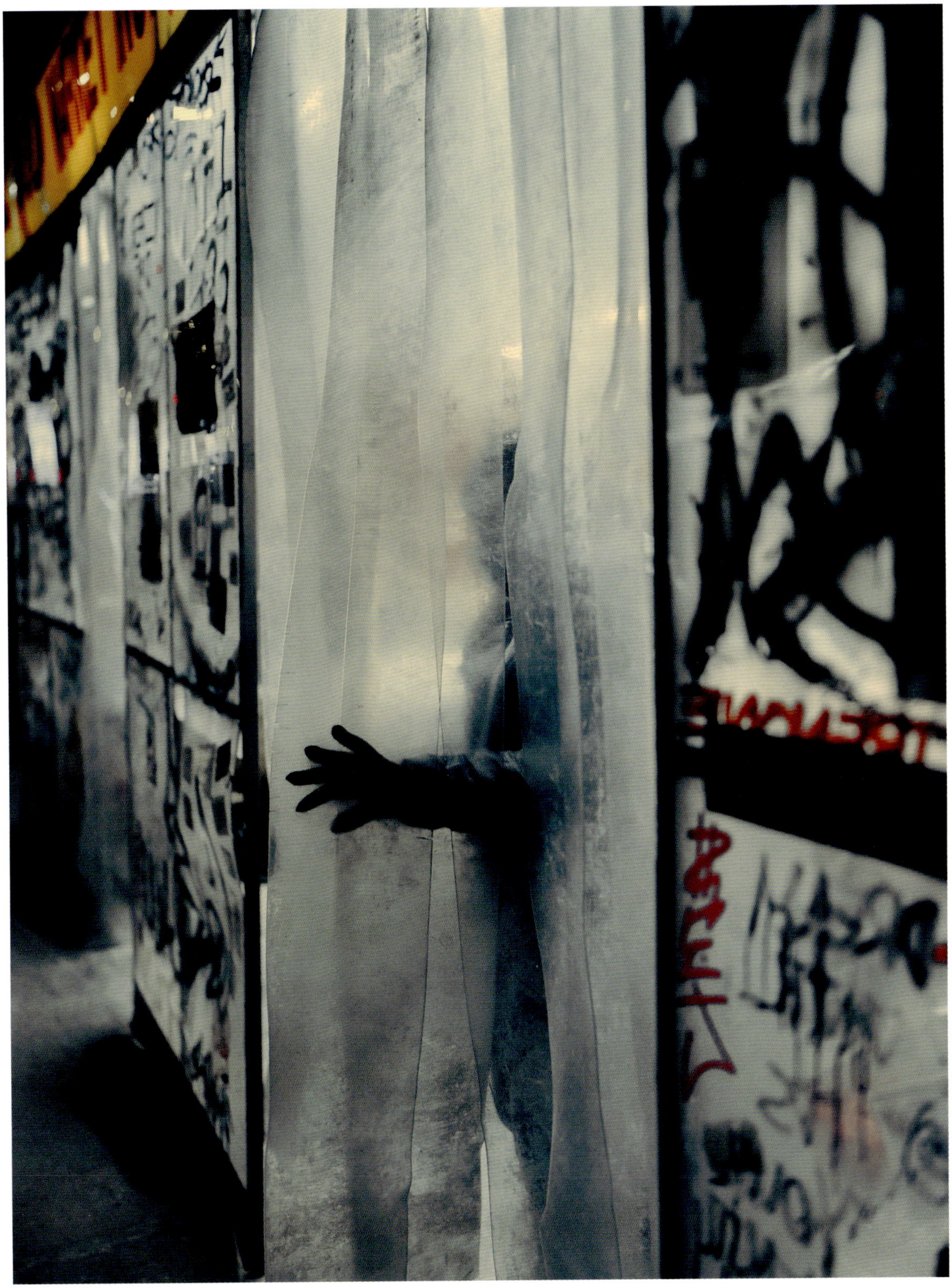

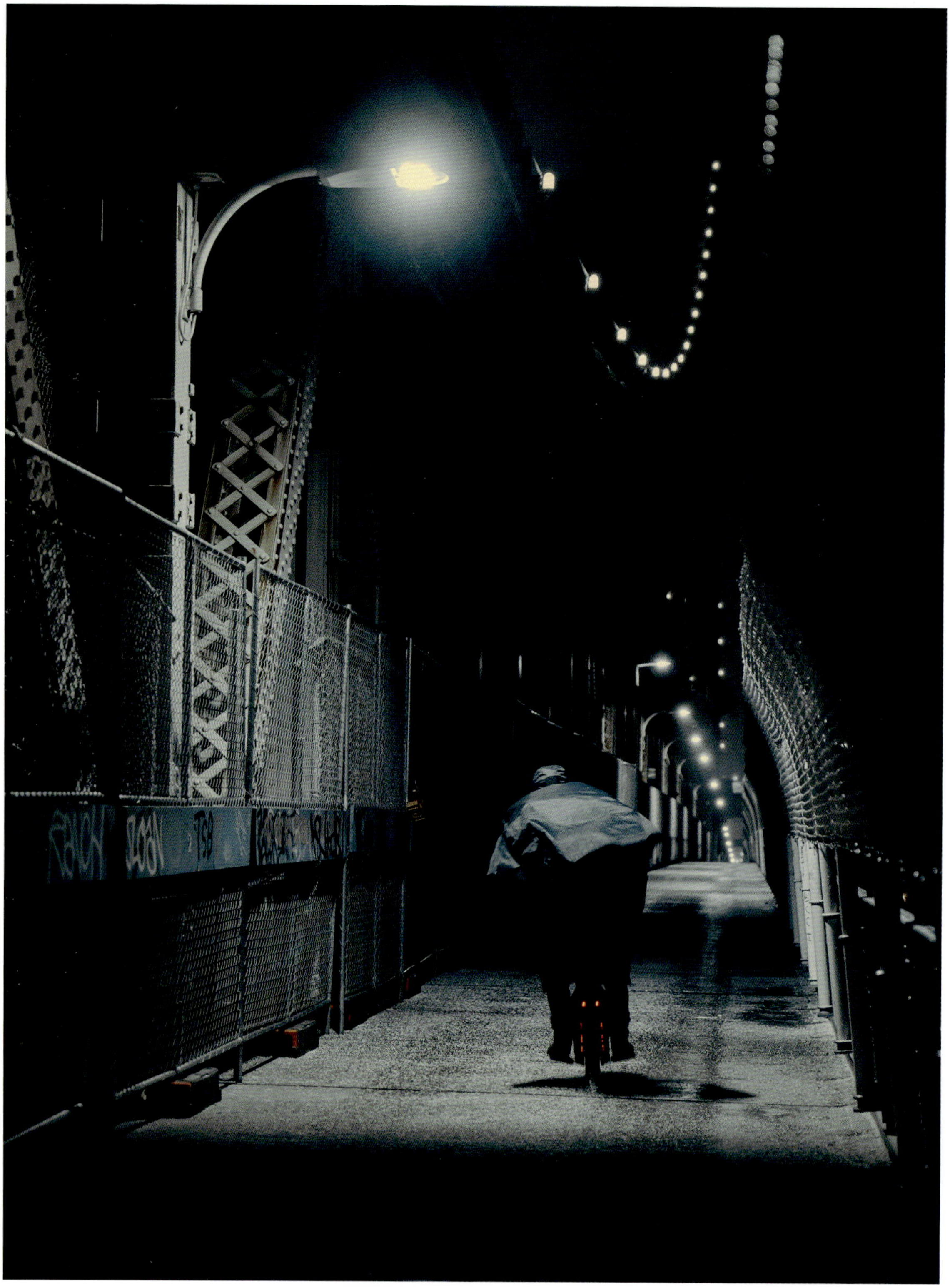

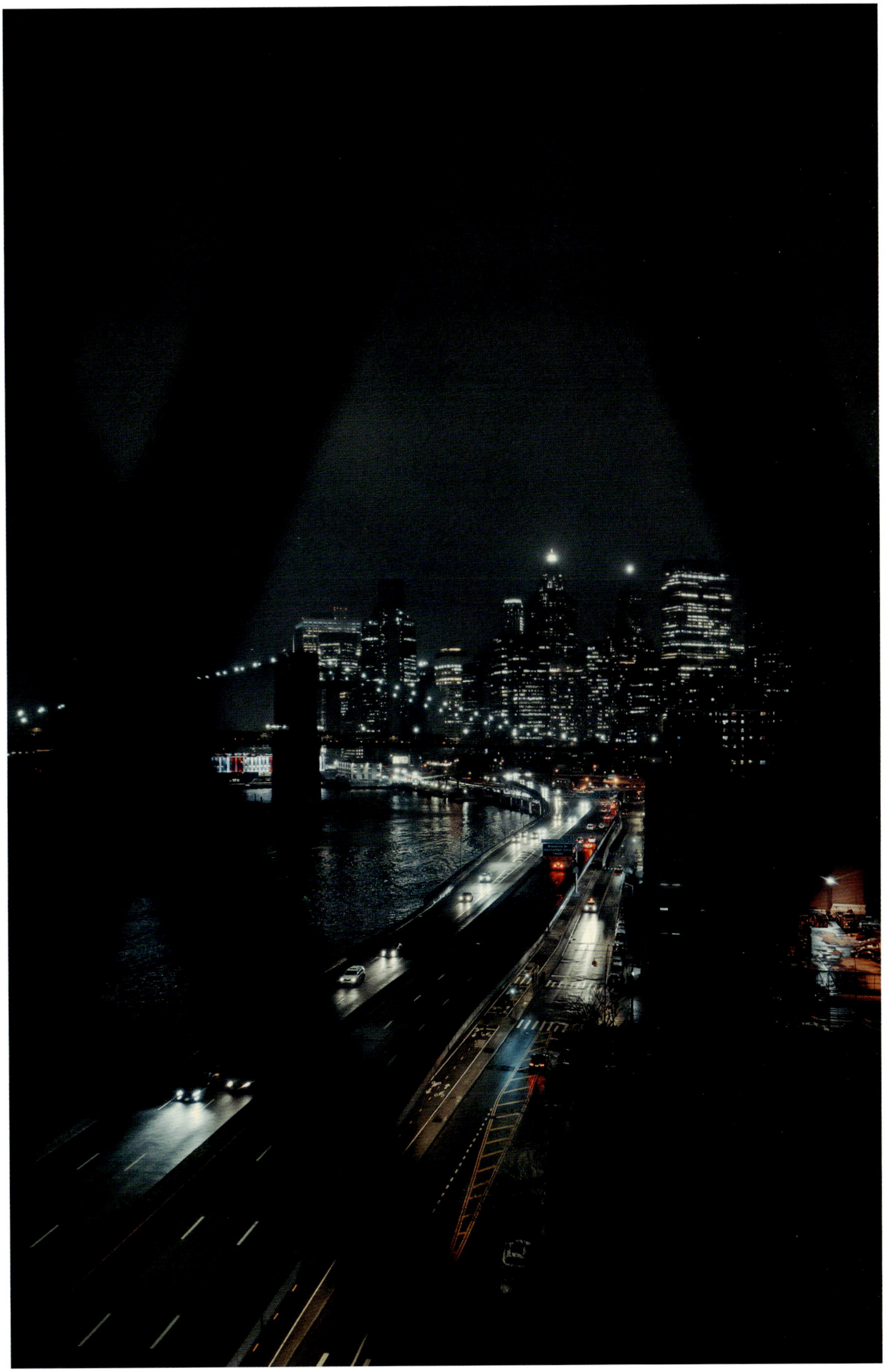

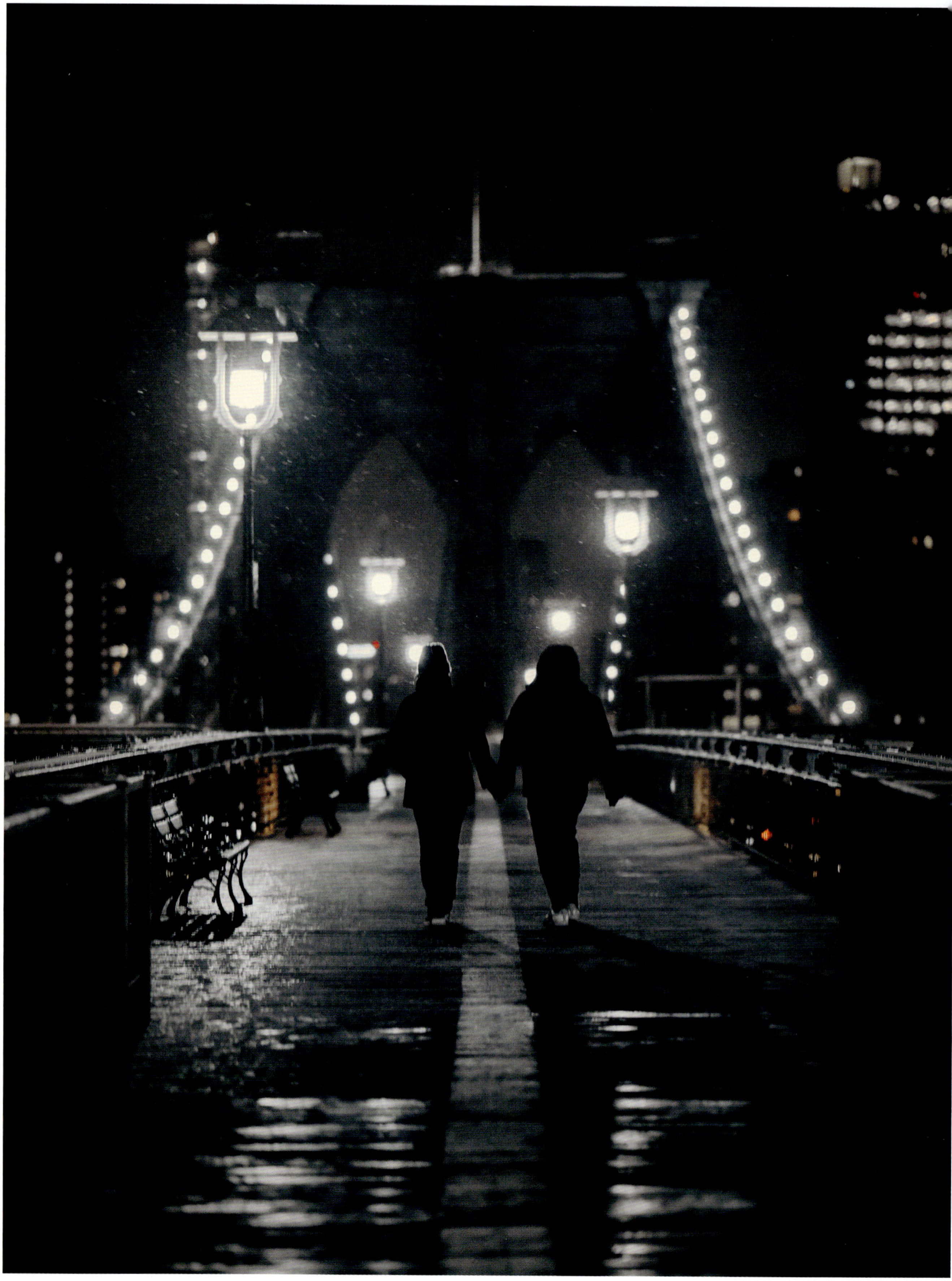

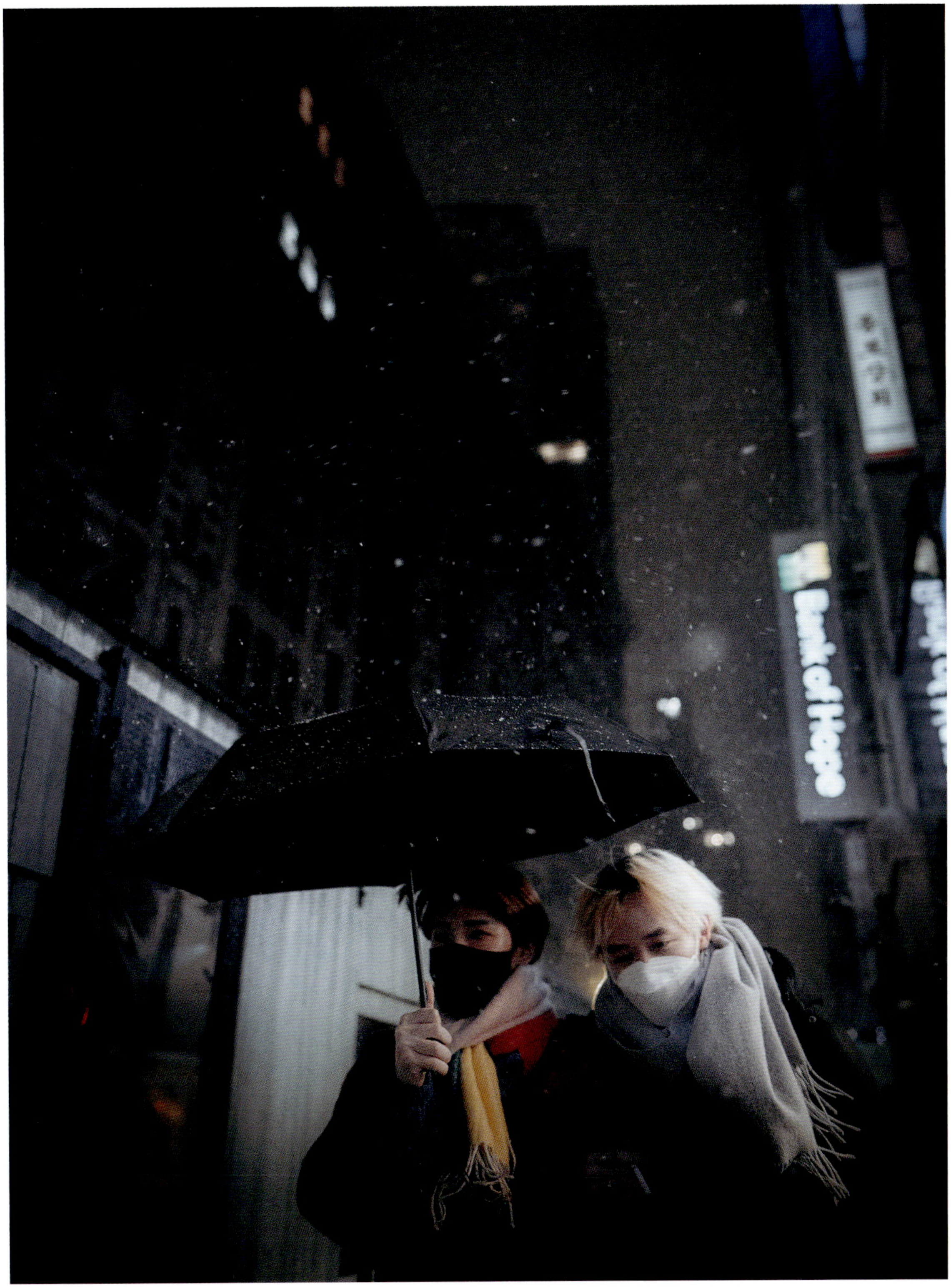
Bank of Hope

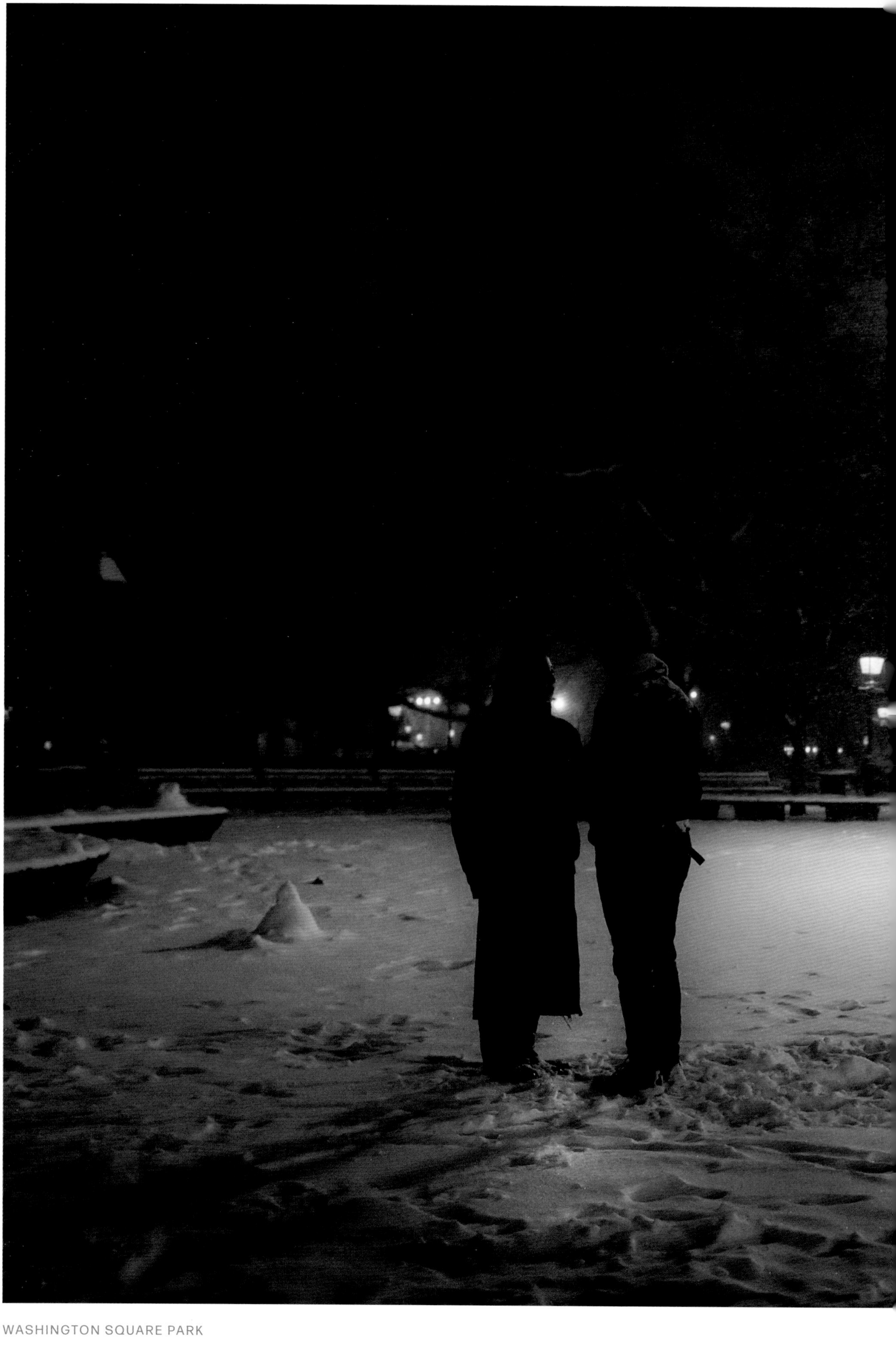

WASHINGTON SQUARE PARK

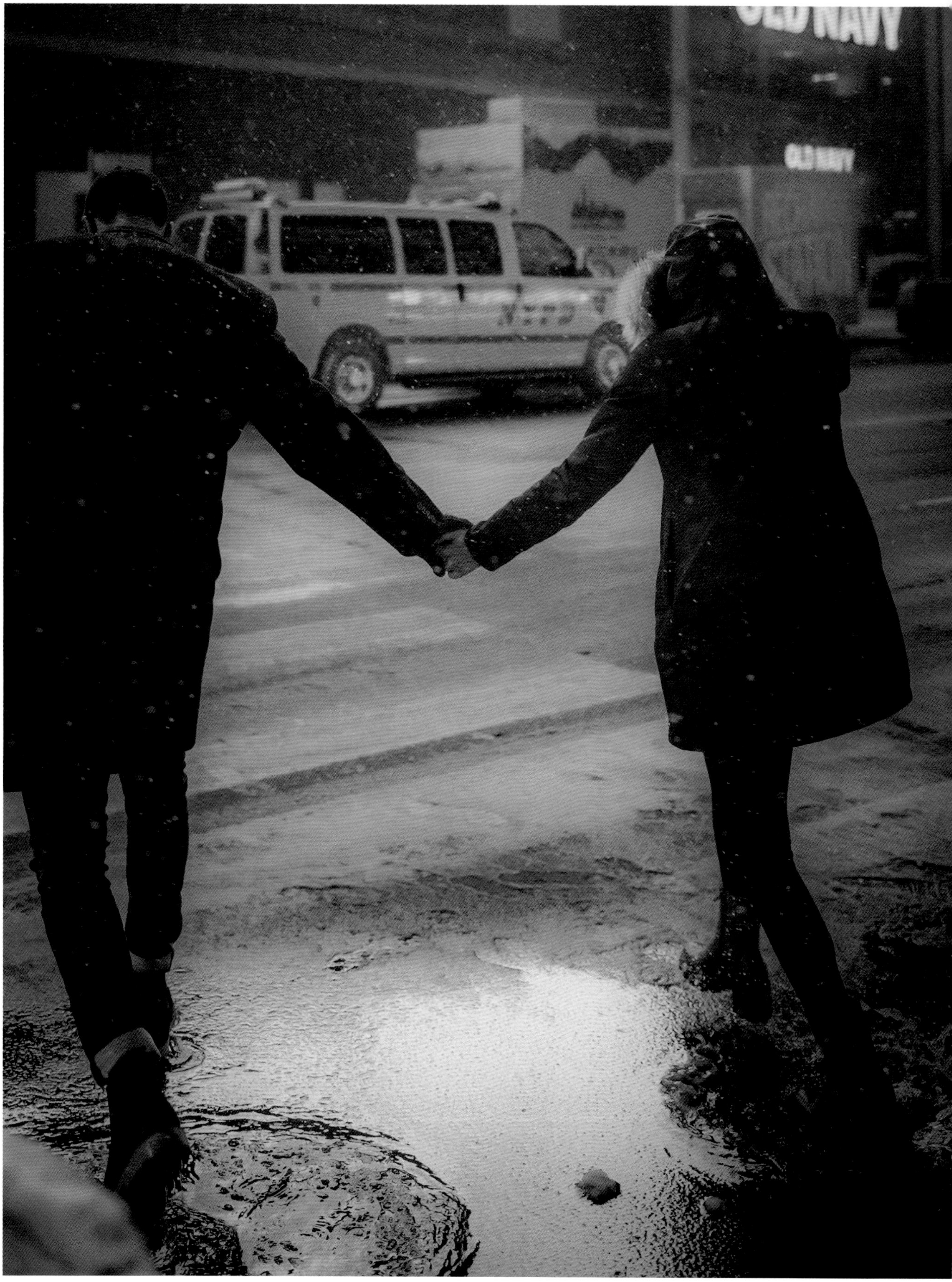
OLD NAVY

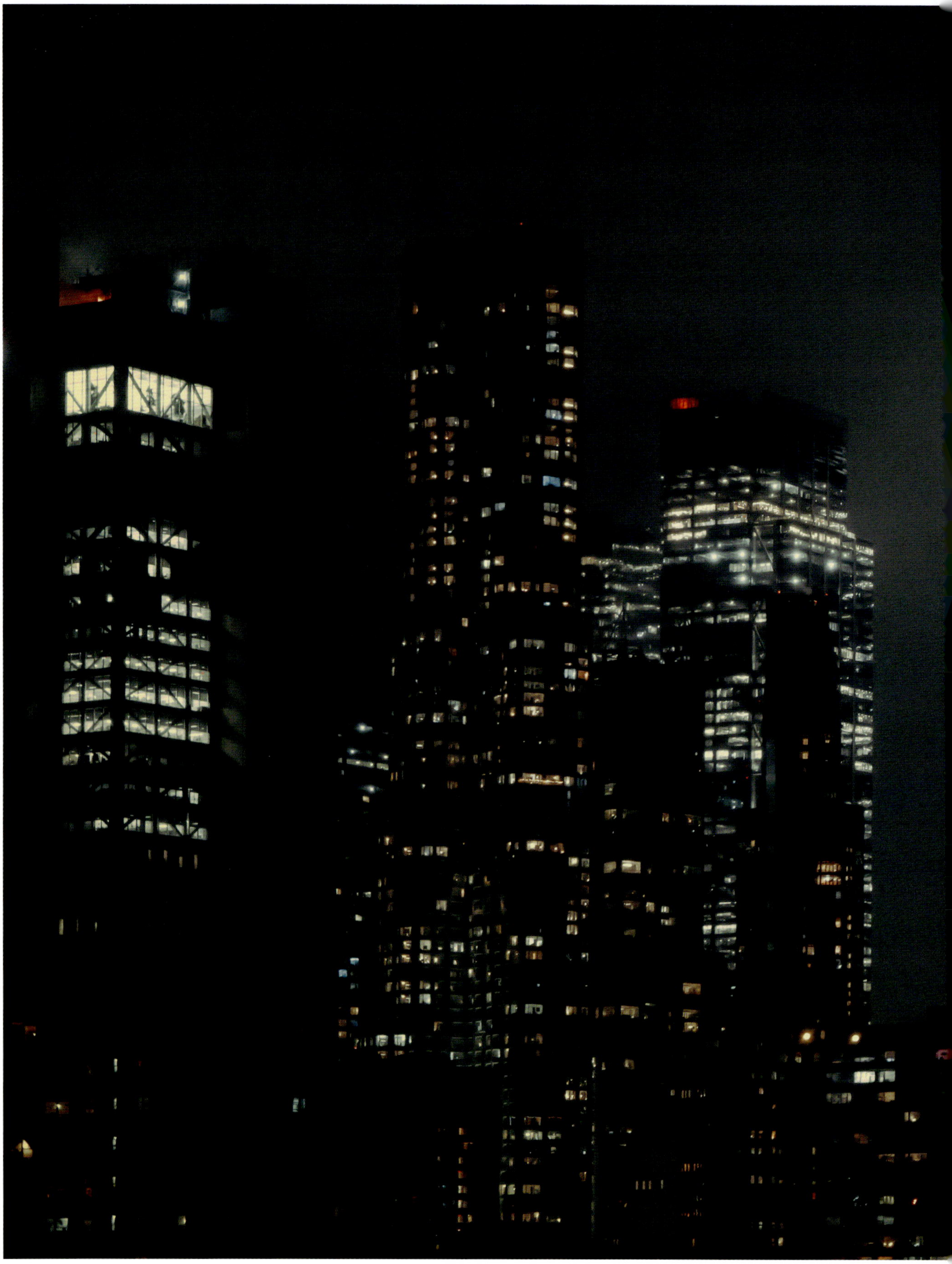

LOWER MANHATTAN

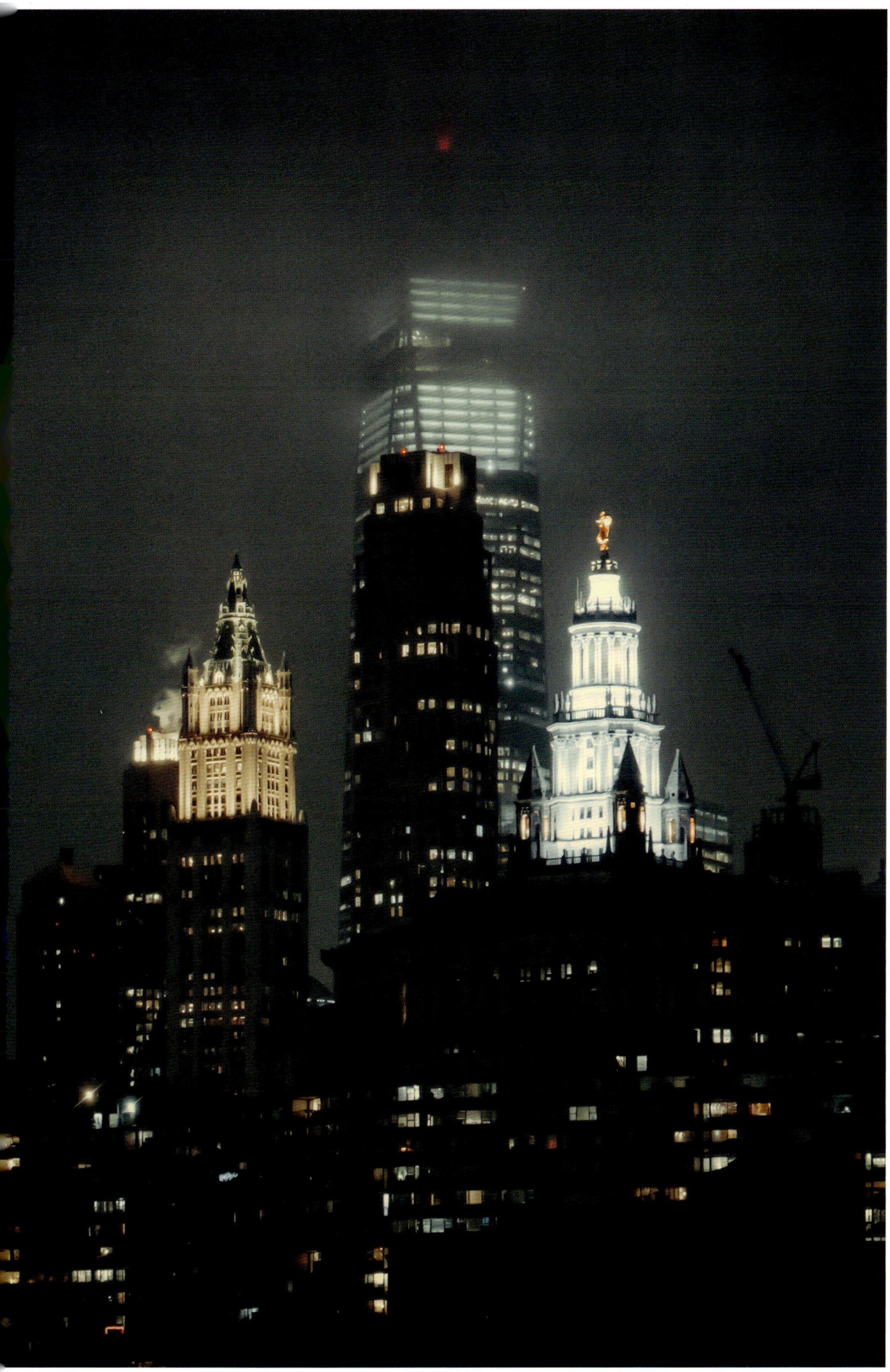

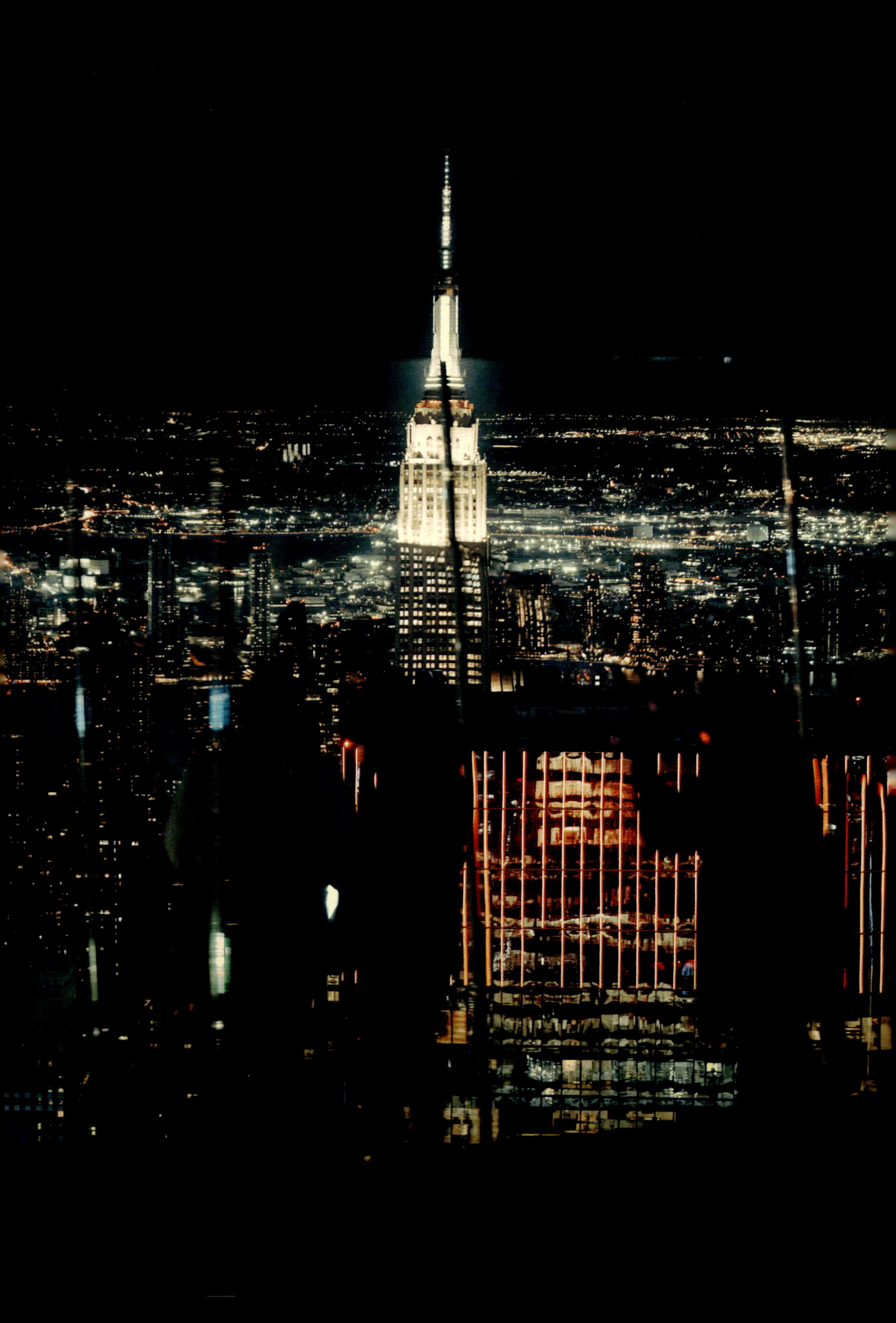

New York's architecture is especially striking at night, when illumination reveals details that can be less noticeable during the day. Exterior lighting, interior office lights, and street-level glow combine to emphasize height, ornament, and structure across the skyline.

Two of the most prominent examples are the Chrysler Building and the Empire State Building, both completed in the early 20th century and central to Midtown Manhattan's silhouette. The Chrysler Building, finished in 1930, is a defining work of Art Deco design. At night, its stainless steel crown—composed of tiered arches and triangular windows—reflects spotlights that accentuate its geometric patterns. The building's illuminated spire and setbacks highlight architect William Van Alen's emphasis on vertical movement and industrial-age ornamentation, including stylized eagles and automotive motifs.

The Empire State Building, completed in 1931, presents a more streamlined Art Deco profile. Its lighting system, installed decades after its completion and periodically upgraded, allows the tower's upper floors and spire to glow in changing colors. These colors are often programmed to mark holidays, civic events, and cultural observances. The building's stepped massing becomes more pronounced after dark, as floodlighting separates each setback against the sky, reinforcing its vertical thrust.

Nighttime lighting plays a significant role in shaping the city's architectural identity in other areas of New York. In Lower Manhattan, the façades of early 20th-century office buildings are often lit from below, emphasizing stone detailing and neoclassical columns. In contrast, contemporary glass skyscrapers in areas such as Hudson Yards and the Financial District create a different effect. Their curtain walls reflect surrounding lights, while illuminated interiors reveal structural grids and floor plates.

Bridges also contribute to the architectural landscape after dark. The Brooklyn Bridge and Manhattan Bridge are outlined by strings of lights that define their cables and towers, creating clear linear forms across the East River. These illuminated structures connect boroughs while visually extending the skyline beyond Manhattan.

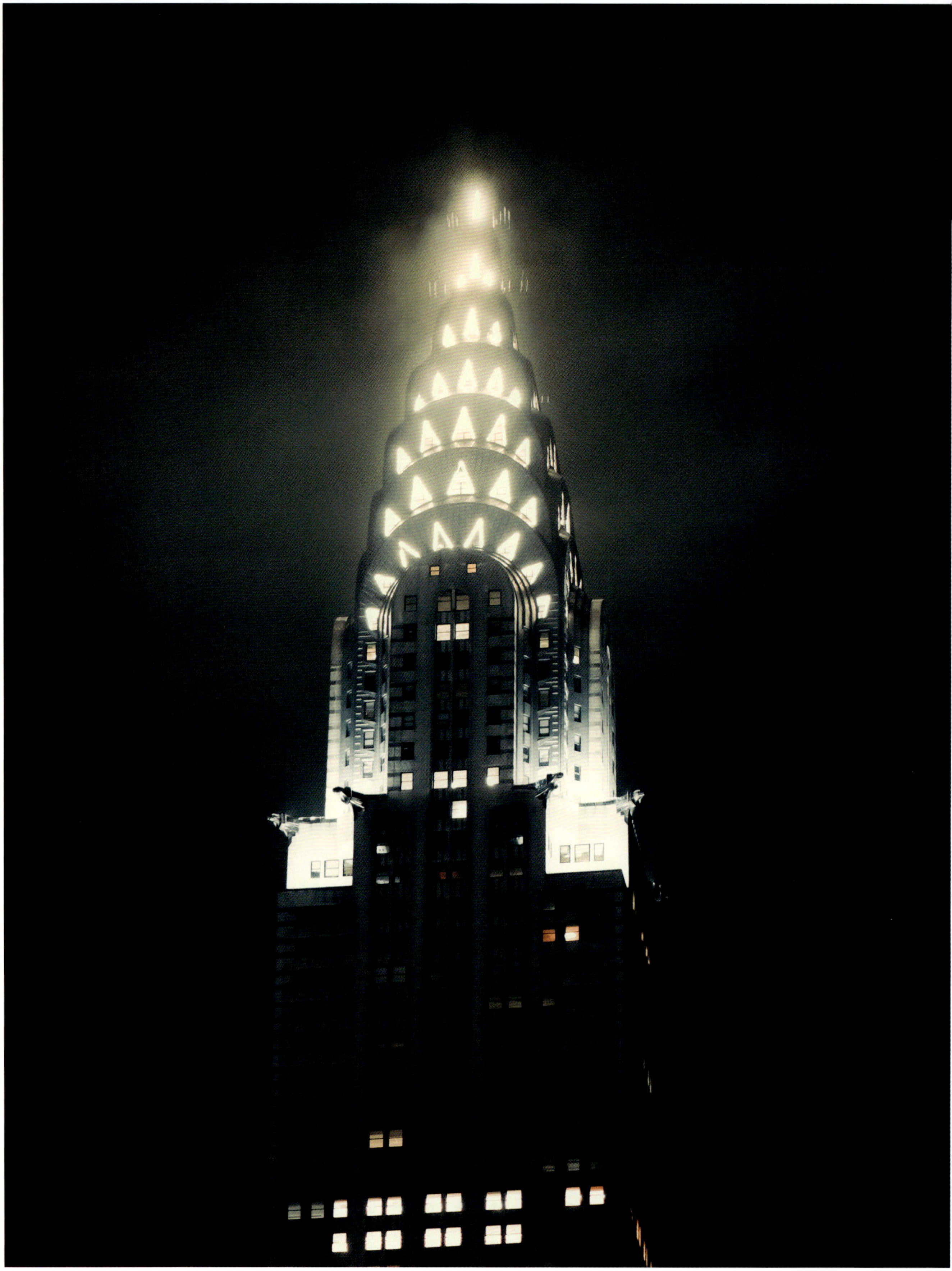

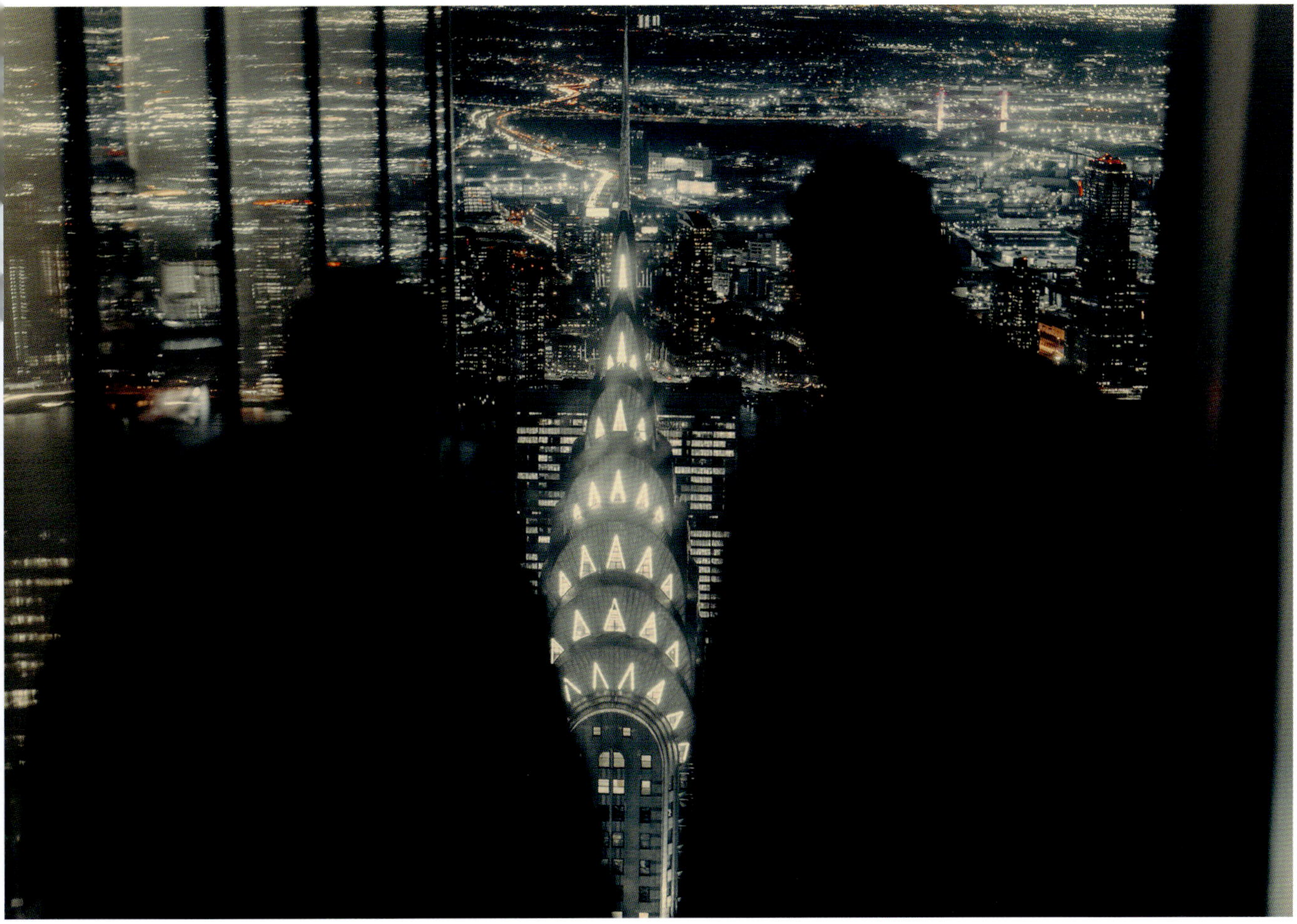

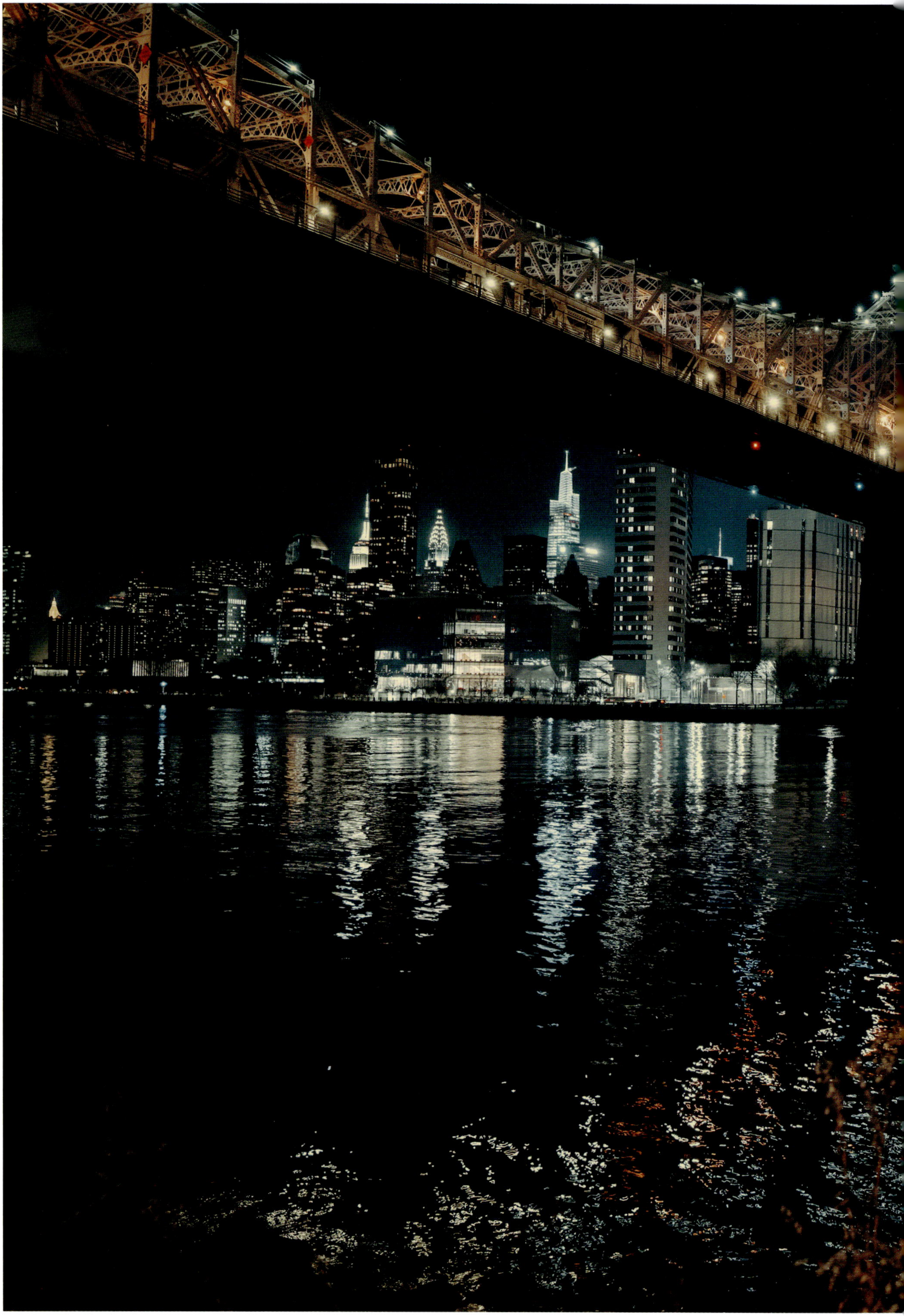

QUEENSBORO BRIDGE

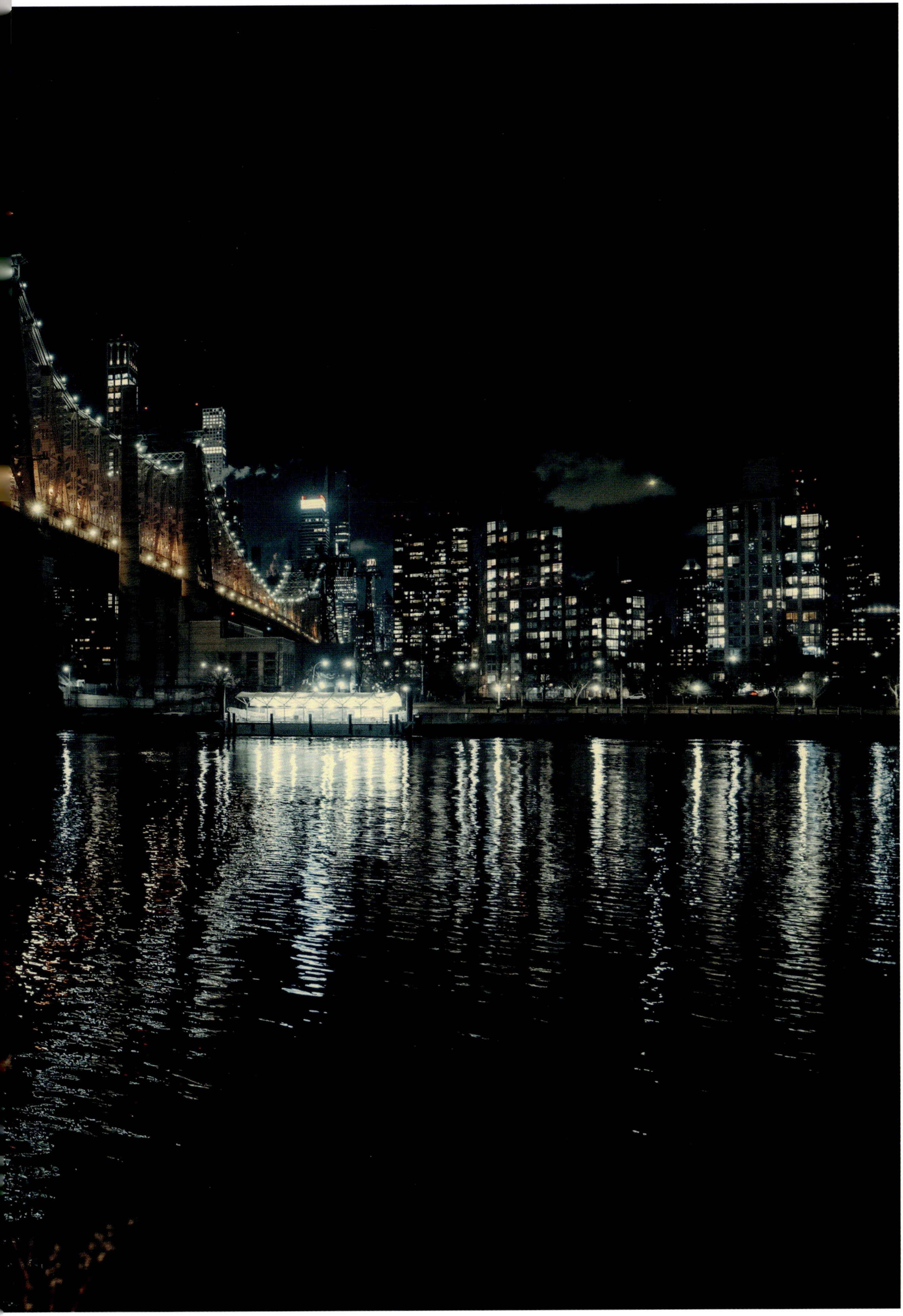

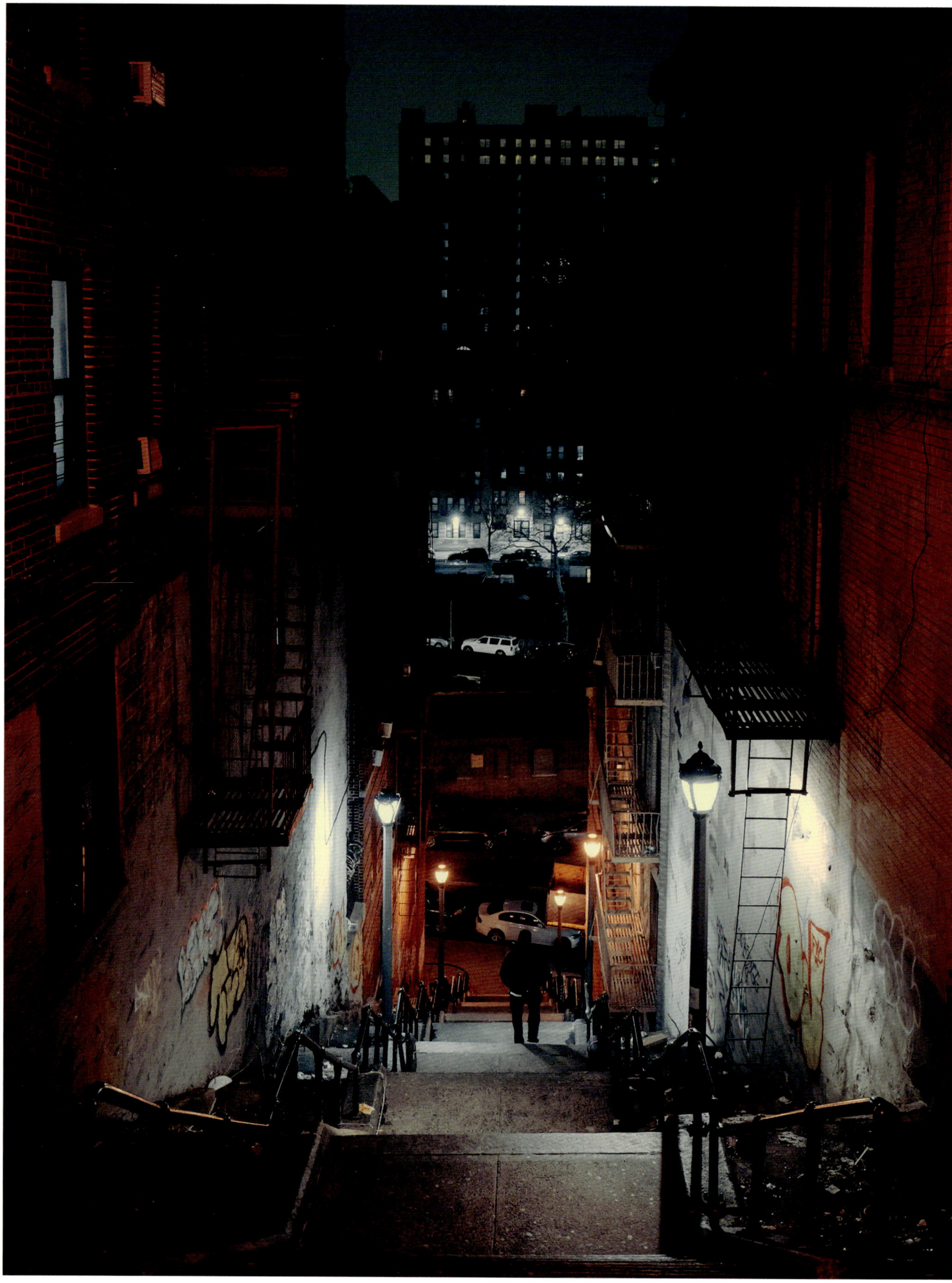

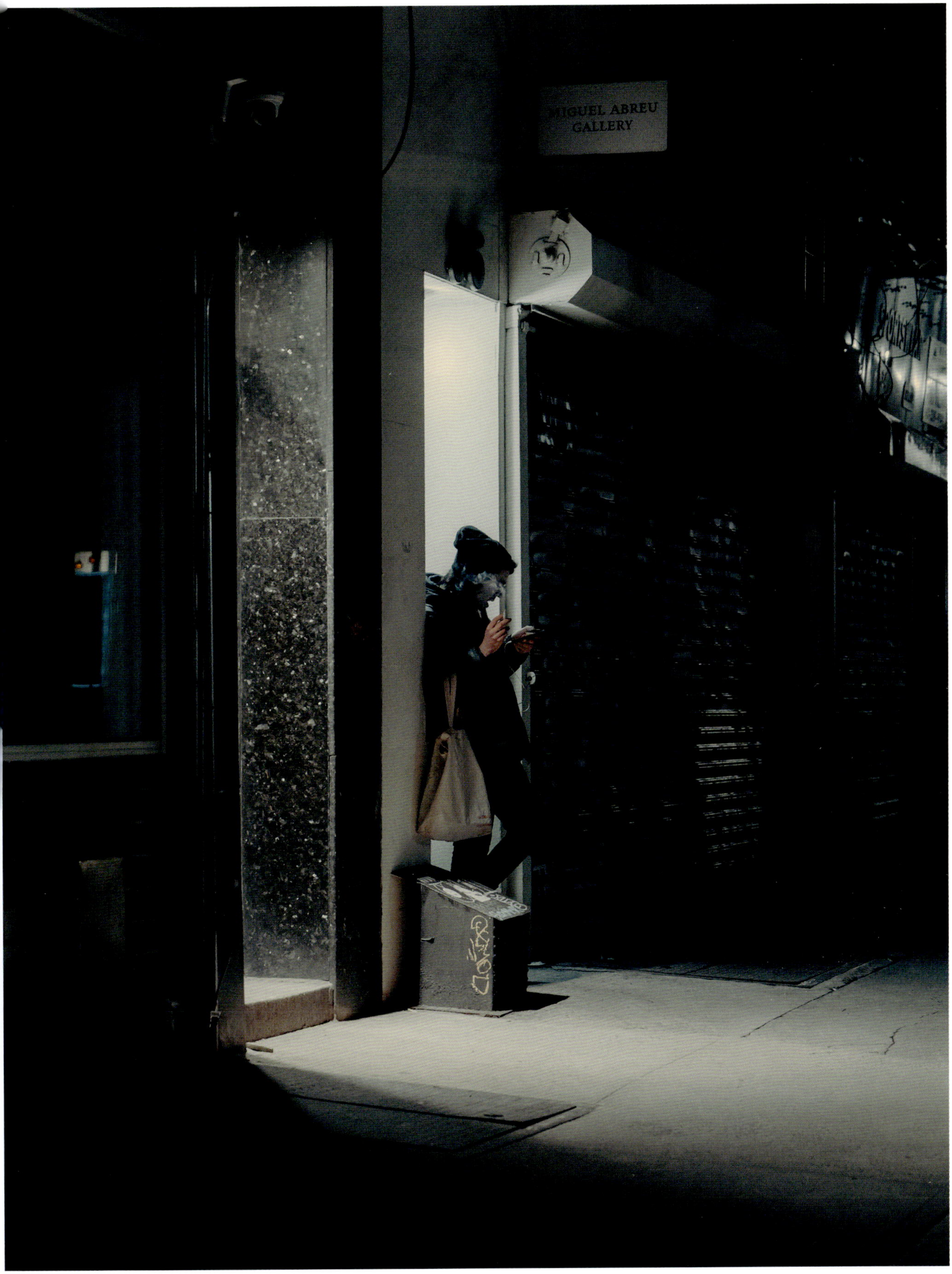
MIGUEL ABREU
GALLERY

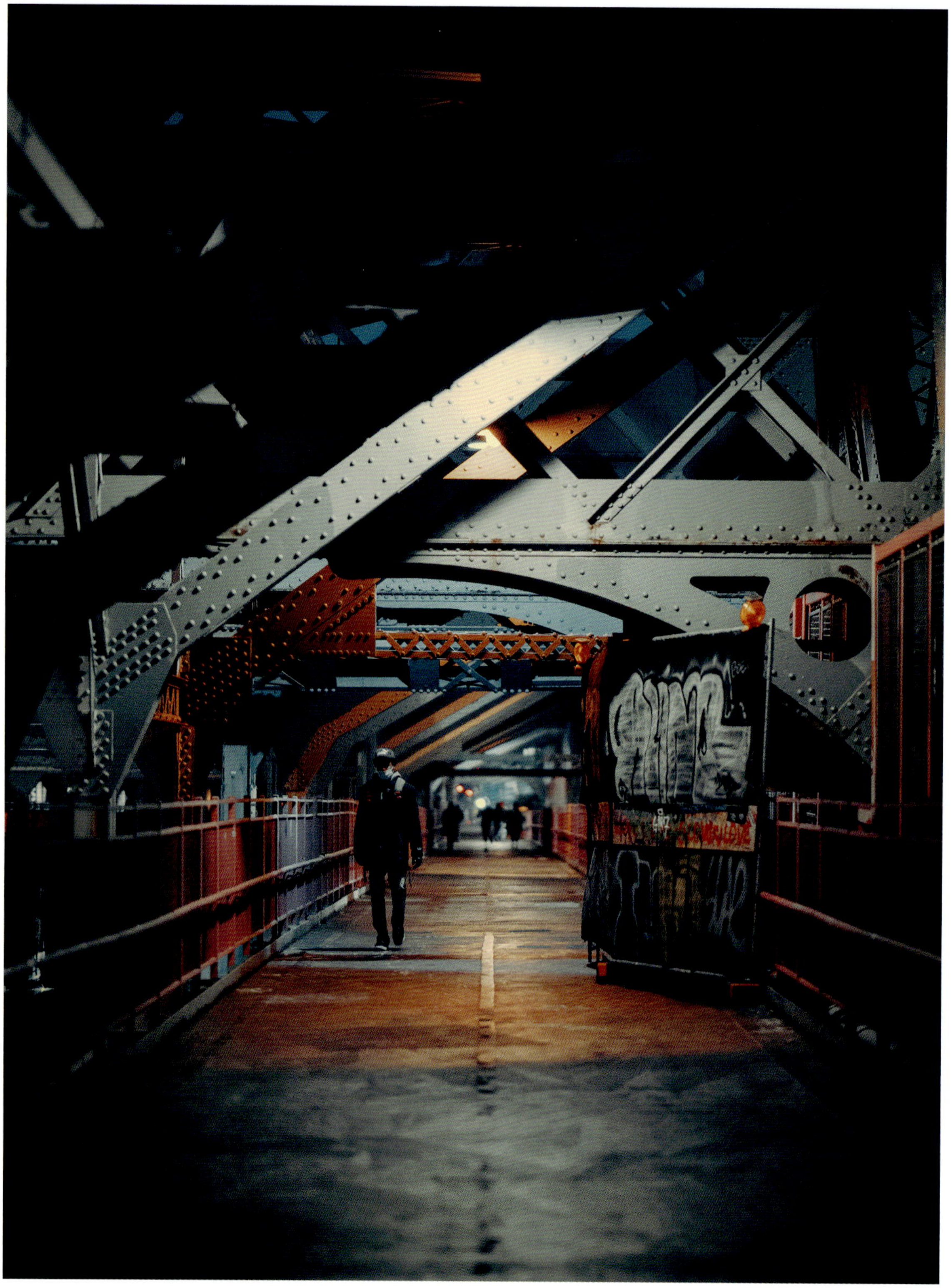

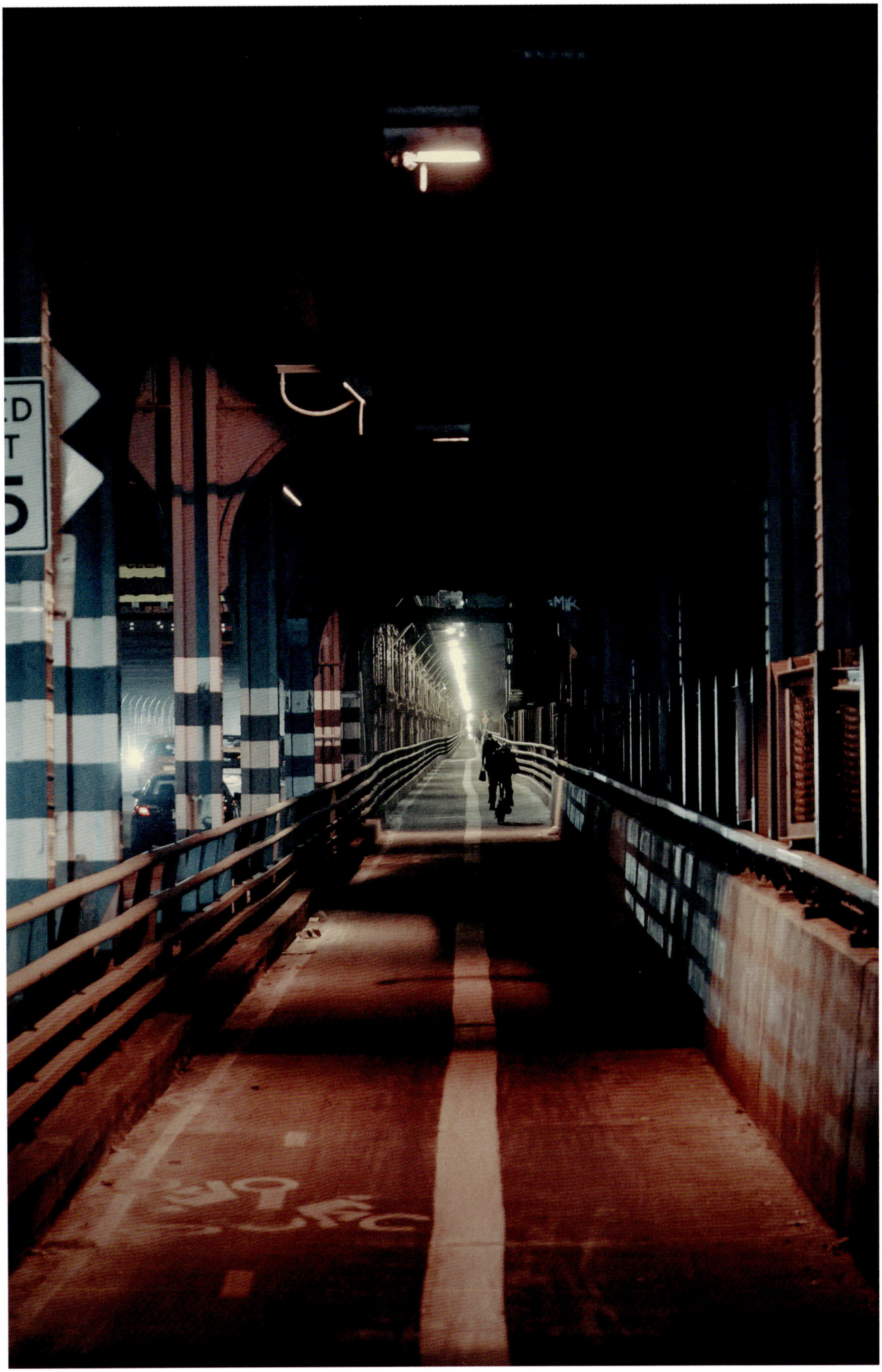

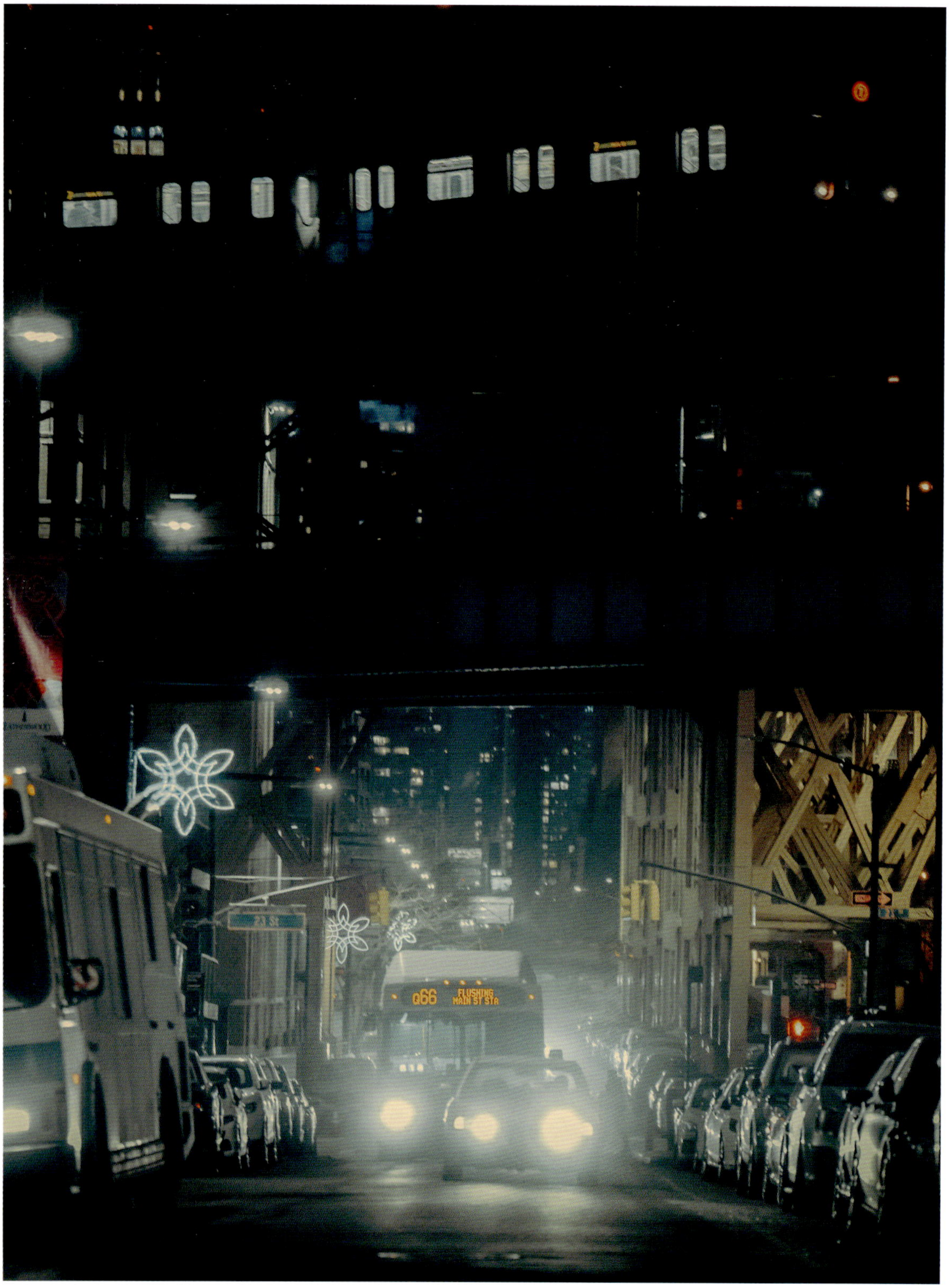
Q66 FLUSHING MAIN ST STA

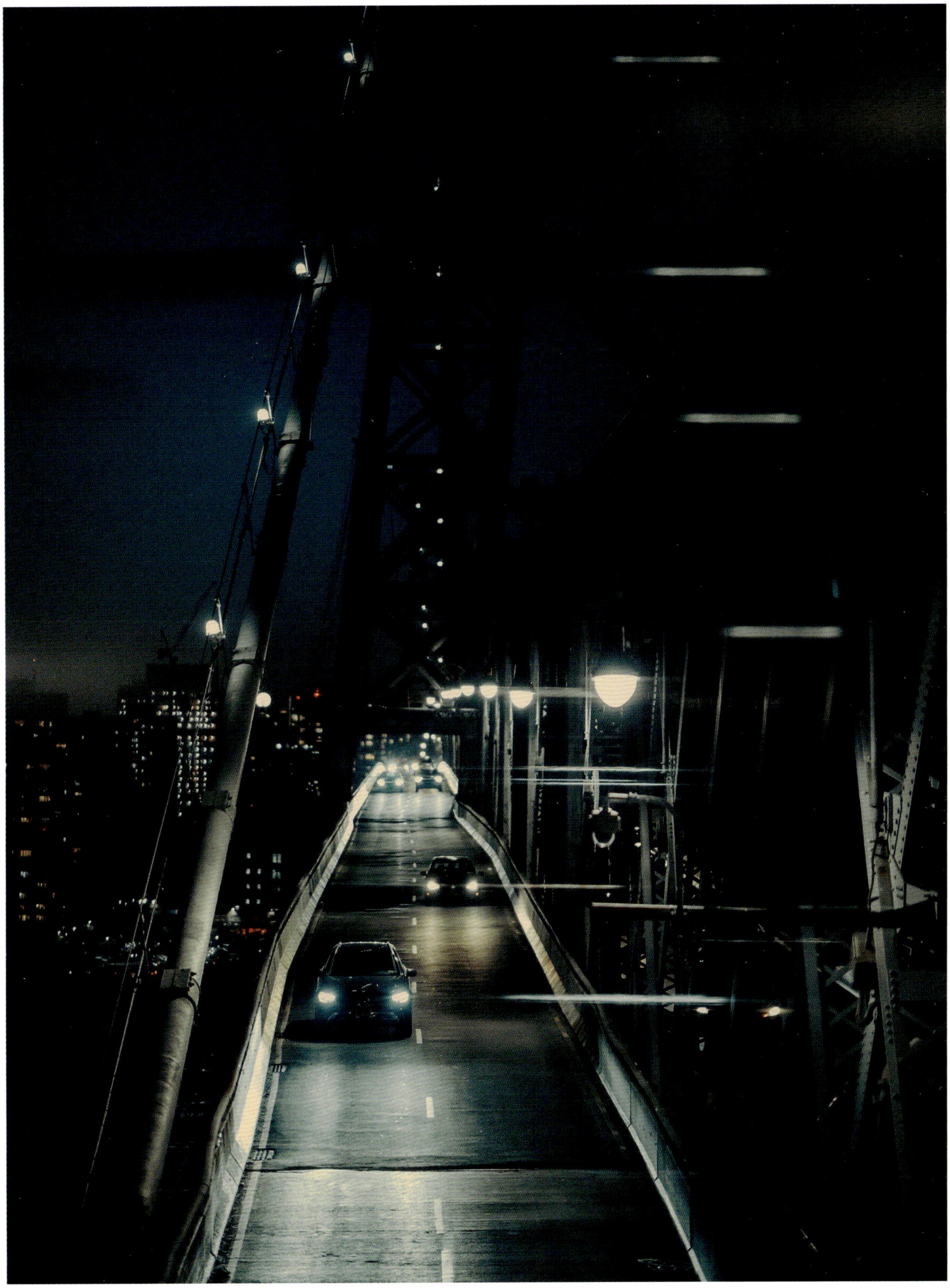

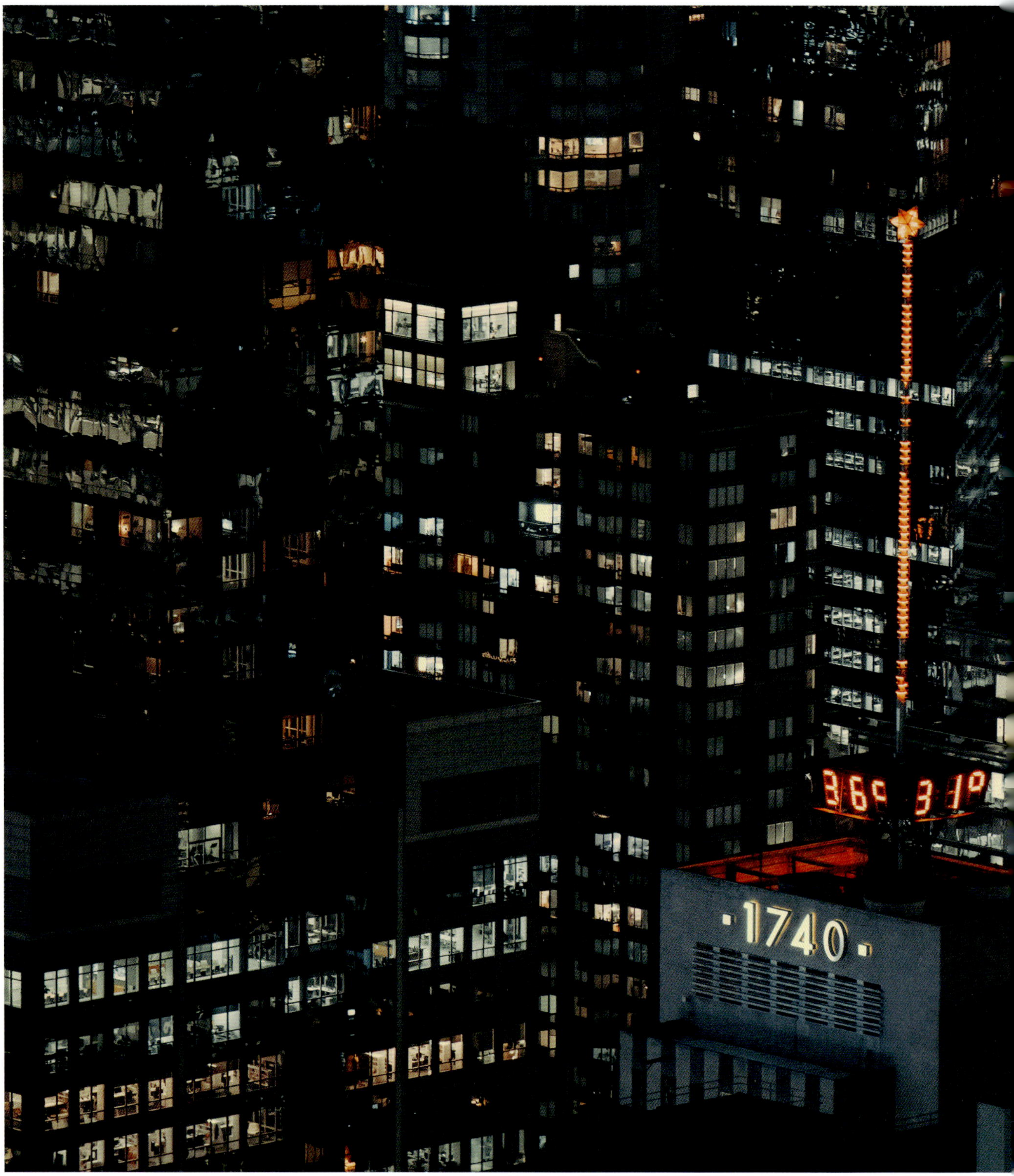
1740

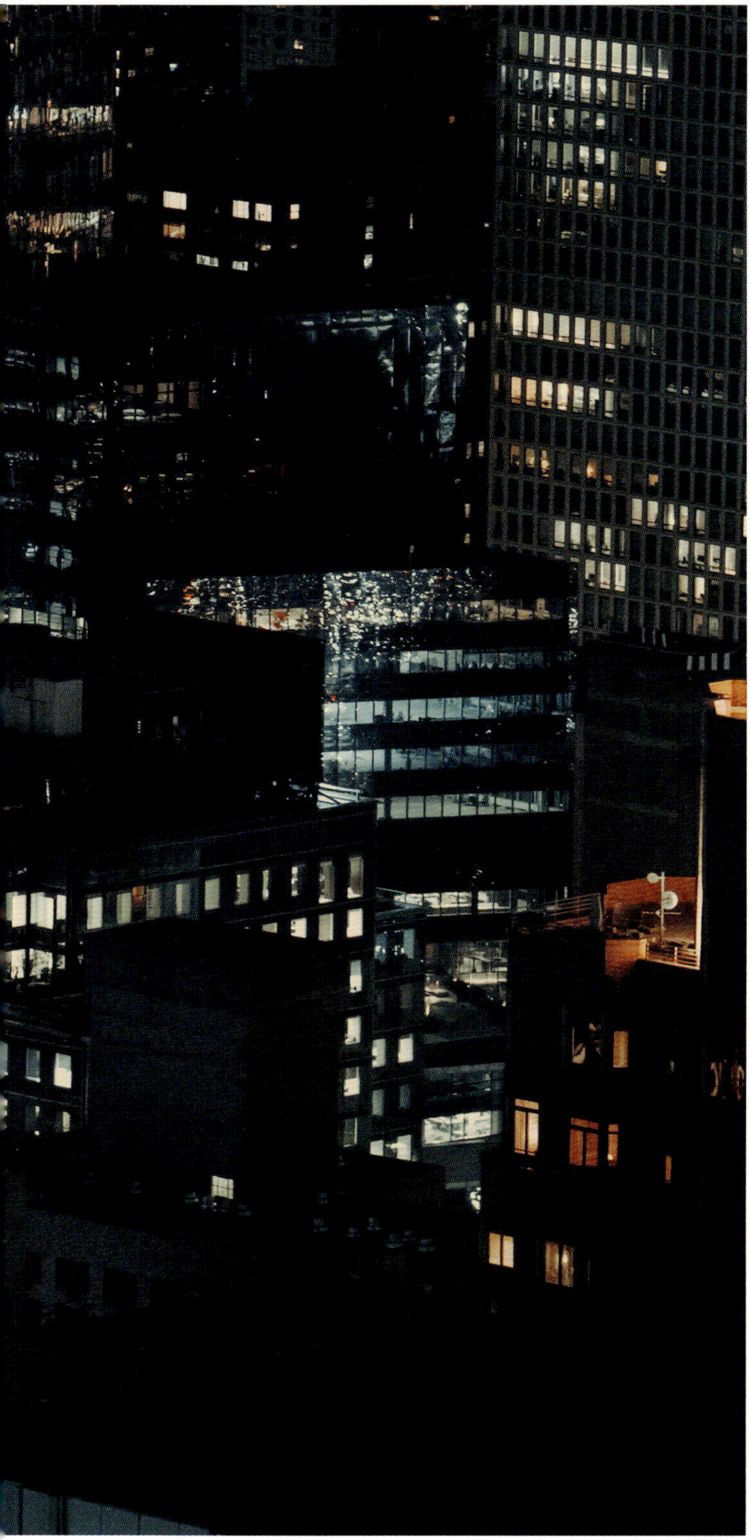

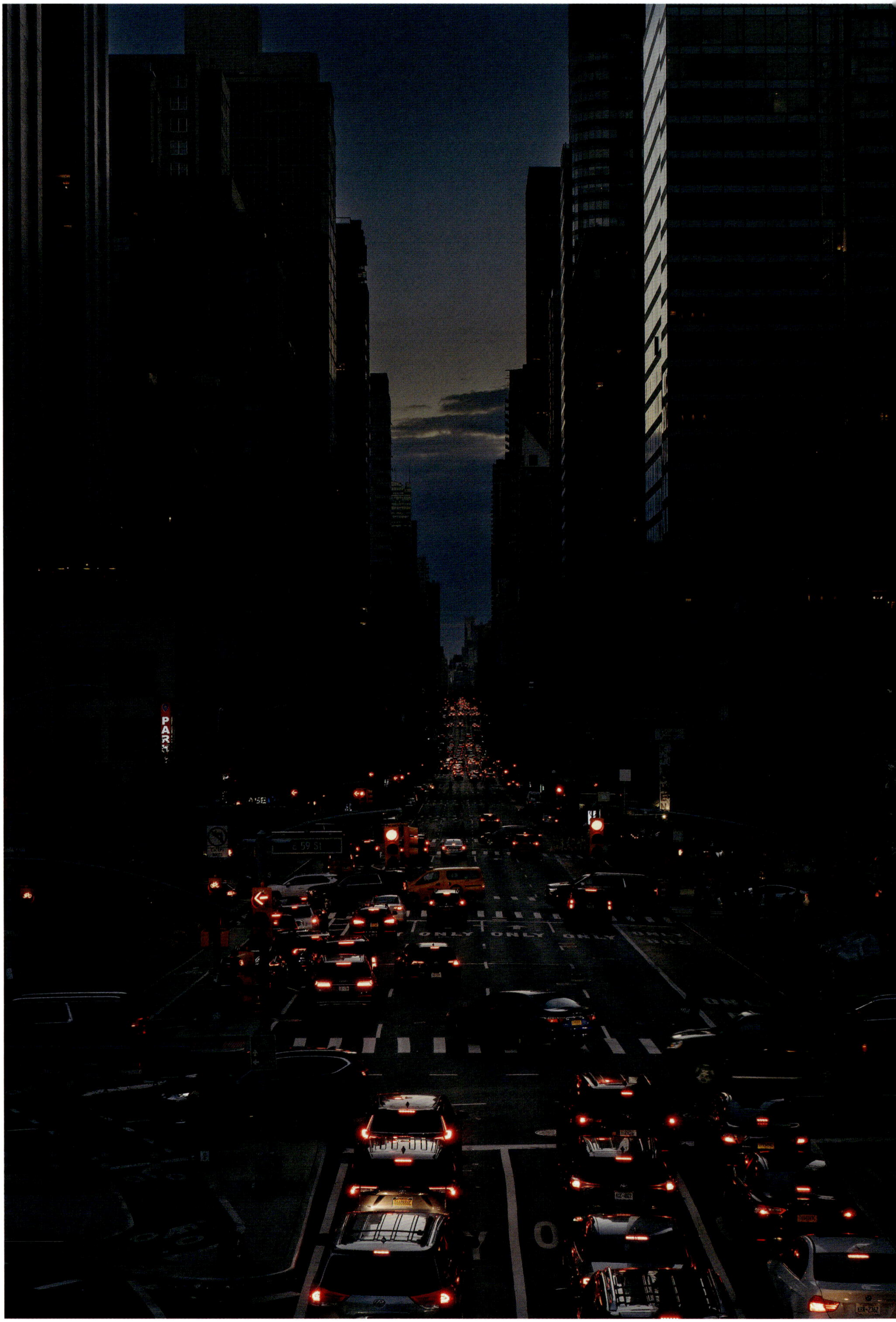

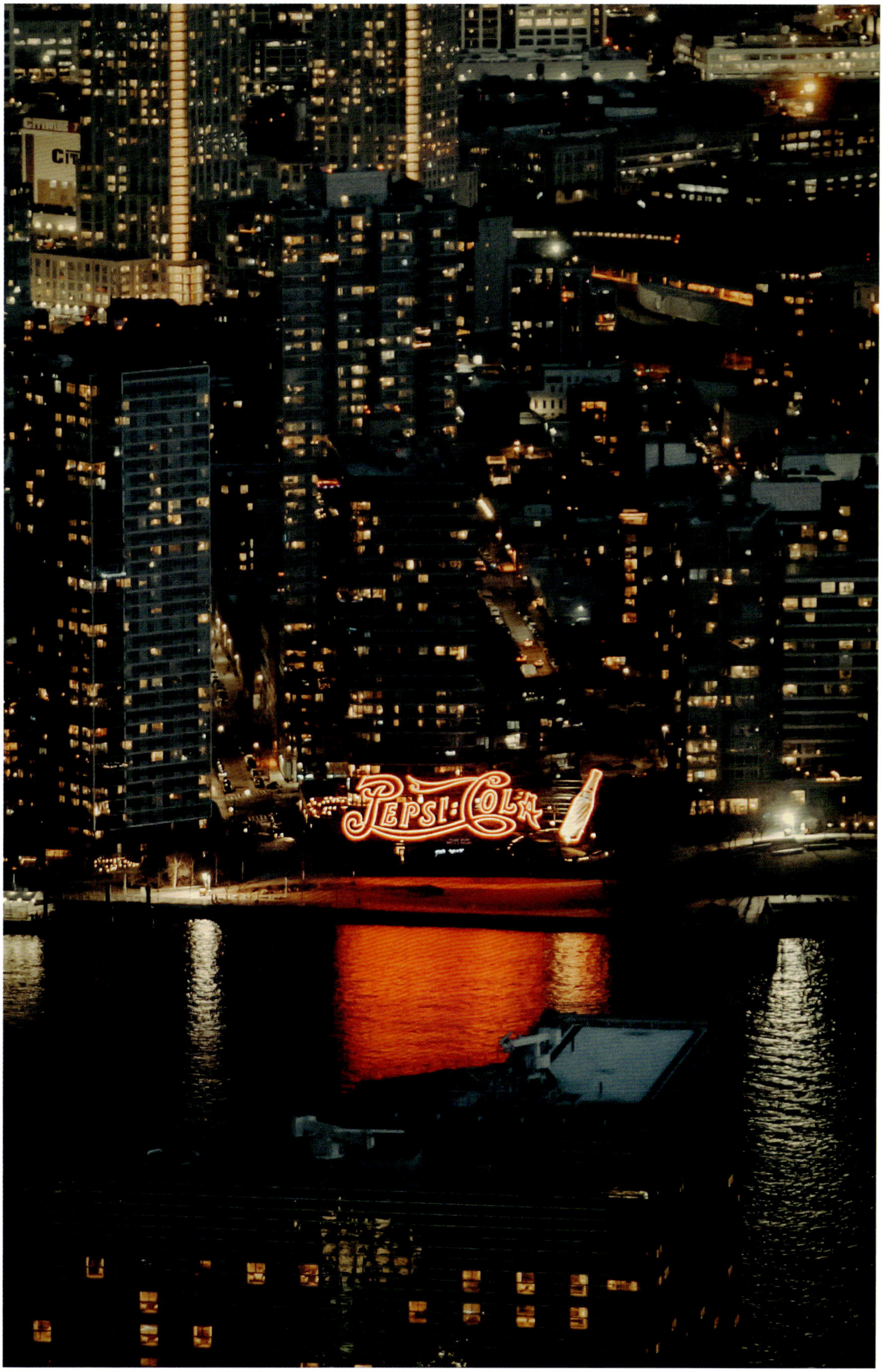
Pepsi-Cola

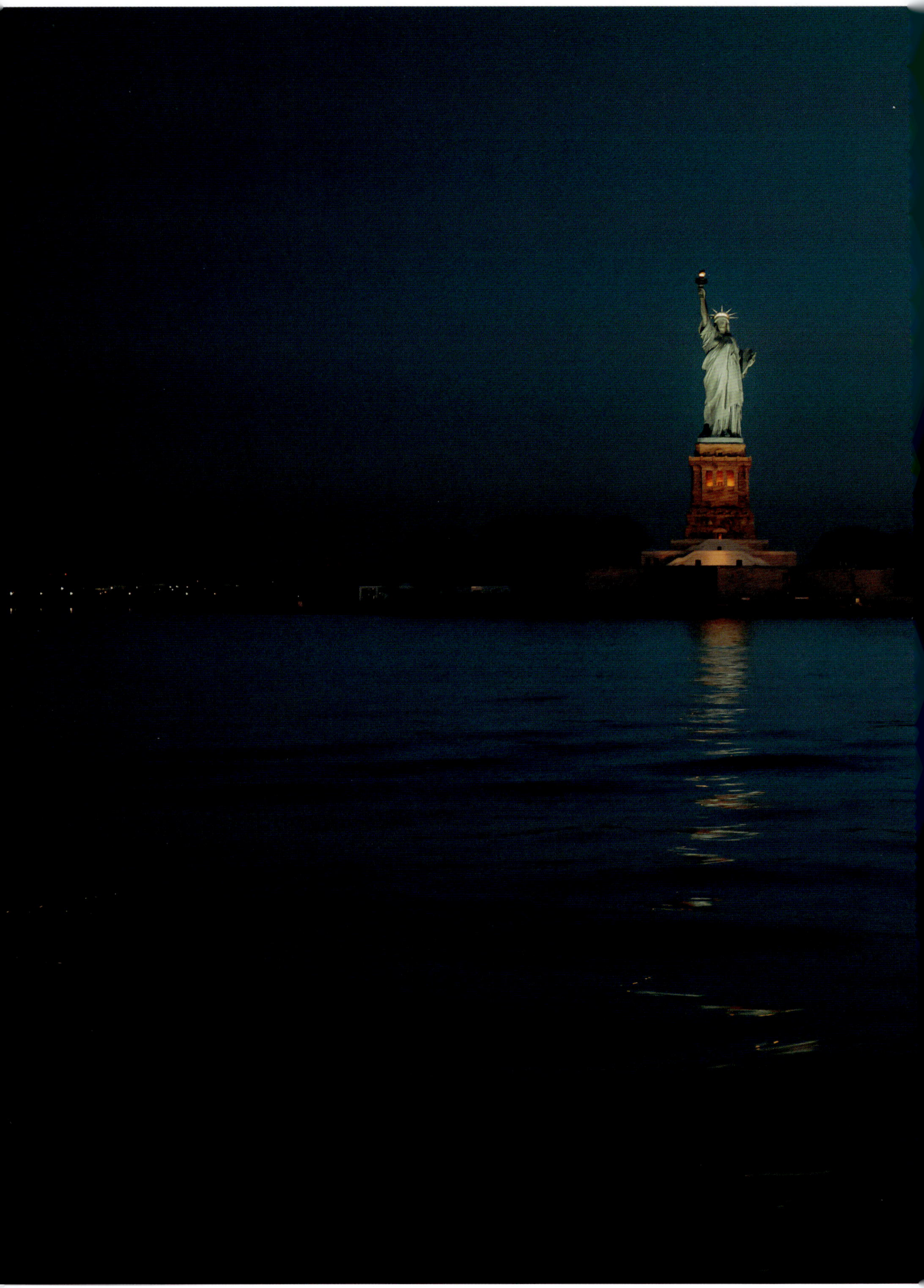

STATUE OF LIBERTY

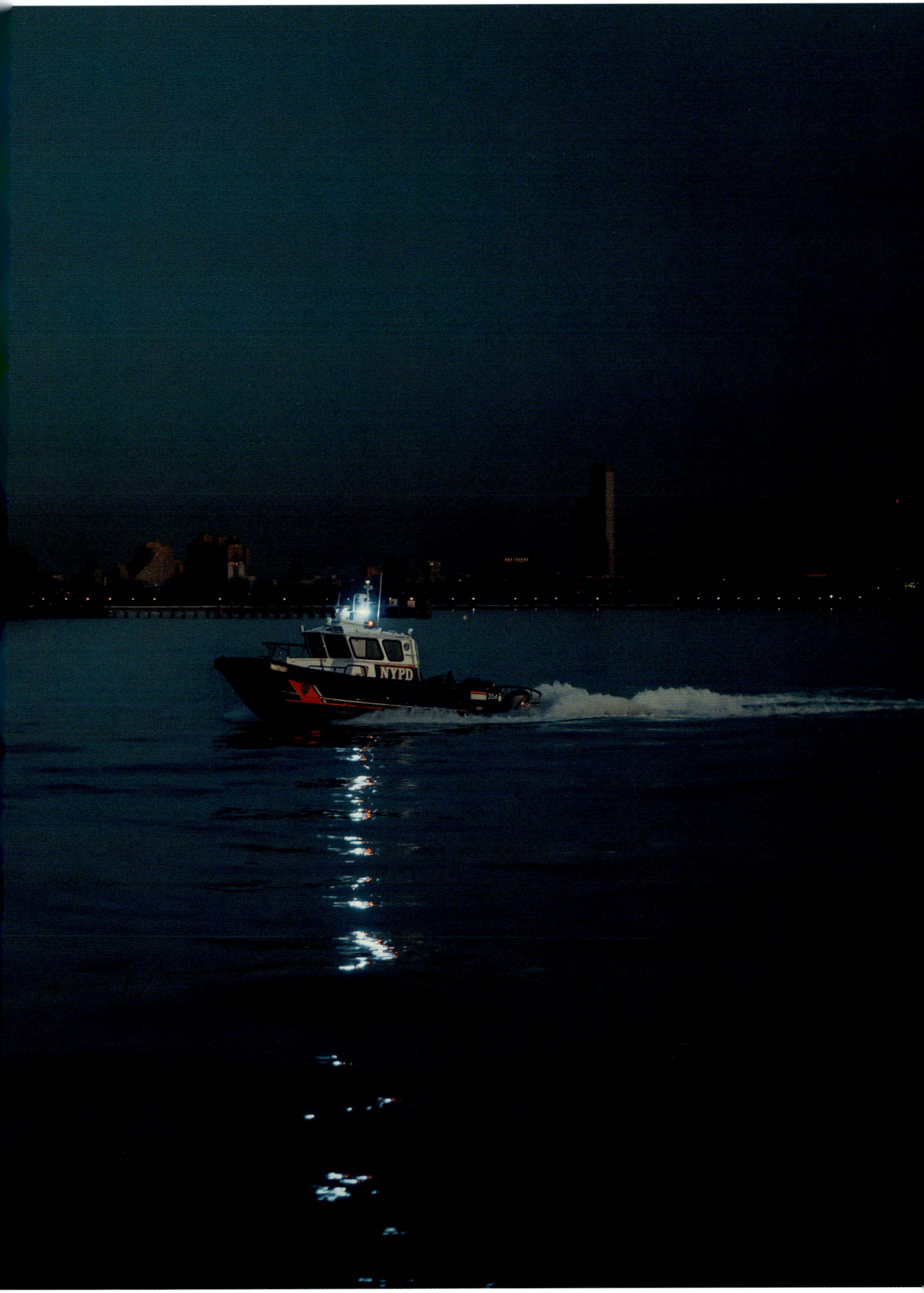
NYPD
354

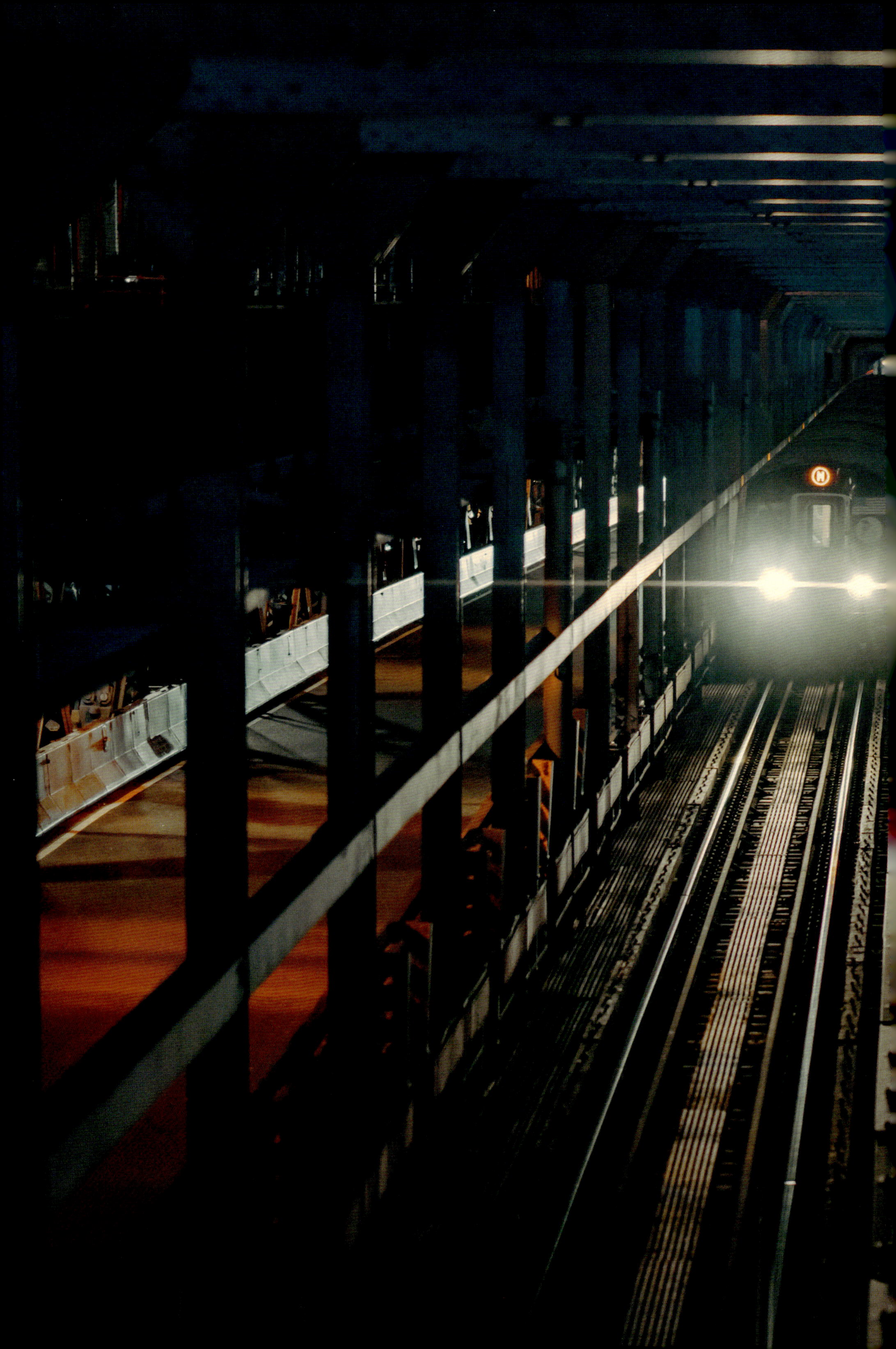

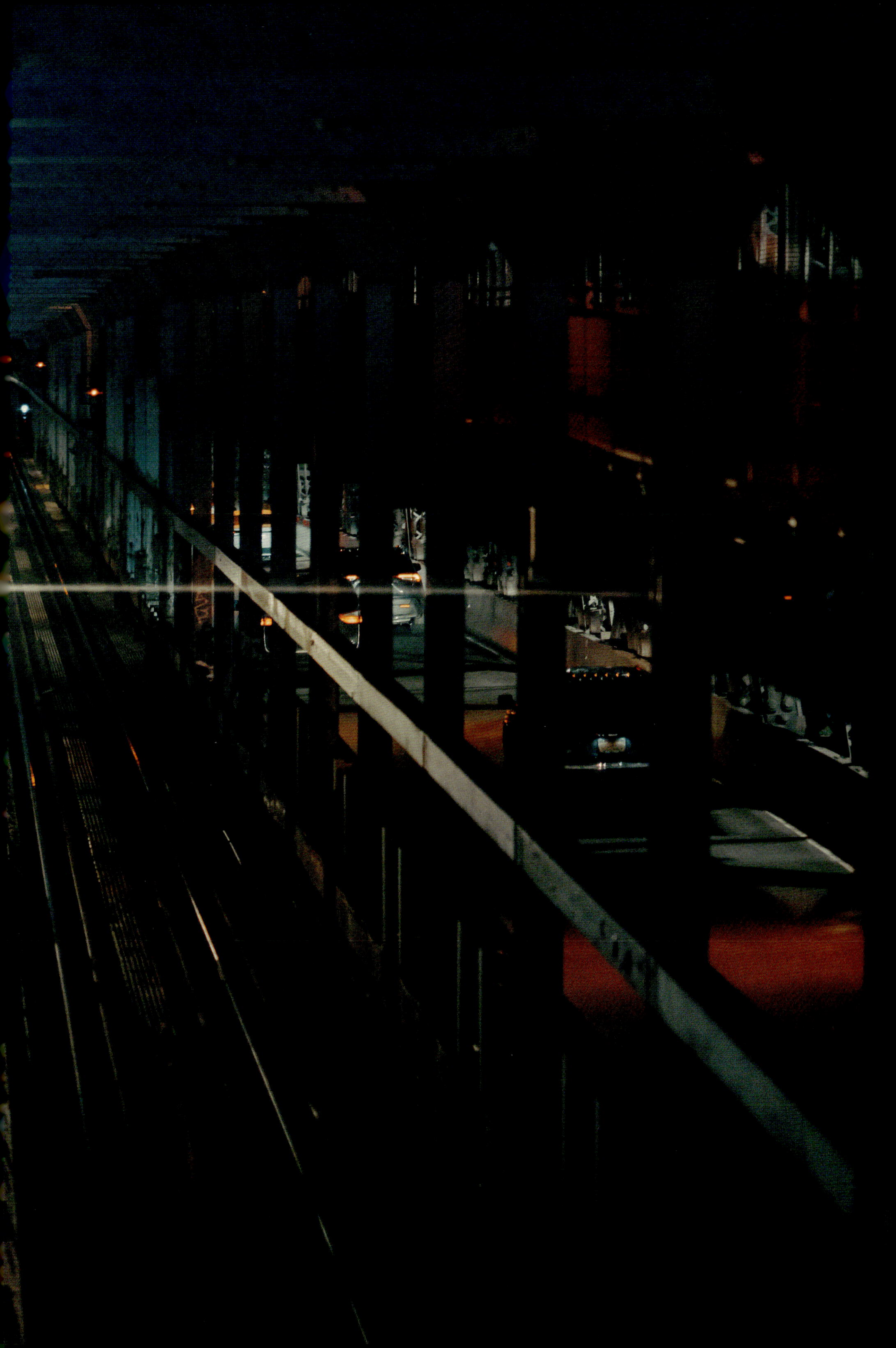

NEW YORK AFTER DARK

PHOTOGRAPHERS

Sanmi Krueger is a self-taught, internationally published photographer and videographer from Berlin who picked up his first camera in March 2018 with the aim to capture moments rather than places.

Since then, he has become passionate about visual storytelling as it allows him to archive reality, transform the ordinary into compelling narratives, and share evocative imagery with his ever-growing community. He has had the privilege of working with industry-leading brands including Mercedes-AMG, Red Bull Racing, and PolarPro.

An essential part of his creative growth process is intentionally remaining genre-fluid—thriving across motorsport action, Arctic landscapes, and street photography. This versatility isn't about choosing a niche; it's about mastering the craft itself, developing an eye that adapts and evolves regardless of environment, all while constantly refining his technical execution and post-processing workflows to create work that resonates.

@capital.shutter

Declan McWhinney is a street and conceptual photographer specializing in visual storytelling where he captures and creates deeply emotional moments in time. He started his creative career as a musician, but when he pivoted to photography, he realized he'd found his calling.

Originally, he was interested in studying psychology to learn and understand more about people. However, he decided not to pursue as he knew he wasn't a strong academic learner. When he picked up his camera after retiring from the music industry, Declan began taking images of anything he found interesting and quickly realized that all of his favorite photos had people in them. He kept practicing and after a year he discovered that he was still learning about people by capturing candid moments of them.

Now, Declan's photography is his lifeblood and he can't imagine living in the world without the eye of a street photographer.

@declanrmc

Cyril Mouty is a Paris-based photographer whose images have appeared in *Trope Paris* and *Trope Rome*. His career began in international luxury and hospitality. Through his various roles in different hotels, Cyril found himself traveling to numerous destinations, immersing himself in a tapestry of countries, cultures, and lifestyles. It was amidst these adventures that Cyril's lens began capturing more than just iconic landmarks and attractions. His focus shifted to the heartbeat of each nation—the people. Street photography and reportage metamorphosed into a profound passion, compelling him to document the essence of every place he visited. Today, for Cyril, the true luxury lies in the exploration of places, cultures, and people. This ideology serves as the foundation for all his work. Cyril endeavors to present photographs that encapsulate the authentic reality of each locale, capturing the scenes as perceived by the human eye.

@cyrilmouty_photography

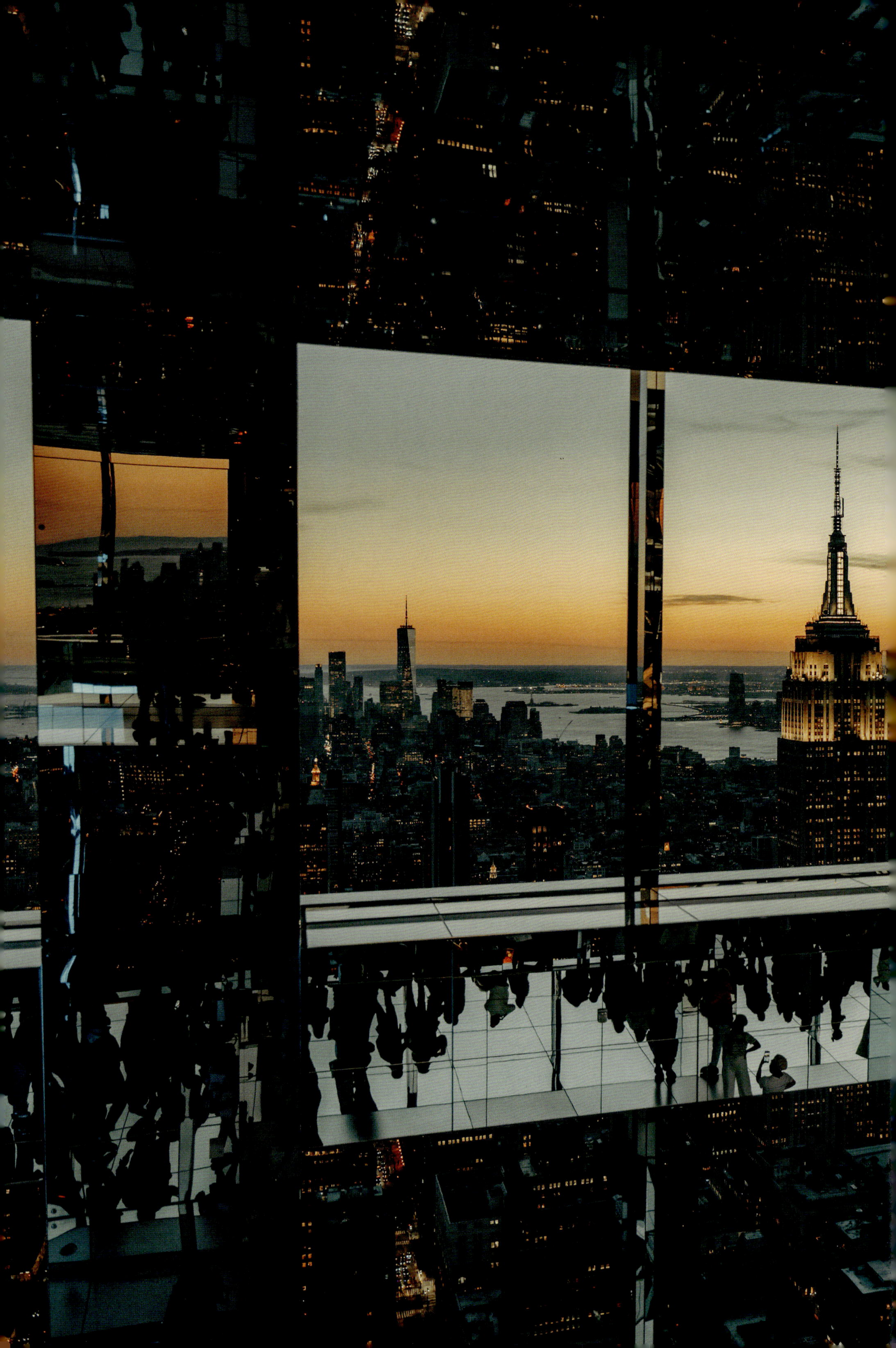

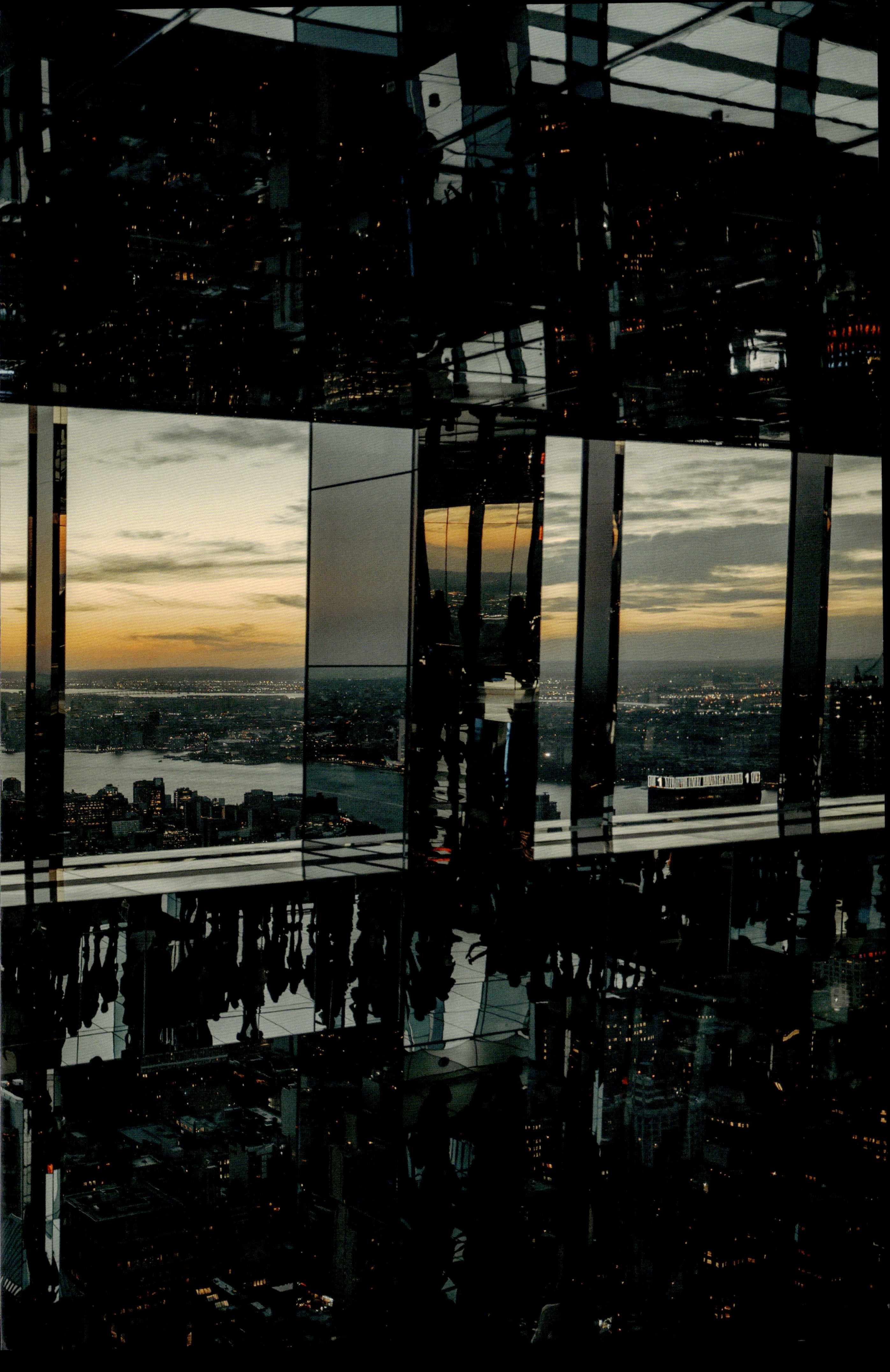

PHOTO CREDITS

Sanmi Krueger

Photographs by Sanmi Krueger appear on the following pages:

006-007, 008-009, 014, 015, 016, 017, 018, 019, 022, 023, 024, 026-027, 028, 029, 030, 031, 032, 033, 034, 037, 040, 041, 042, 043, 044-045, 046, 047, 048, 049, 052, 053, 054, 055, 056-057, 058, 059, 060-061, 065, 070, 071, 072, 073, 076, 077, 078, 079, 087, 088, 089, 090, 091, 092-093, 094, 095, 096, 097, 098, 100, 101, 102, 103, 104, 105, 107, 108-109, 110, 111, 113, 114, 115, 116-117, 118, 119, 120, 122, 123, 128-129, 136, 137, 138, 139, 140, 146-147, 148, 150, 151, 152-153, 154, 155, 156, 157, 158, 159, 160-161, 163, 164-165, 166-167, 170-171, 173, 175

Declan McWhinney

Photographs by Declan McWhinney appear on the following pages:

Front Cover, 002, 004, 010-011, 012, 013, 020, 021, 025, 038, 062, 063, 066-067, 075, 080, 081, 082, 083, 084, 085, 086, 112, 121, 132, 133, 134, 135, 141, 142-143, 144, 145, Back Cover

Cyril Mouty

Photographs by Cyril Mouty appear on the following pages:

036, 039, 050, 051, 068, 069, 074, 099, 124-125, 126, 127, 130, 131, 162

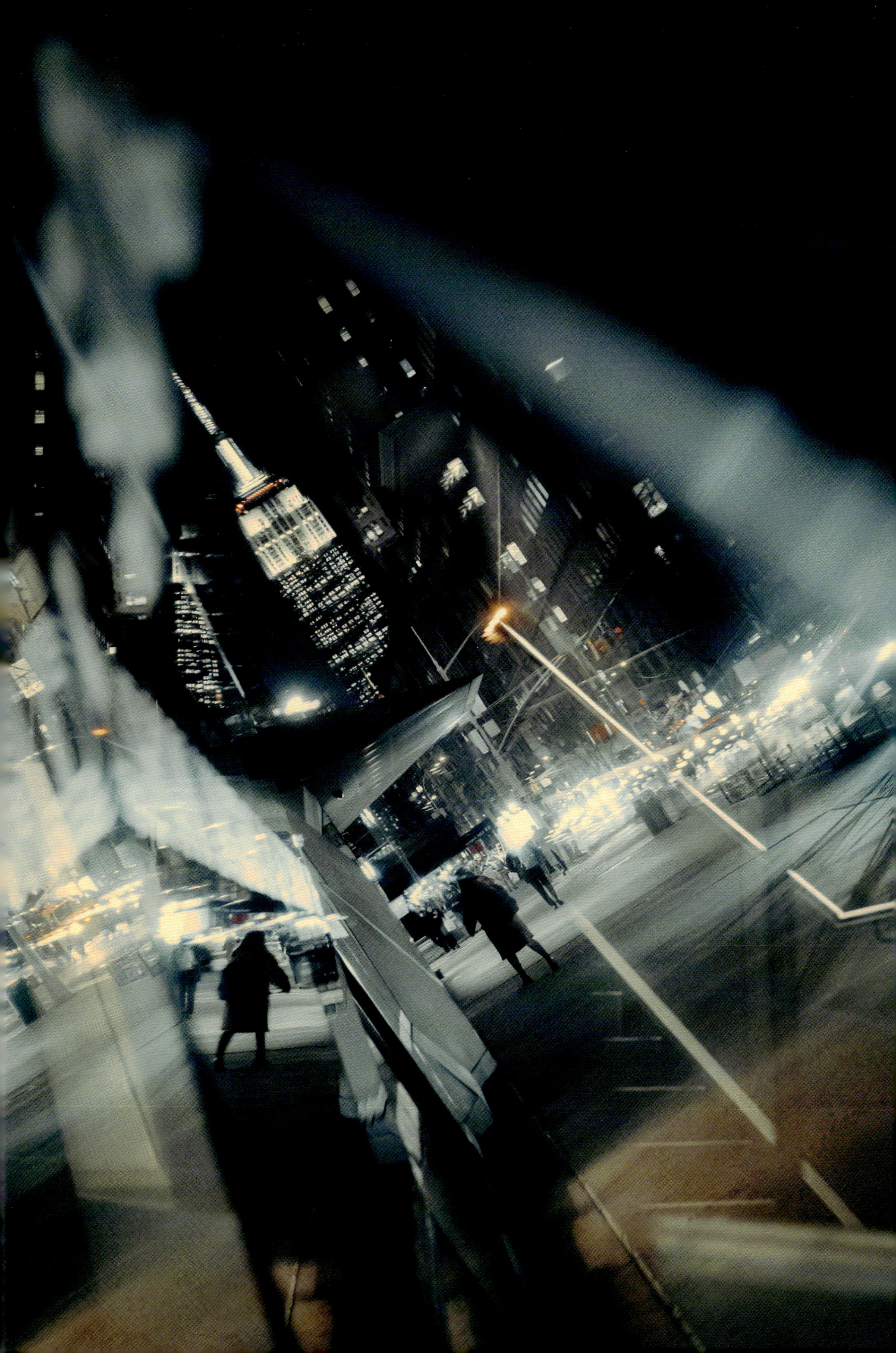

LCCN: 2026934601
ISBN: 978-1-951963-59-0

Printed and bound in China
First printing, 2026

Trope Publishing Co.
Chicago, Illinois, USA

The photographs from *New York After Dark* are available for purchase. For inquires, go to trope.com or email the gallery at info@trope.com

+ INFORMATION:
For additional information on our books and prints, visit www.trope.com

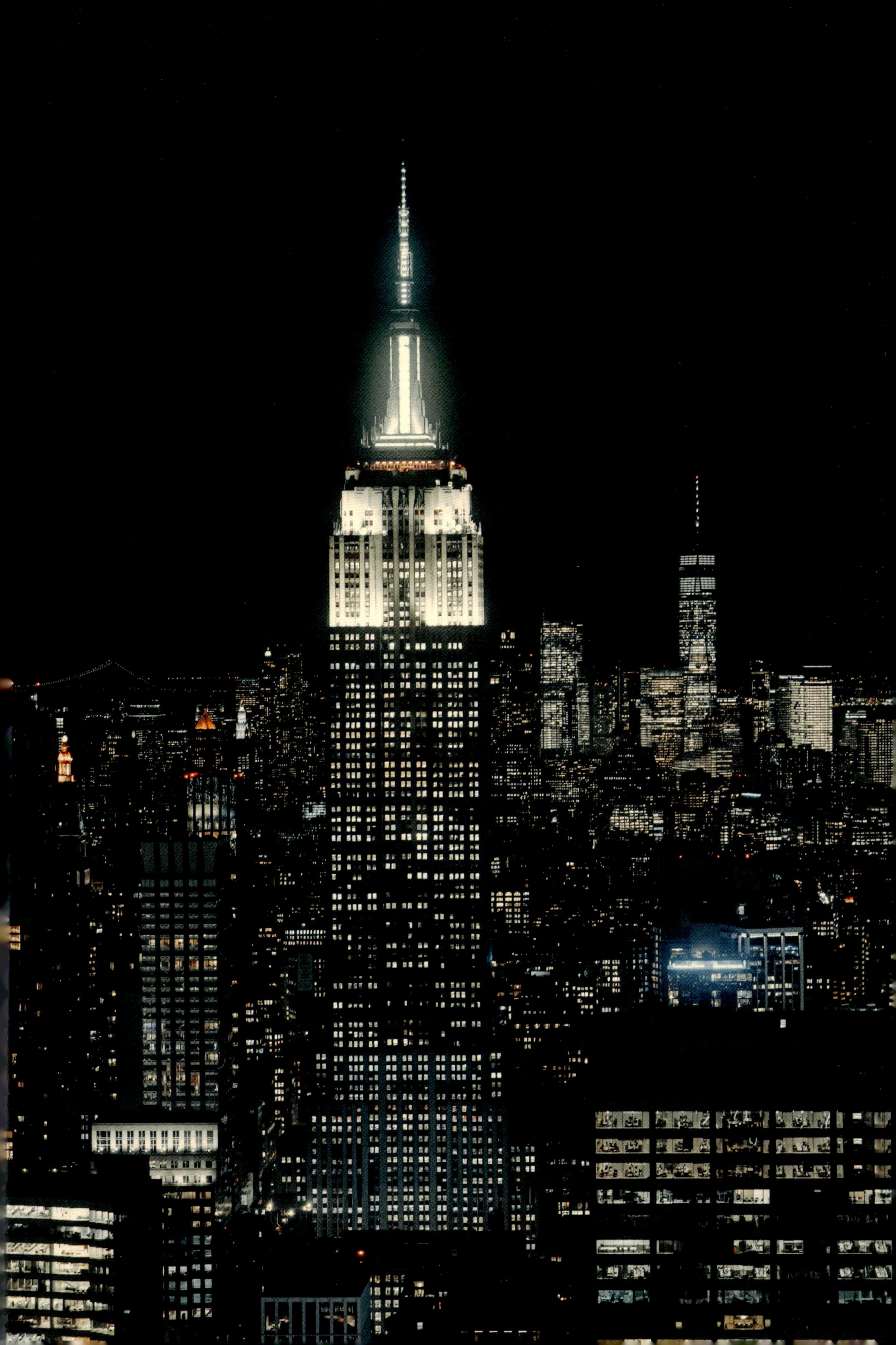

TROPE

TROPE